THE STORY
OF THE CHURCH

THE STORY
OF THE CHURCH

Fourth edition

Allan M. Harman
and
A. M. Renwick

INTER-VARSITY PRESS
36 Causton Street, London SW1P 4ST, England
Email: ivp@ivpbooks.com
Website: www.ivpbooks.com

First published 1958
Reprinted thirteen times
Second edition 1985
Reprinted three times
New format 1992
Reprinted four times
Third edition 1999
Reprinted three times
New format 2004
Fourth edition published 2020

British Library Cataloguing-in-Publication Data
A catalogue record for this book is available from the British Library.

ISBN: 978–1–78974–206–0
eBook ISBN: 978–1–78974–207–7

Set in 11/14pt Minion Pro
Typeset in Great Britain by CRB Associates, Potterhanworth, Lincolnshire
Printed and bound in Great Britain by Ashford Colour Press Ltd,
Gosport, Hampshire

In loving memory of my brother, sister and
brother-in-law

Grant Stewart Harman
(1934–2013)

Marslaidh Anne McClean
(1939–1987)

Murdoch Murchison
(1934–2019)

Contents

Contents

Preface

The first edition of this book appeared in 1958. It soon achieved a reputation as a fine introductory survey to church history, and became well known in both its UK and US editions. Second and third editions followed in 1985 and 1999, with translations into Portuguese, Romanian, Chinese and Korean. Its popularity is shown by the fact that the English text has appeared in more than thirty impressions. Many clearly appreciated its manageable size, and commented also on its readability.

Dr Alexander Macdonald Renwick was a Highland Scot who first entered the British civil service until he felt called to the Christian ministry. He trained at the University of Edinburgh and the Free Church College, and was ordained to St Columba's Free Church, Aberdeen, in 1913. War service as a chaplain in France interrupted his ministry there, and, after returning, he moved to the Free High Church, Dumbarton. In 1926 he was asked to go to Lima, Peru, to succeed Dr John A. Mackay (later of Princeton) as headmaster of the Anglo-Peruvian College (renamed after some years Colegio San Andrés, and retaining that name today), a missionary outreach of the Free Church of Scotland.

While in Peru, Renwick pursued historical and archaeological investigations and graduated in 1931 with the DLitt degree from San Marcos University. His book *Wandering in the Peruvian Andes* was published by Blackwood in 1939.

After a two-year period as the British Council representative in Chile, he returned to Scotland to take up the position of Professor of Church History at the Free Church College, Edinburgh. He was a very popular lecturer and preacher in English, Scottish Gaelic and Spanish, and assisted many Christian Unions in the universities. He was awarded an honorary DD by the University of Edinburgh in

1945. His major writings on church history were both published by Inter-Varsity Press. *The Story of the Church* appeared in 1958, and it was followed by *The Story of the Scottish Reformation* in 1960.

I was a student of church history under Dr Renwick, and then came into closer connection with him when I married my wife, Mairi, who was his step-daughter. It has been my pleasure to edit *The Story of the Church* twice already, and now to give it a pervasive revision and to bring it up to date. While most of my own writing has been in biblical studies, I studied church history at graduate and post-graduate levels, and have written quite extensively on historical subjects in books and journal articles. Among these writings are biographies of Matthew Henry of Chester and Joseph Addison Alexander of Princeton.

Few books of this kind manage to last nearly as long as this one, or achieve so wide a distribution. In travels in many parts of the world my wife and I have come across copies of it, or have heard people speaking of their use of it. My hope is that after having served the church for over sixty years, it will continue to be a most useful tool in introducing readers to the way in which the Lord Jesus established his church and has preserved it down through the centuries. Being members of his church demands faithful service on our part, and in this way so to fulfil our calling, or in the words of James E. Seddon (1915–83):

> Church of God, elect and holy,
> be the people He intends;
> strong in faith and swift to answer
> each command Your Master sends:
> royal priests, fulfil your calling
> through your sacrifice and prayer;
> give your lives in joyful service –
> sing His praise, His love declare.

Allan M. Harman
Ocean Grove,
Victoria, Australia

Acknowledgments

In revising and extending this book, I have had access to many books and journal articles. Since this is a popular survey of church history, I could not interact with other writers. Ideas have certainly entered my thinking and writing over many years, and I trust that readers will be better informed because of the work of others upon which I depended.

Two friends, John and Elizabeth Cromarty of Geelong, Victoria, have helped by reading the complete manuscript and commenting on it. Ken and Anna Harman of Dubai have also been of great help, and I thank them for it.

In all my writing I am aided by my wife, Mairi. She shares my love of church history, and has often helped, not simply by proofreading, but by making suggestions on the text that have improved it. As on many other occasions, she has seen that I have had the time to commit to this project, and aided in many different ways.

Prologue

For more than 2,000 years, the Christian church has exercised a profound influence upon the world. Its moral and spiritual influence has spread, in a greater or lesser degree, to almost all parts of the world. No one, therefore, ought to be indifferent to the story of the church of Christ.

Church history is the story of the Christian community and its relationship to the rest of the world throughout the centuries. It commences with the beginnings of the church in Jerusalem, and its spread to every continent. Christian thought and practice have touched millions of lives, and profoundly affected innumerable countries during the past 2,000 years. Not all that has been done in the name of Christ has been admirable, but generation after generation has witnessed faithful Christians living according to the faith, and witnessing to the saving power of Christ. Study of church history not only satisfies our curiosity as to what happened in past times, but is also of great practical interest for the present. Basic human nature has remained the same in every age, although the circumstances of people's lives may differ. Men and women have had, essentially, the same weaknesses and the same aspirations all through history.

At many times throughout the centuries, the gospel led the church to scale great heights of spiritual achievement, while in other periods, false influences led her out into the dark and arid wilderness of error and decay. Any epoch, including our own, can witness similar times of blessing or despair. Guidance for the present is provided by the study of church history, as lessons from the past are incorporated into our thinking, and warnings from past aberrations from the faith help in current decision-making. Episodes from church history give concrete examples that can serve as guides for the future.

As we look back upon the path by which the human race has arrived at its present position, the question arises 'Have the great events of history happened by chance, or can we trace behind these events the hand of providence guiding all that comes to pass?' Even in secular history there is much that suggests a divine providence directing the affairs of the world, age by age, and out of evil bringing good. This is much more evident in church history. Consider, for example, how the Reformation was preserved, when nothing could prevent Luther and his associates from being crushed. The emperor Charles V, having made a peace treaty with his enemy, the king of France, was trying to stamp out the new movement when there arrived a new distraction: the Islamic Turks came marching up the Danube in their thousands, and were thundering at the gates of Vienna in the very heart of Europe. Thus, Charles V had to make peace with his Protestant subjects and seek their help against the common enemy. As a result, the Reformed Church escaped probable annihilation.

The history of the church is simply an account of its success and failure in carrying out Christ's great commission 'Go therefore and make disciples of all nations, baptizing them in the name of the Father and of the Son and of the Holy Spirit, teaching them to observe all that I have commanded' (Matt. 28:19–20). It may be divided as follows.

1. *Missionary activity*. This is the great story of the spiritual conquest of many lands, showing how the brave little band of disciples, who went forth at Christ's call to preach the gospel, originated forces that progressively influenced nation after nation, in spite of tremendous opposition throughout the centuries. That missionary activity has not ceased, though changes in transport, technology and in societies themselves have produced new methods of evangelistic activity.

2. *Church organization*. Here we see the fulfilment of our Lord's words that, although his kingdom was like a grain of mustard seed, it would become a great tree sheltering the birds of the air (Luke 13:19). The small and apparently weak church became a mighty organization known throughout the world. Its history shows its

moral grandeur. It shows too certain defects arising from human weakness and the love of worldly pomp and power contrary to the spirit of the Christ. Many struggles have taken place between conflicting systems of church government, causing strife and division.

3. *Doctrine.* A part of church history is concerned with the development of doctrinal systems, for questions arose early as to what was the content of the gospel message. Hence, attention must be given to councils, heresies, excommunications, party divisions and similar developments, even when these are not very edifying. Some disputes were central to the faith, because they were concerned with teaching about salvation. Others were about peripheral questions that should have been settled without discord or division. However, accounts of how men and women held tenaciously to the Scriptures in very adverse circumstances are encouraging, even being prepared to suffer as martyrs because of their commitment to the truth.

4. *The effect on human life.* The gospel is shown to be 'like leaven that a woman took and hid in three measures of flour, till it was all leavened' (Matt. 13:33). The lives of innumerable individuals and of many nations have been transformed by the mighty power of the cross. Christian education and philanthropic agencies have exemplified the love of Christ, and throughout the history of the church new agencies have arisen to meet specific needs. Christians have been at the forefront of doing good to all, especially to those of the household of faith (Gal. 6:10). Groups of peoples, and even whole nations, have been taught new moral standards. It is a thrilling narrative, but there is the reverse side. Multitudes have been unfaithful to the great teachings of Christianity, and have fallen back into worldliness and unbelief. Mistakes have been made, and these have brought dishonour on the name of Christ. Looking at the overall picture of the church, the comforting fact emerges that God never left himself 'without witness' (Acts 14:17) and that there have always been some devoted men and women 'whose hearts God had touched' (1 Sam. 10:26).

1

The apostolic age

'In the fulness of time'

The historical situation in the Roman Empire, when the gospel first began to be carried outside Palestine, certainly suggests that God in his providence had been preparing the field, and that all was now ready for proclaiming to many nations the good tidings of salvation through the cross of Christ. A number of factors that greatly favoured the spread of the gospel may be noted.

The political unity of the empire and the long peace had fostered commerce, which in turn sent businessmen all over the Roman world. Excellent roads had been built along the trade routes, and these facilitated passage of goods, easier movement of people and quicker dissemination of ideas. The knowledge of the message of Jesus spread throughout the Roman provinces.

The conquests of Alexander between 334 and 326 BC spread the Greek language far and wide, thus providing a fine medium for expressing theological and philosophical ideas. The translation of the Old Testament into Greek in Alexandria in about 200 BC predisposed many Gentiles to favour monotheism. This translation is known as the Septuagint (often referred to, using Roman numerals, as the LXX).

In the cosmopolitan atmosphere of the empire, where so many races and religions mingled, many people were losing faith in the pagan cults.

The moral condition of the world was deplorable. What it was like is revealed in the first chapter of the letter to the Romans as well as in the works of non-Christian writers. Slavery had produced shocking deterioration not only of the enslaved but also of the homes of their masters.

The fatalism and despair characteristic of the East were moving westward and affecting the outlook of the Roman world.

In these depressing conditions many were looking for hope amid the gloom. They could not find it in the prevailing philosophies of Stoicism and Epicureanism. But at that time, when current religious and philosophic beliefs were not satisfying, a new message of hope entered the scene in the announcement of salvation through Jesus Christ.

Early days

The lives of Jesus and the apostle Paul provide basic information for the study of the history of the beginnings of Christianity. The best source of knowledge is the New Testament. Apostolic and post-apostolic Christian writers also provide considerable information, while secular authors such as Tacitus, Suetonius, Pliny the Younger and Flavius Josephus have references to Christian beliefs and practices.

The day of Pentecost brought significant change to the apostles. As promised by Christ, they were 'clothed with power from on high' (Luke 24:49; see Acts 2), and then went out to spread the Christian message in God's strength. Disciples who had been very timid now became almost fearless (see Acts 3 – 4). Very soon the number of men converted in Jerusalem alone numbered 5,000, exclusive of women and children (Acts 4:4).

Beginning at Jerusalem, the Christian faith soon spread far and wide. In Roman times communications by sea as well as by land were relatively easy, a factor that greatly helped the early missionaries. Jews outside Palestine, who spoke Greek and were influenced by Greek culture, began to receive the gospel. Barnabas, a friend of Paul, a native of Cyprus, is typical of this very important group. Soon the good news was being carried to Samaria, and to Caesarea, on the Mediterranean coast of Palestine, and was being proclaimed freely to the Gentiles (see Acts 8, 10, 11). This was a veritable revolution. The gospel then went to Phoenicia, to Cyprus and to the very important city of Antioch in Syria.

The conversion of the apostle Paul (about AD 35) was of surpassing importance to the church, for he became the outstanding 'apostle to the Gentiles' (Rom. 11:13). At Antioch, known as 'the Queen of the East', he and Barnabas did a most fruitful work among Jews and Gentiles. As this was a very important commercial centre, the gospel spread from there into wide areas both east and west. Among the Jewish groups encountered in every city, Paul and the other apostles found starting points for their work of empire-wide evangelization, even though the majority of the Jews rejected the gospel.

The conversion of so many Gentiles soon raised serious problems as to how far these new converts ought to be bound by the laws and ceremonies of Jewish belief and traditions. Those known as 'Judaizers' wanted the male Gentiles to be circumcised (to become Jews first); thereafter they might become Christians, but Christians with a strong Jewish flavour. Fortunately for the Christian church, Paul set his face resolutely against these tendencies (Gal. 2:7–16; 3:1–11). The whole problem was debated and resolved at the Council of Jerusalem in AD 49. There Paul gained a significant victory over those opposing him (see Acts 15:1–19). In spite of this, however, the question vexed the church for a long time. The Judaizers continued to attack Paul's position to the end of his life.

Tracing Paul's missionary journeys on a map, and following the account in the book of Acts, helps our understanding of the early spread of Christianity. He proclaimed the gospel in Antioch, Cyprus, Pamphylia, central Asia Minor, Cilicia and Syria. Then he pushed on to Troas and across to Europe. Arrival in Thessalonica (modern Thessalonika) and Philippi was significant because he was at the crossroads of Roman highways that opened the way into northern Europe (see Acts 16 – 18).

After long years of incessant missionary labours, Paul was arrested at the temple in Jerusalem and conveyed to Caesarea for his own security (see Acts 21:27–40, 23–27). For two whole years, he was unjustly kept in Rome for trial and, for another two years, was kept a prisoner, though at his own expense (Acts 27 – 28). He preached his message freely to all who came to him – even to the soldiers who took their turn in standing guard over him. It was not long before many, even 'of Caesar's household' (Phil. 4:22), believed in Christ. During this period, also, Paul wrote some of his profoundest letters. He seems to have been set free in AD 61 and to have visited once more the regions such as Crete, where he had evangelized so successfully in previous years. He was again in prison when he wrote the second letter to Timothy prior to his execution about AD 64 during the persecution under Nero (AD 58–66).

All we know about Peter suggests he was no less active than Paul. His eager, impulsive heart kept him constantly engaged in the service of Christ all his days. As Paul was the apostle to the Gentiles in a special sense, so Peter was pre-eminently the apostle to the Jews. This would have led him to the great cities of the empire, where vast numbers of his countrymen were to be found. The small amount of evidence available points to Peter's being in Rome towards the end of his life and having died there as a martyr. Perhaps he died at the same time as Paul, or at least in the same year. No foundation exists for the claim that Peter was Bishop of Rome for twenty-five years – from AD 42 to 67. Had Peter been there before AD 61, Paul could not have failed to mention him in the letters he wrote from that city just prior to that date. The fact that Peter probably visited Rome as an apostle would not make him Bishop of Rome, much less pope of Rome. Apostles were not settled in one place like diocesan bishops. Indeed, at that time, and for long afterwards, there were no such bishops. It is, therefore, incorrect to speak of Rome as the 'See of Peter', or of the pope as occupying 'the chair' of Peter.

Remarkably, little reliable knowledge is available about the personal history of the various apostles. Their work has endured, but in many cases details about their lives have perished. The same applies to the founding of some very great and important churches. Thus, we have only a vague tradition that Mark founded the church at Alexandria. No historical information is available as to the foundation of the famous churches in Rome and Carthage. After the day of Pentecost, many returned to their own countries from Jerusalem, taking with them the gospel. Likewise, a little later, much was done by Christian businessmen to spread it (Acts 8:26–40).

The apostolic message

What was the message delivered by the church in those days? It is briefly summed up by Paul in 1 Corinthians 15:1–11. The early believers never forgot the fact of sin – that men and women are lost. The very name 'Jesus' reminded them of this, for it means 'Saviour'. The resurrection was to them the crowning evidence that Jesus was all that he claimed to be – the Son of God who had all power given to him. In their preaching they appealed to the testimony of many eyewitnesses who had seen Christ after his resurrection. The evidence was overwhelming. They also appealed to the miracles performed in his name by his apostles, and pointed to the wonders of his saving grace as seen in themselves and in many others. So successful were they in spreading their teaching that, eighteen years after the resurrection of Christ, his followers were accused of having 'turned the world upside down' (Acts 17:6).

Through this 'good news' that the apostles preached, the lives of men and women were transformed. As the whole narrative in the New Testament shows (Acts and the letters), the chains of vice were broken and sinners were cleansed and raised to a higher spiritual plane by the work of God. The broken-hearted were comforted, the weak were made strong, the selfish learned to love their fellows and sacrifice themselves for the cause of Christ. Superstitions were swept away and idolatry vanished (Eph. 4:24–32). Even slaves, who up to that time were treated as less than human, and who could be sold or killed at the pleasure of their owner, were now given a place in the Christian church. They were children of God, and sat down at the same Communion table as their master. The effects of all this on first-century communities was immense.

Early persecutions

Christ warned his disciples, '"A servant is not greater than his master." If they persecuted me, they will also persecute you' (John 15:20). The earliest persecutions came from the Jews, not from the Romans. At first, the civil authorities scarcely distinguished between Christians and Jews. The authorities extended the privileges that had already been granted to Jews to the Christians as well, including protection under Roman law. One of the worst of the Jewish persecutions was the one that followed on from the death of Stephen, the first Christian martyr (Acts 7:1 – 8:4). The accounts of Paul's travels given in the book of Acts shows how bitter was the Jewish opposition to the gospel.

The Roman authorities could not understand the claim that Christ was supreme and that all, even kings and emperors, must submit to him. The Christians refused to conform to many accepted customs. They would have nothing to do with idolatry, and condemned the public games, where gladiators fought in mortal combat to make sport for the spectators, and where innocent prisoners were thrown to the lions for the entertainment of vast multitudes. The Christians refused public office and certain public duties, such as the burning of incense to the gods or the pouring of libations, because such things were associated with pagan rites. The result was that they were regarded as a morose and intolerable group in the community. Matters came to a crisis when, in AD 64, the emperor Nero accused the Christians of setting fire to the city of Rome. The public feeling against them was such that they were universally reviled. Even a writer such as Tacitus, who disliked Nero intensely, wrote of Christianity as a 'most mischievous superstition'. He accused Christians of 'abominations', and declared that 'they were put to death as enemies of mankind' (*Annals* 15.44).

The cruelties perpetrated at Rome in the Neronic persecution were unspeakable, and a vast number of Christians were killed. Some were wrapped in the skins of wild beasts so that they would be more savagely attacked by dogs. Some were crucified; others were placed in barrels of pitch or smeared with pitch and set on fire, and these living torches were used by Nero to illumine his gardens as he drove about, enjoying this dreadful spectacle.

The destruction of Jerusalem

Before the Neronic persecution of the Christians had died down, terrible events in Palestine compelled the Romans to enter a life and death struggle with the Jews. For these events, the Christians had no responsibility. The struggle was precipitated by the Zealots, a Jewish nationalistic party that had resolved to deliver their land from the Romans, by violence and massacre if need be. After AD 60, the Zealots had become so powerful that no other Jewish group could counteract their fierce and desperate anti-Roman propaganda.

The people had good cause for their discontent, for Roman administration had become very corrupt, and this presented the Zealots with their opportunity. At this time, the Christians in Palestine were in an exceedingly difficult position, for they were hated equally by the Romans and by the Jews.

The day of God's wrath, so often foretold, was about to break. The conflict began when, in May AD 66, the Zealots massacred the Roman garrison in Jerusalem. In spite of some early Jewish victories, Titus surrounded the city four years later. Remembering Christ's warning (Matt. 24:15), the Christians fled to Pella beyond Jordan and were saved. The terrible siege of Jerusalem began at Easter, when the city was crowded with the pilgrims who had come to observe the Feast of the Passover, and went on till September. Never have men fought with more desperate heroism than did the Jews then. Hundreds of thousands were slain by the sword; many others died from famine and pestilence. At last the Romans took possession of the temple and ransacked all its treasures, including the most sacred vessels of the divine service. Finally, even the Holy of Holies was set on fire, and six weeks later all Jerusalem was completely subjugated (see Christ's prophecy: Luke 19:41–44; Matt. 24:2; Mark 13:2).

It was the end of an epoch. The old order had fulfilled its day and perished. The fanaticism and violence of the Zealots had been the occasion of bringing this destruction upon the beautiful, but unrepentant, city that had so often killed the prophets and stoned those who were sent to it (Luke 13:34), and had 'crucified the Lord of glory' (1 Cor. 2:8). The removal of the temple, with its priests, ritual and ceremonial, was a further indication that old things had passed away and that a better day had dawned. Christ, by his death, had opened the way to God and brought in a more spiritual worship.

7

The organization of the early church and special gifts

A careful study reveals that in the apostolic age some officers in the church were temporary and others permanent. To the first group belonged apostles, prophets and, in one sense, evangelists; to the second, the office of elder (*presbyteros*) or bishop (*episkopos*); and that of the deacon (*diakonos*). To understand certain developments in church history it is important to know something about these offices.

The most outstanding of all was the *apostle*. The word means one who is 'sent', a messenger. In the wider sense this applied to men such as Barnabas and Epaphroditus (Acts 14:4, 14; Phil. 2:25). The 'twelve apostles', however, were in a special class. The New Testament tells us of their qualifications. They were chosen directly by Christ and commissioned personally by him to spread the gospel, organize the church and work miracles. They received particular revelations and authority directly from the Lord, and were empowered by God to communicate inspired teaching to the church for all ages. Their utterances were accepted as Scriptures inspired by the Holy Spirit (1 Cor. 2:13; 7:40; 1 Thess. 2:13).

The apostles were a unique class appointed by Christ to establish his church in the world at a time when special guidance and instruction were needed. Their supernatural gifts and authority were such that they left no successors. When the last apostle died, he left behind him no one else of equal authority.

The New Testament prophets were inspired announcers of the truth, whether dealing with the present, the future or the past. There were many of them in the early days of the church, and they are classed as next to the apostles (1 Cor. 12:28; Eph. 2:20). They gradually disappeared from the scene and ceased to function after the third quarter of the second century. It is now realized that the prophetic function was of immense importance in the church in the days before the canon of the New Testament was formed, and before there was a trained ministry.

From a biblical point of view, the *evangelist* was temporary only in the sense that he preached the gospel to those outside the church and planted churches where they did not previously exist. He differed from an apostle in not possessing of necessity any supernatural powers. He travelled about, and his duties were mainly the conversion of sinners and the building up of a congregation that he left afterwards to a settled ministry. Throughout the ages, evangelists have done a great work in times of moral darkness and spiritual decline by acting as auxiliaries to the regular ministry. Philip and Timothy were typical evangelists.

When we turn to consider the permanent officers of the church in the days of the apostles, elders and deacons were appointed and their duties defined (1 Tim. 3:1–13; Titus 1:5–9; 1 Peter 5:1–4). The office of *elder* is variously described in the New Testament as bishop, pastor, teacher, preacher, minister, steward, angel (messenger). The various terms mentioned refer to the same office but each presents a different aspect of its work. Thus 'pastor' indicates their duty to 'shepherd the flock' of Christ. 'Bishop', a word used to translate the Greek *episkopos*, indicates that they were 'overseers', and Paul shows that as 'overseers' they had to 'care for the church of God' (Acts 20:17–28). That the *presbyteros* and *episkopos* (elder and bishop) were the same is demonstrated by many facts. Thus, Paul addressed his letter to the Philippians to 'the bishops and deacons'. It was a small church in a small city, yet it had a plurality of bishops. It was not uncommon in the early church to find a large number of bishops in a small area. They could not be bishops in our modern sense. Then, again, the elders (*presbyteroi*) at Ephesus are expressly called 'bishops of the flock' (*episkopoi*). Furthermore, the qualifications of elders and bishops were the same. There is scarcely any difference among scholars today in accepting that in the New Testament the same officer is called both bishop and elder.

The term 'deacon' comes from the Greek *diakonos*, meaning a *servant* or *minister*. In the various English versions of the New Testament, whenever the reference is to those who were administering the funds and property given for the poor, the word is rendered *deacon*. In this sense it refers to a definite class composed of men of high Christian character (Phil. 1:1; 1 Tim. 3:12–13). The office was very well known in the early church, and it has been generally believed that the 'seven' set apart by the apostles were the first members of this order (Acts 6:1–6). This is now doubted by certain scholars, but it is in accordance with the view of Irenaeus in the second century. The seven were appointed expressly to attend to the administration of charitable relief among the poor, so that the apostles could be freed from serving tables and give themselves constantly 'to prayer and to the ministry of the word' (Acts 6:4). This certainly expresses the reasons why deacons were given a place in the church, whatever view we may take of the seven. They were appointed as helpers in the administration and general business of the church, so that the other ranks of the ministry might dedicate themselves more fully to the higher spiritual exercises of their calling. In the course of history, the various bodies that make up the Christian church have differed considerably in their teaching regarding the position and functions of the deacon.

While the apostles lived, their authority was decisive; but even in their day councils were held, as in AD 49, at Jerusalem. Later the councils were of a regional character, but the churches in the various regions (although autonomous) kept up a correspondence with one another and maintained fraternal unity in the love of Christ. Later still, from AD 325 onwards, came the great ecumenical councils that sought to lay down laws for the church universal.

The worship of the early church was modelled upon the simple service of the synagogue rather than upon the ritualistic service of the temple, and the worshippers really came into vital touch with God. The result was a most powerful and effective church. The early Christians accomplished much. With no worldly grandeur, with little social influence, without even church buildings, they went on from strength to strength. This was in spite of the opposition of the great Roman Empire and the bitter animosity of a sinful, pagan world that hated them because the purity of the Christians' lives condemned their own lack of moral standards.

The very essence of church organization and Christian life and worship in the first two centuries was simplicity. There was an absence of that formalism and pomp that took possession of the field in later times when spiritual life declined. Christians met for worship whenever they could, often in private homes and sometimes in more public places, such as 'the hall of Tyrannus' (Acts 19:9). Their worship was spontaneous under the guidance of the Holy Spirit, and had not yet become inflexible in its form through the use of manuals of devotion. The church was vigorous. Not only the pastor but also many of those present took part in the services, for to them the priesthood of all believers was a tremendous reality.

By the end of the first century, the gospel had been carried far from its starting point in Jerusalem. No amount of persecution could stop it. Towards the East, it had reached Mesopotamia and Parthia. In the West, it had spread to Gaul and Spain. The church was growing already in the great cities of Rome, Alexandria and Carthage. In Antioch and Ephesus, as well as in Corinth, it was very strong. Christian groups were to be found scattered throughout Syria, Arabia and Illyricum. Such was the record of seventy years' work in the face of constant opposition.

2

The second century

The first seventy years of the second century constitute one of the most obscure periods in church history. The beginning of this period coincided with the death of the apostle John at Ephesus. He had returned from his exile in the lonely isle of Patmos when the persecution ceased upon the death of Emperor Domitian (AD 81–96). Through personal disappointments, Domitian had become suspicious and embittered, and had established a reign of terror throughout the empire. Near the end of his life, he turned fiercely on the Christians, especially in the East. Later ages looked back upon him as almost a second Nero.

The writings of the early church

The passing away of the apostolic band made it more difficult for the church to tread with confidence the path that led into an unknown future. Although Clement of Rome tells us that the apostles, knowing that difficulties would arise as to the oversight of the church, had made provision for the appointment of ministers (bishops, or presbyters, and deacons), there was a great change in the quality of those who led the church in this century. They were good men up to a point, and their writings compare favourably with those of the secular authors of the period; but they were obviously neither so spiritual nor so lucid as those who wrote the books of the New Testament. They did write some significant books, however, and a brief account of them can be given.

The *Epistle of Clement of Rome* is interesting as being probably the earliest of the sub-apostolic writings. It was written in AD 96 to the church at Corinth, where there had been certain unpleasant divisions. Irenaeus, writing about a century later, says that Clement was the third Bishop of Rome. There is, however, no suggestion in Clement's letter that he had authority over any church other than his own. This is striking in view of the claims for supremacy always made by the Roman Catholic Church for the Bishop of Rome. In fact, Clement himself, like Paul and Luke (in the Acts of the Apostles), always uses the terms 'bishop' and 'presbyter' as being interchangeable. He traces the offices back to apostolic times, and this fact underscores his rebuke of those at Corinth who were rebelling against those who had been chosen by the church (1 Clement 44.1–2). We cannot read Clement's lengthy letter without being deeply impressed by his earnestness, by the constant appeal to Scripture, both Old Testament and New, especially the Pauline letters, and by his deeply evangelical tone whenever he touches upon atonement for sin.

The next two sub-apostolic writers are chiefly interesting as showing the vagaries of churchmen who laid aside the divine Word given by apostles and prophets and followed their own imaginations. These are Barnabas, who wrote about AD 132, and Hermas, who wrote *The Shepherd* between AD 140 and 150. Their imaginations ran riot. They both cherished strange ideas, the former about the Mosaic law, and the latter about the forgiveness of sins after baptism.

The Teaching of the Lord through the Twelve Apostles to the Gentiles (the *Didache*) is regarded by some scholars as very early because of its primitive outlook. Others maintain that it was written somewhat later than the middle of the second century in some remote quarter of Syria or Palestine, and that this accounts for the primitive element. Early features remained largely unchanged in this backwater of the church. It is very much coloured by Jewish views, is in parts legalistic and unspiritual, and lays great stress on fasts and ascetic practices such as abstaining from bodily desires. In this, especially, it goes quite beyond what is laid down in the New Testament. Baptism, it is interesting to note, may be performed by immersion or by pouring of water on the head three times, with cold running water preferred. Both the minister and the candidate ought to fast previously. As in the case of *The Shepherd*, prophets still have a place in the church but are losing influence, and rules are laid down for a very close scrutiny of their claims, to save the church from impostors. The same tendency was noticeable everywhere, and by the end of the second century the work of prophets had virtually ceased.

Ignatius, Bishop of Antioch, who was martyred at Rome between AD 110 and 117, is one of the most remarkable and puzzling figures in church history. He wrote seven letters to various churches when on his way to Rome to be put to death. He dealt with the atonement and the incarnation (but more especially with the early heresy known as Docetism then threatening the church), with the Judaizers and with the subject of the episcopate. Docetism taught that Christ, during his life, had only an apparent body and not a real one, and that his sufferings were therefore illusory. To meet the heretics, Ignatius stressed the importance of unity and extolled obedience to the authority of the bishop as the best means of maintaining it. He wanted to have the *episkopos* in undisputed control, and, because he did not see this in any church other than his own, emphasized the virtues of monarchical episcopacy as strongly as possible. The bishop, he held, had the mind of Christ ('The Epistle to the Ephesians', *The Early Christian Writings*, p. 62). To the Trallians he wrote, 'Respect the bishop as a type of God, and the presbyters as the council of God, and the college of the apostles. Apart from these there is not even the name of a Church' ('The Epistle to the Trallians', III). This, like similar statements of his elsewhere, is almost blasphemous. He assigns a most important place to the presbytery as well as the bishop, and in this we may have a clue as to his real meaning.

We have already seen the sense in which the terms *presbyter* (elder) and *bishop* were understood in early days, and noted that these terms referred to the same person. By the time of Ignatius, in Antioch and other places in the East, one of the presbyters had been chosen to preside over the others. He had become a permanent pastor and president of the other presbyters or elders, who helped and advised him in the work of the church. This president is the man whom Ignatius calls *bishop* because he is *episkopos* (overseer). This view is borne out by the fact that each of Ignatius's seven letters is addressed to the church concerned and not to a bishop. Even in writing to Rome, he makes no mention of any bishop there.

Polycarp of Smyrna is easily the greatest saint and martyr of the second century known to us. Smyrna is the modern-day Turkish city of Izmir. Polycarp was a disciple of John the apostle, and, since he was burnt at the stake in AD 156, was some 86 years of age. He must have been about 30 years old when John died. Irenaeus, who was his pupil, related that Polycarp often referred to the apostles, and especially to John. He was a man of simple and beautiful faith, and of a loving heart. In AD 155 Polycarp visited Rome to discuss the vexed question of the date of Easter. While there, he met Bishop Anicetus of Rome on equal terms, and although they failed to agree on the matter under discussion, they remained excellent friends. Polycarp was invited to take some of the most solemn services. According to Irenaeus, his ministry there was greatly blessed. It is obvious that the Bishop of Rome did not then claim any authority over other churches.

Polycarp was burnt at Smyrna in the reign of the emperor Antoninus Pius. A letter from the church of Smyrna to the church of Philomelium dwells upon his kindness to his captors and his calm bearing at the stake. Most striking of all is his famous reply to the proconsul who offered to save his life if he would curse Christ. 'Eighty and six years have I served Him, and He hath done me no wrong; how then can I blaspheme my King who saved me?' (quoted in Eusebius, *Ecclesiastical History*, iv, ch. 15).

Correspondence between Pliny the Younger and the emperor Trajan furnishes valuable information as to the position of the church in the early years of the second century. When Pliny became governor of Bithynia (south of the Black Sea) in AD 111, he found that Christianity had progressed so much that the pagan temples were almost deserted. He was deeply concerned at the rapid spread of this 'depraved and extravagant superstition', and began taking steps to stop its advance. He seemed surprised, however, at the character of the Christians. He found that on an appointed day they had been accustomed to meet before daybreak, and to recite a hymn by turns to Christ, as to a god, and to bind themselves by an oath, not for the commission of any crime but to abstain from theft, robbery, adultery and breach of faith, and not to deny a deposit when it was claimed.

Although this moral standard is basic teaching with Christians nowadays, it must have seemed to him, in that hard Roman world, an almost incredibly high plane of morality. Pliny consulted the emperor as to how he should deal with these people. His plan had been to ask in the first place if they were Christians. If they answered affirmatively, he repeated the question two or three times, threatening them with death.

Trajan's reply approved of the line taken by the governor. He ordered that no attention be paid to anonymous accusations, which lent themselves to abuse. Christians were not to be sought out for punishment. If they were openly informed against and the charge proved, they must be punished; but if they recanted and worshipped the pagan gods, they were to be pardoned. Trajan's successor, Hadrian, took the same approach, reinforcing the position that the practice of Christianity was unauthorized, though no anonymous accusations were to be accepted by the authorities.

At first sight, there seems to be little consolation for the Christians in the directions of Trajan and Hadrian. But in reality they brought considerable alleviation of the Christians' position, for it very much lessened the number of charges levelled against them.

The work of the early *Apologists* merits attention. The constant and widespread slanders against the Christians, and the misunderstanding of their position by the rulers, compelled them to write treatises, known as 'Apologies', defending their religion. The two earliest Apologists seem to have been Quadratus and Aristides of Athens in the first half of the second century. We know of their work only from the pages of Eusebius, and even then the reference is very brief.

The greatest of the early Apologists was Justin Martyr, a most earnest Christian and a true lover of learning. He was born at Shechem in Palestine around AD 100, and died as a martyr at Rome in AD 163 in the reign of Marcus Aurelius. His *First Apology* was addressed to the emperor Antoninus Pius, the Senate and the whole Roman people. The *Second Apology* is short and is to the Senate only. His lengthiest work is the *Dialogue with Trypho the Jew*, which aims at explaining the Christian faith to the Jews.

Justin's works reveal throughout a love of culture, a spirit of reverence and an earnest desire to spread the knowledge of the faith. Born a pagan who became a keen student of philosophy, he went from place to place earnestly seeking truth, visiting Rome, Athens, Alexandria and other important cities in his search. One day, walking near the shore at Ephesus, he met an old man 'of meek and venerable manners' who pointed him to the Scriptures and Jesus Christ. The flame of a divine love took possession of Justin, and he found the true philosophy.

In the *First Apology* he refutes in a masterly fashion the usual charges against the Christians – their supposed atheism, their alleged disloyalty, their licentiousness in secret meetings, their cannibalism. His attitude to the thought-systems of his day is of great interest. For him, philosophy, especially Platonism, was good as far as it went. He insists, however, that Christians are saved by the power of Jesus and not by knowledge and philosophy, excellent though these are. It is heartwarming to read his expositions of the Scriptures to show that 'Christ was delivered up for our transgressions' (see *First Apology*, chs 50–52; *Dialogue with Trypho*, ch. 95).

His account of the Christian weekly worship is worth attention:

On the day called Sunday, all who live in cities or in the country gather together to one place, and the memoirs of the apostles [Gospels] or the writings of the prophets are read, as long as time permits; then, when the reader has ceased, the president verbally instructs, and exhorts to the imitation of these good things. Then, we all rise together and pray, and when our

prayer is ended, bread and wine and water are brought, and the president in like manner offers prayers and thanksgivings, according to his ability, and the people assent, saying Amen; and there is a distribution to each, and a participation of that over which thanks have been given.
(*First Apology*, ch. 67)

The second-century service of worship was marked by simplicity. It consisted of the reading of the holy Scriptures, the address by the president and his prayers 'according to his ability', which indicates that he was one of the brethren chosen to preside and not a member of a priestly caste. In AD 163, or soon after, Justin and several companions were sentenced to death at Rome by the bullying prefect Junius Rusticus. They were asked in a severe tone, 'Do you suppose that you will rise again, and live for ever?' Justin's noble reply was, 'I do not suppose it. I know it.'

Under Marcus Aurelius persecution raged for years. One of the worst outbreaks was in AD 177 at Lyons and Vienne, in Gaul. A large number of Greeks had come from Asia Minor to the Rhône Valley, where they had established a strong church. It was ministered to by men who came from their old homeland. Eusebius presents us with a terrible picture of the sufferings of the faithful in this church. The mobs, possessed of a satanic spirit, committed shocking atrocities, such as the murder of Bishop Pothinus, aged 90. The heroic witness of Blandina, a martyred slave girl, who was fragile in body and timid in spirit, can never be forgotten. Day after day, she was subjected to every kind of torture but her tormentors could not compel her to deny her faith. She seemed clearly sustained by God, and even that diabolical crowd said, 'Never woman in our time suffered so much.' In the end she was butchered by an official. The Christians saw in her the crucified Lord Jesus, and acknowledged 'that all who suffer for the glory of Christ have ever fellowship with the living God' (Eusebius, *Ecclesiastical History*, V.1.42).

Many heresies arose and flourished during the second century. No history of this period would be complete without some consideration of them.

The Nazarenes

This name was at first given derisively to the whole church. Later it was applied to the sect that carried on the tradition of the early Judaizers, who caused Paul so much trouble. Before the destruction of Jerusalem in AD 70, as mentioned above, the Jewish Christians fled across Jordan and found refuge at Pella. Their descendants clung tenaciously to their Jewish customs for a long time. They scrupulously kept the law of Moses, and carefully observed circumcision and the rabbinical rules as to the Jewish Sabbath. Their influence was never powerful, but they lingered on till at least the end of the fourth century.

The Ebionites

These resembled the Nazarenes in a number of ways but were much more extreme and desired to impose the Jewish law on every Christian. They rejected all the writings of Paul, and of the four Gospels recognized only Matthew's. From even this Gospel they cut out all references to the Saviour's miraculous conception and pre-existence. Like the Gnostics (see below), they believed that it was only at his baptism that Jesus became divine when the Spirit descended on him. The Spirit, they said, left him before his death, and so it was just an ordinary man who suffered on the cross. They believed he would come again in glory as the Son of Man from heaven.

The Gnostics

This was a heresy far more subtle and dangerous than any that had appeared so far. It became so widespread that by the beginning of the third century most of the more intellectual Christian congregations throughout the Roman Empire were, to some degree or other, infected by it. It took many forms and in the short space available it is exceedingly difficult to do more than indicate some of its main features.

Gnostics gave a version of Christ's work that was devoid of any real Christian content, and proceeded to develop a system that combined their very nebulous Christian ideas with elements taken freely from the mythologies of Greece, Egypt, Persia and India, and from the philosophies and theosophies of these lands. The word 'Gnostic' comes from the Greek word *gnōsis*, 'knowledge'. This knowledge, they claimed, was esoteric or secret, and could be possessed only by that section of men who are 'pneumatic', spiritual – the superior people. There was another class made up of the 'psychic', those who cannot get beyond faith. The prophets and other good Jews belonged to this class that was inferior to those having *gnōsis*. The great mass of the human race was 'hylic' (subject to matter) and so were in hopeless bondage to Satan and their own lusts.

The Gnostics taught that as matter was utterly and irretrievably evil, salvation consisted in overcoming and eliminating it. This could never be done except by those who had *gnōsis* and practised asceticism, and this knowledge could come only to the 'pneumatic' class. To resist matter and overcome it, they abstained from material enjoyments. They saw in God's best gifts sources of danger, and rejected the most innocent enjoyments for fear of contamination with what was material. On this ground, their morals were at first exceedingly strict but, as so often happens when men live unnatural lives in contravention of the deepest cravings of their nature, they frequently degenerated into shocking licentiousness.

The two most brilliant Gnostic teachers were Valentinus and Basilides, both connected with Alexandria in the second century, though Valentinus was in Rome by about AD 140. Another leading figure was Marcion of Sinope, who died at Rome in AD 170. He was an earnest man and approximated to the orthodox Christian position in some respects. He rejected, however, the Old Testament and taught that the God of the Old Testament was not the Father of the Lord Jesus Christ. He was excommunicated, but his purity of life and sincerity gathered around him many followers.

According to the Gnostics, the Supreme Being is self-existent, infinitely remote and unknowable. He is the First Principle but without attributes, and is beyond time and change. The problem for them was how this ineffable Being, whom they called Bythos, could create matter that they regarded as evil, or have anything to do with it. They got over the difficulty by postulating a series of thirty emanations from Bythos, each emanation originating the next in order. When one of these was sufficiently distant on the borderland of light and darkness, he created the world and did it badly. This was the Demiurge, or God of the Old Testament who was worshipped by the Jews.

All the Gnostic systems were wildly speculative and exceedingly complex, and do not lend themselves to treatment in a short work such as this. At least one Gnostic school of thought that claimed to be Christian, yet turned the Scriptures upside down, taught that Pharaoh and Ahab were saints, while Moses and Elijah were sinners, and even regarded the God of the Old Testament as very evil.

Some Gnostics wrote commentaries on the Bible, and this stimulated Christian scholars to study the criticism of the Scriptures more carefully and led to the writing of able treatises in defence of the faith. On the other hand, Gnosticism greatly fostered asceticism, which was an importation from the East, and so the way was paved for the rise of monasticism in the church.

Montanism

At the time when Montanism arose, things were not well with the church. Gnosticism was offering a serious challenge and undermining the foundations of Christianity. The apostles were all dead, and the remarkable gifts of the Holy Spirit that characterized the early church were dying out. Many false prophets had arisen, and prophecy itself was falling under suspicion. The church was settling down to an easy formalism. The pulsating spiritual life of an earlier day was lacking, and rigidity, if not frigidity, was becoming the order of the day. Montanism arose as a strong reaction against all this, and particularly against Gnosticism. There was an urgent need for its witness to the fact of the dependence of the church on the Holy Spirit, but unfortunately Montanism too, like the Gnosticism it criticized, fell into the temptation of placing human speculation above divine revelation.

This striking movement was started by Montanus, a native of Ardabau in Mysia. He claimed to have received a special revelation from the Holy Spirit, and started a wild and frenzied revival campaign. He was joined by two rich ladies, Priscilla and Maximilla, who had deserted their husbands. In some aspects of their teaching the Montanists were similar to some of the followers of Edward Irving in Britain in the nineteenth century. They also professed to have authority to impose a more rigid discipline on the church, forbade second marriages and stressed the superiority of celibacy to the married state. In their pride they thought they surpassed even Christ in their teaching. The accession of Tertullian of Carthage to their ranks was a great triumph for them. Nevertheless, the sect disappeared from Africa by AD 370, and from other places by the beginning of the sixth century.

The Montanists were severe in their church discipline, dividing sins into remissible and irremissible – sins that could be forgiven and those that could not be forgiven in this world. This parallels the distinction made later by the Roman Catholic Church between venial and mortal sins, although the list of sins was not quite the same. The extremism of Montanism produced some violent reactions. Because of the vivid descriptions they gave of a millennial epoch of sensuous enjoyment, the doctrine of Christ's second coming, with which this was identified, was laid aside by the church as a whole. Once preaching was discredited, Christ came to be regarded as far away, and the clergy were seen as having his affairs in their hands, and doing his work on earth through the sacraments. This led to the exaltation of the ministers of the church. Especially after the time of Cyprian, they were regarded as priests offering again the sacrifice of Christ at the altar.

The Montanists had also brought impassioned preaching into disrepute, together with all forms of emotionalism in religion. Preaching ceased to play such a prominent part in the life of the church. A direct result of this was that the role of the one priest was magnified because he ministered the awe-inspiring mysteries at the altar, and it was supposed that only through him could men do business with God. Outside the church where he ministered, there was no salvation. It was a sad departure from the faith of the apostolic church, even though the priests vociferously claimed to be in the apostolic succession.

3

The early Catholic fathers
(AD 180–250)

Difficulties facing the early church

By the last quarter of the second century, the position of the church had sadly been undermined, on the one hand, by the cultured and heretical Gnostics, with their fanciful speculations, and by the Montanists, on the other, with their dislike of learning and fanatical extremism that largely nullified what was good in them. Spiritually, the church had become weak. It was just at this time that the Catholic fathers began their notable work. They were a remarkable group of brilliant and devoted men – Irenaeus, Tertullian, Cyprian, Clement of Alexandria and Origen. Three great difficulties confronted them: the New Testament canon, the 'rule of faith' and apostolic succession. They tackled them with considerable determination, but some of their solutions raised grave problems that had to be faced in future centuries or later ages.

The New Testament canon

The list of books to be accepted into the canon of the New Testament was not fixed. The Gnostics put forward gospels and letters of their own and demanded their acceptance. Many of these were fantastic and mischievous, and the problem was how to find a standard of truth that would be accepted by all. Irenaeus stressed that the real test was whether the books were by the apostles, or at least by men closely connected with them. Those that were apostolic, in this sense, were called 'Scriptures' by Irenaeus. A little later, Tertullian wrote of the 'New Testament', which he placed on a level with the Old as regards divine inspiration. God, by his Spirit, led his people to recognize the books that were inspired, while many of the apocryphal books, by their contents, excluded themselves.

The rule of faith

It was difficult to argue with the Gnostics, because they used spurious gospels and letters, and, with their allegorical method of interpretation, could make even the genuine Scriptures appear to bear any meaning they wished. To protect the church from this sort of thing, candidates for baptism from an early period were asked to accept a certain simple creed, or 'rule of faith'. Thus grew up what we now call the Apostles' Creed. Irenaeus appealed to the doctrinal beliefs of the various churches that dated back to the days of the apostles to find a true creedal basis. He appealed to the 'tradition' of these churches to establish the true doctrine (*Against Heresies*, III, ch. 4). This served its purpose then, but afterwards became a serious stumbling block as people got further away from apostolic times, and traditions became vague and unreliable.

Apostolic succession

Irenaeus also appealed to the idea of an apostolic succession of office-bearers in the church. These were viewed as guarding the sacred deposit of the faith that had been given through the apostles, and the tradition that reached back to the days of the apostles. Lists were made of the succession of bishops in the larger churches. It is noticeable, however, that Irenaeus, like the early church, makes no distinction between 'bishops' and 'presbyters'. For example, he refers sometimes to Polycarp as 'bishop', sometimes as 'presbyter'. He deals similarly with the whole list of bishops at Rome. The presbyter (or elder) was by now, however, imperceptibly passing into a bishop in more or less the modern sense. When we come to Tertullian and Clement in the third century, the transition has been made. The church has come to find its unity in the episcopate, and now appeals to the supposed 'tradition' that has come down through the bishops. This subsequently led to the prominence given by the Roman

Catholic Church to tradition, which resulted in their placing it side by side with the holy Scriptures.

Irenaeus of Gaul

Irenaeus, the first of the great fathers, or teachers, of the period AD 180–250, was born in the province of Asia about AD 130. He was a disciple of Polycarp of Smyrna, who was, in turn, a disciple of John the apostle. Thus, at the end of the second century, he was only at one remove from those who knew directly one or more of the apostles. He was, therefore, in a unique position to appeal to tradition in his arguments with the Gnostics, for the lives of John, Polycarp and his own covered among them about 200 years. The tradition, therefore, was likely at this stage to be reliable. Not so later tradition, the authenticity of which became very dubious.

Irenaeus was at Lyons in Gaul in AD 177. After the brutal murder by the mob of the aged Pothinus in that year, Irenaeus was called to succeed him as bishop. His greatest service to the church of God was through his extensive writings, and especially his work *Against Heresies* in five books. The importance of this work in saving the church from the insidious and pernicious doctrines of the Gnostics cannot be exaggerated.

Tertullian of Carthage

There is nothing to show when the gospel was first carried to North Africa. All at once, in AD 180, there appears on the page of history a vigorous church, with its members suffering martyrdom fearlessly in the remote communities of Madaura and Scilla. Tertullian, Cyprian and Augustine were all members of this church, and left an indelible impression on the ages that came after them. Here the first Latin Christian literature was developed, for Carthage, a large and beautiful city, was pre-eminently a centre of Latin culture.

It was in Carthage that Tertullian was born between AD 155 and 160. His parents were pagans, and he lived the usual life of cultured pagans in that city of corrupt theatres and brutal gladiatorial contests. He was trained as a lawyer. This naturally had a great effect upon his manner of expressing theological concepts, and later influenced deeply the forms of thought and the theological terms of the church as a whole. He was the first to use the term 'Trinity' in writing of the Godhead.

The church at Carthage and the church at Alexandria represented opposite tendencies. The one distrusted philosophy and emphasized Christian dogma; the other loved philosophy and liked to speculate and express theological ideas in philosophical terms.

Tertullian demonstrated great energy, dash and daring. His brilliant forensic gifts were used to the utmost in defence of Christianity. His courage was unlimited, and he attacked with vigour and invective the highest authorities in the empire. His writings were voluminous, and thirty treatises besides other works have come down to us. His *Apology*, written in AD 197, in the reign of Septimius Severus, is one of the ablest ever written. As a great lawyer, he brings out with crushing effect points never dealt with by other Christian Apologists. In his *De Idolatria* he discusses questions such as 'What should a Christian do when invited by a pagan neighbour to a wedding, or other social event, where some pagan rite may be performed?' He maintains that a Christian could not enter the army or hold public office because he would be called on to participate in pagan rites, such as pouring out libations.

A book that had very far-reaching and mischievous effects was his *De Praescriptione*. It was aimed at the Gnostics and other heretics. Tertullian fell back on a practice of the law courts – to raise a 'prescription' or preliminary objection that cut off the opponent at the beginning. Tertullian cuts off the heretics by insisting that the churches founded by the apostles have the deposit of truth. They, and they alone, have the correct tradition. Hence, the church should not admit heretics to discussions on the Scriptures. The door is thus slammed in their faces.

This was dangerous doctrine, and led to much ecclesiastical despotism and intolerance in later ages. He falsely assumed that tradition must be in accordance with, and therefore equal with, Scripture, and developed the views of Irenaeus on this subject. In time, there evolved from this the full Roman Catholic doctrine of church authority and tradition. Tertullian, like Irenaeus, held to the teaching of Paul in Romans 5 that in our first head, Adam, all men sinned and fell, and that in Christ, the second Adam, believers are redeemed from all evil. The point he dwelt upon most, however, was the inherited sinfulness of the human race. His thoughts on this theme were very suggestive, and prepared the way for Augustine's profound treatment of the subjects of sin and grace. Tertullian, however, fell far short of Augustine in this field, for while he regarded grace as opposed to nature, he did not regard it as opposed to merits. So he opened the way for a doctrine of salvation by 'good works', at least in part.

He favoured very rigid penance in the church, was very ascetic in his outlook, and utterly condemned second marriages. Because of the prevailing immorality, he condemned in the strongest terms attendance at the theatre and at public amusements. For a man with his stern, gloomy, passionate nature, Montanism was congenial, and it is not strange that in his later years he joined this sect. In spite of this, his great gifts continued to secure for him the respect of the church generally. He had, however, grave faults, and could be unfair, fanatical and vindictive.

Cyprian of Carthage (c.AD 200–58)

Cyprian is important not only for his strong emphasis on tradition, in which he resembled Tertullian, but because he brought forward far-reaching claims for the episcopate, and also introduced sacerdotal conceptions that brought about revolutionary changes in the worship of the church. He was born at Carthage about AD 200 of cultured, noble and wealthy parents. When 46 years of age, an aged presbyter whom he had befriended won him for Christ, and directed him to the study of the Bible. He then sold his beautiful estate in literal obedience to the words of Christ, and gave the money to the poor. He was baptized, and two years later became a presbyter. Very soon afterwards he was elected Bishop of Carthage by popular acclamation. He did not want to take so high a post but the people insisted, and he felt it was a revelation of the divine will. This election by the people of such a recent convert aroused bitter feelings among presbyters who were passed over, and this led to schism.

In the year AD 250, under the emperor Decius, a persecution began that was more severe than any that had preceded it, and decimated the church. It sifted out the unfaithful, nominal Christians, who were now numerous, and left the loyal and robust members to carry on a witness to the gospel. Cyprian had to withdraw from Carthage but returned in AD 251. He is important in church history for the following reasons.

1. *His strenuous insistence on the high place of the episcopate.* This originated in the considerable opposition from schismatics that he had to face. In Carthage opponents led by Novatus set up a rival bishop. This party, supported by the 'confessors' (as those honoured by the church for enduring persecution were called), wanted a relaxation in ecclesiastical discipline. They wished to receive back into church membership, without any proof of repentance, those who had denied Christ in the day of trial, and had made shipwreck of their faith. The party of Novatian (a rival bishop at Rome) stood for extreme severity in discipline, and insisted that no one who had denied the faith, or been guilty of a 'deadly' sin, should ever be restored again to church membership. Cyprian encountered very strong opposition from both sides. To meet it, he insisted on the unity of the church, and denounced the sin of not rendering obedience to the bishop who had, he said, his authority directly from God. He made great claims for the absolute supremacy of the bishop as a God-appointed ruler of the church. In succeeding ages this claim was accepted far and wide, and as a result church government became almost completely autocratic.

2. *His concept of the clergy as sacrificing priests.* He was the first to give this idea concrete shape in the Christian church. The Lord's Supper he regarded as the offering up on the altar of the very body and blood of Christ. The change was serious and led in time to the doctrine of transubstantiation and the abuses of the supposed sacrifice of the Mass. Until Cyprian's time, the church continually

boasted, in its dealing with pagans, that it had neither altar nor sacrifice.

3. *His strong belief in the autonomy of each bishop in his own church.* Bishop Stephen of Rome, finding that he could not bring all the churches to agree with him as to the baptism of heretics, sent forth a despotic decree demanding submission from the other churches, especially those at Carthage and in Asia, which opposed him. Cyprian rose in his strength and did battle against the usurpation of Rome, as Polycarp and Irenaeus had done before him.

In 258, in the Valerian persecution, Cyprian was beheaded 40 miles from Carthage. The great multitude who looked on, and included many pagans, were deeply moved at the faith and courage he displayed.

The influence of the Alexandrian Church

The situation in Alexandria was totally different from that in Carthage. Founded by Alexander the Great in 332 BC, Alexandria became one of the greatest cities in the world, with a population of possibly 2.5 million people. There was no more cosmopolitan city anywhere. Its commerce was vast, for it did business with all the nations from India to the Atlantic. Its culture was Greek, and second only to that of Athens. Its illustrious men were many. In about 200 BC, in this city, the Septuagint, or Greek version of the Old Testament, which prepared the way for the gospel among Greek-speaking people, had been completed. The monotheism of the large Jewish population, Platonism, Neoplatonism and Gnosticism all affected the life of thinking men in Alexandria.

In the second and third centuries AD the church in this great city produced a series of outstanding leaders, men such as Pantaenus, Clement and Origen. The Catechetical School, over which these Christian teachers presided in turn, came to be very highly regarded, not only for its theology but also for its philosophy and science. It had been founded because they realized that in these spheres the church must face up to the world of learning around them. At first, it was intended only for catechumens, but it soon established courses in philosophy, grammar, literature, mathematics and science. Crowds of students flocked to this centre of learning. They came not only from among the Christians but from among those pagans who were earnestly seeking the truth. Pantaenus, Clement and Origen were men of noble Christian character. Surrounded by a restless intellectual community, and living in a very cosmopolitan city notorious for its turbulence, they all suffered much for the faith and were ready to die for it if need be, so great was their love for Christ.

Clement (c.AD 150–215)

Clement became head of the school about AD 190. Unlike Tertullian, he considered that pagan philosophy could not be ignored by the Christian church. He maintained that it had elements of great value, but held at the same time that all true learning was given by God to lead men at last to the holy Scriptures, where we have the final revelation of himself. Clement aimed at gathering in the treasures of wisdom and knowledge from all sources and using them for Christ. He was driven from Alexandria in AD 202 in the fierce persecution under Septimius Severus. He died in AD 220 in Caesarea. His extensive works included *Hortatory Address to the Greeks*, *The Instructor* and a large collection of *Miscellanies*.

Origen (AD 185–254)

Origen was one of the most brilliant teachers and writers ever known in the Christian church. The son of a martyr, and reared in a fine spiritual atmosphere, he became head of the Catechetical School at the age of 18, and raised it to its highest fame in spite of persecution. He loved the Scriptures and showed remarkable ability in interpreting them. He went to considerable extremes in his asceticism – fasting, refusing wine and all delicate food, and sleeping on the bare floor. He toiled incessantly and, according to Jerome, 'produced more books than any other man could read in a lifetime'. Some estimated his works at 6,000, including letters and articles. His best-known books are the *Hexapla*, his voluminous *Commentaries*, *First*

Principles (the first work on systematic theology) and *Against Celsus*, a brilliant apologetic treatise.

While believing strongly in the divine inspiration of the Scriptures, he fell into the snare of allegorical interpretation so typical of Alexandria. He stressed the deity of Christ and the doctrine of the Trinity as against various heretical schools, which resembled somewhat modern Unitarians. He saw that the doctrinal questions at issue were of vast importance, especially that which concerned the true divinity of our Lord. The early church had regarded Christ as unquestionably Lord and God. He was adored with a simple reverence, and believers did not speculate as to the mode of his divine being or the relationship between his deity and humanity. From the end of the second century, however, new theories began to present themselves, the chief of which was Monarchianism. This word meant for the Greek theologians that there was only one person in the Godhead. The names Father, Son and Holy Spirit could be applied indiscriminately to this one person. Two views prevailed as regards the nature of Christ.

Some believed that a divine power descended on the man Jesus and enabled him to do the works of God. This was *dynamic Monarchianism*, from the Greek word *dynamis*, 'power'. This view was maintained by Theodotus, Artemon and Paul of Samosata, as well as by the Alogi, who denied the Logos teaching of John.

The other belief was that all the fulness of God dwelt in Christ, and that this was a *mode* of God's manifestation. Hence the system was called *modalistic Monarchianism*. Sometimes God manifested himself as the Father, sometimes as the Son and at other times as the Holy Spirit, but it was always the same divine person, although differently manifested. Praxeas, Noetus, Beryllus and Sabellius took this view. The last mentioned was the best known and his name is often given to Monarchianism in general, although there were minor differences between him and the other exponents of the heresy. The Monarchian theory was severely criticized because it implied that the eternal Father had suffered on the cross. On this account, its supporters were called *Patripassians*. The teaching of Scripture, accepted by the church catholic, was that Christ was truly God and that at the same time he had a personality distinct from the Father and the Holy Spirit, and yet was one with them. Origen rendered invaluable service in his powerful and clear defence of this great article of the faith. In particular his exposition of the doctrine of the Son's eternal generation paved the way in AD 325 for the decision of the Council of Nicea as to Christ's deity, as well as for later pronouncements in the ecumenical councils of the fourth century.

In the field of speculation Origen's imagination ran riot. He claimed that he was loyal to the rule of faith adopted by the church, while exercising ample liberty of expression on matters not covered by the accepted creed. His bold, pioneering spirit caused him to be regarded as a heretic in many quarters. His theory about the successive incarnations of the human soul illustrates how freely he could speculate on what he thought was an open question. It is, he said, of the very nature of God to be ever creating. There must have been a series of created worlds, and souls must have been created from the beginning. The unequal state of men, angels and devils now must be due to their experiences in the various worlds they have been in, for all at first must have been equal because God is just. Souls are always rising or falling. They go up or down as a reward or punishment for their actions in each successive state of existence. Even the devil himself can yet ascend to higher worlds. Punishment, he believed, is purely remedial, and finally, in the long cycle of the ages, every soul must be gathered home to the bosom of the divine Father. Those who taught in the nineteenth century the doctrine of the 'larger hope' were following, with faltering steps, the trail blazed by Origen.

Bishop Demetrius of Alexandria became very jealous of his brilliant subordinate and had him excommunicated and exiled after he had been, for twenty-eight years, the distinguished head of the Catechetical School. At Caesarea in Palestine, Origen established another centre of learning and, for twenty years more, continued to influence all classes in society. He was thrown into prison at Tyre during the Decian persecution and was broken down by his terrible suffering there, dying soon after his release in AD 254.

4

Trial and triumph

Fresh persecutions

In the reigns of Alexander Severus (AD 222–35) and Philip the
Arabian (AD 244–9), the church was treated by the civil power in a
friendly way. It was a period of syncretism, when men were trying
to find a common faith by extracting the best from all religions.
Origen kept up a friendly correspondence with Philip, and for thirty-
eight years the church was left in peace. As a result, it greatly
increased in numbers and prestige. But then came the terrible
persecutions under Decius and Valerian that continued, with some
intervals of relaxation, from AD 250 to 260.

This period was a time of great calamity for the empire. The
barbarians were pressing in on all sides. The invasions by the Goths
were especially serious. Decius (AD 249–51) believed that safety lay
only in reviving the ancient virtues of the Roman people, and
decided therefore that Christianity must be rooted out. In the reign
of Valerian (AD 254–60) the political situation became still more
perilous. The emperor was persuaded to renew the persecution,
which, once begun, was systematic and terrible. Some of the outstanding victims were Cyprian of Carthage, and two bishops of
Rome, Stephen and Sixtus II.

After the Valerian persecution, the church was allowed to go un-
molested for more than forty years. Before the end of the century,
there were Christians in every sphere of life, and for eighteen years
Diocletian, who succeeded to the throne in the East in AD 284,
refrained from any persecution because it might bring down the
empire. At last, however, he was persuaded by Galerius, his relentless
colleague in the East, to begin the most ruthless of all attempts to

stamp out the church. It began in AD 303 with an edict to destroy Christian places of worship and all the sacred books of the Christians. When the prefect and his men entered the large and beautiful church at Nicomedia, the capital of the Eastern part of the empire, they were amazed to find no image of the deity. They burnt the holy Scriptures, pillaged what they wanted and razed the building to the ground.

In the region administered under Diocletian by Galerius, the persecution was especially brutal, with scourging and tortures before death. The Western emperor, Maximian, also carried out the edicts with full force in Italy and Africa. Constantius, however, the 'Caesar' under Maximian of Gaul, Britain and Spain, refused to inflict death on anyone for his religion, maintaining that 'the temple of God', the human body, must not be so maltreated. He continued this policy even when he and Galerius succeeded Maximian and Diocletian as emperors in AD 305.

Dramatic change under Constantine

In AD 306 Constantius died and was succeeded by his son Constantine, who marched victoriously against several rival claimants to the throne. Before the battle of the Milvian Bridge, 27 October 312, when Constantine defeated Maxentius, he passed through a remarkable spiritual experience. The story goes that he claimed he saw in the sky a flaming cross with the inscription in Greek 'By this sign conquer.' Whether this was an optical illusion due to his excitement at the time, it is hard to say. The whole incident may just be pious legend. What is certain is that something affected him profoundly. While his motives were sometimes mixed, and he retained some old superstitions, he now showed that he fervently believed in the God of the Christians.

This conversion of the emperor was an event of surpassing importance to the church, for not only was it productive of great good, but it led also to certain evils. Only a few years earlier such an occurrence would have been regarded as quite impossible. In 312 Constantine became joint emperor with Licinius. A few months later, in March 313, they issued from Milan their epoch-making decree giving full toleration to the Christian faith, and restoring to the church all places of worship that had been confiscated, and making good all losses. This was indeed a historic day. A notable fact about this proclamation is that it was based upon the rights of the individual conscience, and granted unconditional religious liberty to all in the West, a truly remarkable decision in such an age. Eleven years later Constantine, having quarrelled with Licinius, defeated him in battle at Adrianople and became master of the whole empire, East and West. Christianity now enjoyed complete freedom throughout the Roman world. With his growing power, Constantine became vainer and more self-complacent. He liked to array himself in splendid robes. It is not surprising, therefore, to find him presenting the Bishop of Jerusalem with a set that vied in splendour with the best vestments of the pagan high priests. This is the first instance of the use of vestments in the Christian church.

The emperor maintained close friendship with the bishops and did his best to settle the various controversies that arose in the church at that time. This led to an intervention by the state in church affairs, and created a precedent that proved a very serious problem in later ages. There were, however, solid advantages as well. They are seen, for example, in the greatly improved status of women, in the mitigation of the horrors of slavery and in the keeping of the Lord's Day (Sunday) for rest and worship. At the same time, the favours of the state, welcome though they were, tended to produce an arrogant spirit in the clergy.

Constantine's successors were by no means equal to himself in either character or ability. His sons had troubled reigns and, for the most part, favoured Arianism. His grandson, Julian the Apostate (361–3), because of the evil treatment meted out to him by the sons of Constantine and the massacre of his relatives by them, renounced Christianity, and did his best to restore a reformed kind of paganism. Polytheism was, however, rotten to the core, and the attempts to restore it proved a fiasco.

At the beginning of this fourth century, Christianity, as already noted, had suffered under Diocletian the greatest of all persecutions, but by the end of the century paganism had virtually disappeared in the Roman Empire. Jerome could declare in his time that every pagan altar in Rome was forsaken and every temple was desolate. Yet, in the Christian church itself there were at work tendencies towards priestcraft, sacramentalism and monasticism that were ominous for the future.

5

Great councils, great men, great events (AD 325–500)

Bitter theological controversy marked the following period in the life of the church. The time had come for it to clarify its attitude to certain great doctrinal questions. The points at issue were thoroughly debated in gatherings attended by the majority of church leaders, and the decisions of the first four ecumenical councils, as they are called, were embodied in creeds that are still accepted, at least nominally, by the Christian churches. It was a peculiarly turbulent age in the theological sphere. In the fifth century, in particular, it was not uncommon for opposing parties to seek victory by force, and shameful fights ensued. Many unworthy things were said and done. Yet, out of all the strife, declarations of faith emerged that were priceless for succeeding generations.

The Arian controversy

This controversy split the church for a time and had repercussions that were felt for about three centuries. Arius, who originated the dispute, was a presbyter in Alexandria. About the year 318, he began to propagate views as to the divinity of Christ that were contrary to the accepted doctrine of the church. He taught that Christ 'had come into being out of nonexistence', that 'once He was not' and that 'He was created and made' (Sozomen, *Ecclesiastical History*, I, ch. 15). On this view, the Son was inferior to the Father in nature and dignity, although the first and noblest of all created beings. Alexander, the Bishop of Alexandria, took action in 320 and declared that he believed the Son to be 'consubstantial and coeternal with the Father'.

Arius was not straightforward in his controversial methods, and cleverly tried to cloud the issues. He was deposed in 321, but, being an able and charming man, was befriended by eminent ecclesiastics such as Macarius, Bishop of Jerusalem, Eusebius of Nicomedia and Eusebius of Caesarea, the historian.

Every effort at reconciliation between Bishop Alexander and Arius having failed, the emperor Constantine in 324 called the *First General Council* at Nicea, in north-west Asia Minor, to deal with the situation. This ecumenical council was attended by 318 bishops from most of the lands from Spain to Persia. It was a remarkable gathering, with the emperor in attendance, and a fine Christian, Hosius of Cordoba, presiding. Many of those present bore the scars of persecution, with maimed limbs and blinded eyes. They had known the deepest suffering for Christ's sake, and now the emperor himself welcomed them. It was, indeed, a new epoch, as Eusebius recounts in his history (I, chs 6–7).

The discussion resolved itself into a debate on the question whether Christ was *homoousios* (of the same essence as God), or *homoiousios* (of similar essence with God). The chief protagonists were Athanasius (a deacon) and Arius (a presbyter). These, and not the bishops, were the men who really counted in the council. At first, many sought to procure a vague pronouncement that would commit them to neither side. In the end the orthodox party secured a large majority and the council declared that Christ was 'the Son of God, only begotten of the Father . . . of the substance of the Father . . . very God of very God'. This decision has been of immeasurable importance in the history of the church.

Arius was anathematized and banished with two companions to Illyria. Two years later, however, the strife was renewed in all its bitterness when Constantine received Arius back into favour, and banished Athanasius, now Bishop of Alexandria, to Treves when Athanasius refused to reinstate Arius. No fewer than five times was Athanasius exiled to distant regions and then recalled, and each time on returning to Alexandria was received with delirious joy by his devoted flock. The intrigues of the Arians were innumerable. Often it was a case of 'Athanasius against the world, and the whole world against Athanasius'. After having known suffering and exile for the greater part of his active life, his last six years (367–73) were spent in peace and honour in his diocese of Alexandria.

The Council of Constantinople in 381 was the Second General Council, and was attended by 186 bishops. It emphatically asserted the deity of the Holy Spirit as against the views of Macedonius and Sabellius. The latter taught a kind of Unitarianism (see pp. 32–3).

The Council of Ephesus (in 431) condemned and deposed Nestorius, the eloquent Bishop of Constantinople, who in his opposition to the Monophysites so stressed the two natures of Christ that he was accused of teaching that Christ was two persons. Monophysitism held that our Lord had one nature only, the divine having absorbed the human. One result of the growing stress on celibacy in the church was an insistence on the perpetual virginity of the Virgin Mary. To glorify her, she was given the title *Theotokos*, 'Mother of God'. With good reason Nestorius protested, maintaining that Mary was mother of 'the Man, Christ Jesus', but not of his deity. The council was glaringly unjust, and Nestorius was banished to the desert of the Thebaid (the district near the ancient Egyptian capital of Thebes). He had many followers in Syria and Persia, and they formed the Nestorian Church. In its early days this church expanded rapidly. It established itself strongly, first in Persia and then in Armenia. Its missionaries then pressed on further eastward, and by 625 had reached China by way of Central Asia. This church (now known by its preferred title, the Assyrian Church of the East) still exists in Iraq and Armenia, in spite of terrible persecutions from the Muslims. It is currently represented strongly outside the Middle East, especially in the USA. Twenty years later Eutyches, the implacable opponent of Nestorius in the Council of Ephesus, was charged, to his great astonishment, with being himself a heretic, and with teaching that Christ had only one nature – the divine. Though defended by the turbulent Synod of Ephesus in 449 (known as the 'Robber' because of its injustice), he was condemned at the *Council of Chalcedon* (451). This council, with an attendance of 500 bishops, affirmed that Christ has 'two natures inconfusedly, unchangeably' but that are united in one person. To this day, the opposite doctrine of one nature ('Monophysitism') lingers on among the Jacobites of Syria, and the Copts of Egypt and Ethiopia.

Outstanding churchmen

The references to these must be very brief, but even to know their names and periods is of some value.

Hilary of Poitiers (295–368). He stands out as the great champion of orthodoxy in the West, as against the Arians of his time. His theological writings were many and very able.

Ambrose of Milan (340–97) was, in character, one of the most unbending men ever known. His courage never failed, and he withstood the strongest rulers. He would not allow the setting aside of any place of worship in Milan for the Arians, even when this was demanded by the mother of the emperor Valentinian II. Later he not only refused Communion to Maximus, who had usurped the throne of the Western empire, but even to the great emperor Theodosius, who was denied admission to church for eight months after he had ordered a massacre of rebels in Thessalonica. The emperor made a complete capitulation.

Aurelius Augustine (354–430) is so important that he must receive fuller treatment than others. He was born at Tagaste in Numidia, his father being then a coarse pagan, while his mother, Monica, was a Christian of outstanding saintliness. To her self-sacrifice, noble faith and incessant prayers, Augustine owed more than can be estimated. His *Confessions* form a classic of self-revelation, and show the sensuality of his early years among the licentious students of Carthage. At the age of 17, he took a young woman as a concubine. When a son was born, he called him Adeodatus (by God given), a strange name in the circumstances.

He was influenced successively by the *Hortensius* of Cicero, the Bible, the Manichaeans, Aristotle and Neoplatonism. For years he prayed, 'O God, grant me chastity and continence, but not yet.' Then, at Milan, where he was holding a post as a government teacher of rhetoric, he fell under the spell of the great bishop Ambrose. Finally, his internal conflict became intolerable, and under a fig tree in the garden, in a paroxysm of weeping, he found the Saviour of whom his mother had so often told him. The spiritual change was complete. He knew it was all from the sovereign mercy of God, and henceforth, like Paul, the marvels of divine grace became his chief theme.

In 395 he was made Bishop of Hippo in North Africa, a place to which his name gives lustre still. His fertile brain brought forth book after book, such as *De Vita Beata* (On the Blessed Life), *De Ordine* (On Providence) and *De Baptismo* (On Baptism). His most notable works were on sin and grace and were called forth by the Pelagian controversy in 312, when Pelagius, a British monk, denied original sin and refused to believe that the sinner was helpless to save himself. Augustine insisted that sin wrought such ravages in man that he cannot save himself. He maintained that no man can really love God or believe in him savingly until the grace of God comes to him. These teachings profoundly affected both Martin Luther and John Calvin at the Reformation. The claim has been made that his great apologetical treatise *The City of God* entitles Augustine to be regarded 'as the one great philosopher sprung from the soil of Christianity proper'. He died in 430 while the barbarian Vandals were besieging his beloved city of Hippo.

Although Augustine was the greatest Christian of his age, he sanctioned certain beliefs and customs that were afterwards productive of much evil in the church. Thus, he taught that there was no salvation outside the visible Catholic Church (with its traditionalism and sacramentalism). He also favoured ascetic monasticism, fostered the use of relics and encouraged belief in purgatory. Nevertheless, no other mind since the time of the apostles has made such a deep impression on Christian thought, whether Protestant, Roman Catholic, scholastic or mystic.

The Three Cappadocians is the name given to Basil the Great, Bishop of Caesarea in Cappadocia (329–79), his brother, Gregory of Nyssa (332–94), and their great friend Gregory of Nazianzus (330–90). They were men of the highest character, ready to devote themselves and their riches unreservedly to the cause of Christ. In the fourth century, when Arianism was strongly aided by the secular power and many theologians were unscrupulous in their attacks on those who supported the Nicene Creed, they stood out boldly in the Eastern Church in defence of the cause for which Athanasius had earlier suffered.

John Chrysostom (347–407), Bishop, first of Antioch and then of Constantinople, was a saintly man, an outstanding scholar and one of the greatest orators of all time (hence his name, which means 'John of the golden mouth'). His faithfulness in preaching repentance offended the empress Eudoxia, and he was deposed and banished in 403. He died through ill-treatment on his way as a prisoner to Pityus (a large and wealthy Greek city on the north-east of the Black Sea).

Jerome (340–420), one of the most interesting and picturesque figures in church history, was born in northern Dalmatia. He produced the Latin Vulgate Bible version of the Roman Catholic Church. He started a monastic community at Aquileia, but it broke up in a 'whirlwind' of dissension. He was a man of hasty temper and never suffered fools gladly. Nevertheless, because of his scholarship and force of character, there was much that was attractive about him. He spent thirty-four years at Bethlehem, where he lived mostly in a cave as a hermit, and there carried out his immense literary and scholarly labours. He defended monasticism and celibacy with extravagant enthusiasm, but found that the world always invaded even the loneliest retreats.

Leo I, known as Leo the Great (390–461), stands out as the first truly great churchman to appear in Rome since apostolic times. The Council of Chalcedon (451) agreed that the term 'pope' be reserved exclusively for him and his successors at Rome. It is remarkable that, before Leo, only one Roman bishop could be regarded as outstanding. This was Hippolytus (died 235), who was bishop of a sect and much opposed to the official Roman bishops. The personality of Leo made so great an impression upon the rough pagan conqueror Attila that he turned back from the gates of Rome at Leo's behest. Leo was a man who bent all his strength towards gaining recognition for the Bishop of Rome as universal bishop. He based the claim on the primacy that was supposed to have been granted to Peter (Matt. 16:18). He gave a new interpretation to these words, a meaning that differed from that placed on them by Ambrose, Jerome and Augustine. His claim was conceded in the West, with the exception of the Celtic church, and was strongly backed up by a decree from the emperor Valentian III, who made it an offence against the state to resist the dictates of the pontiff. Leo took up the extraordinary attitude that 'Peter has never quitted the guidance of the Church which he received'.

The church in the East emphatically repudiated his claims. Even the Council of Chalcedon, where he exercised much influence, refused his request to be recognized as universal bishop. His assertion of papal supremacy, however, produced a profound effect in later ages.

A changing world (400–500)

The fifth century is forever memorable as the period when the Roman Empire fell before the barbarians of the north and northeast. Love of luxury, rural depopulation and other ills had weakened the empire. Little by little the Teutonic tribes had been pressing across the frontiers. Devastating conquests shocked the Roman Empire. The Burgundians, Suevi, Vandals and Alans pushed west and overran Gaul in 408. Most of the conquering barbarian tribes were Arian Christians. Although they were not orthodox, it was fortunate for the church in the Roman Empire that their conquerors professed any kind of Christianity, for it saved many Christian lives and much church property, not only in Rome but elsewhere as well.

Alaric the Visigoth, after various victories and setbacks, entered Rome and sacked it in 410. Rome, 'the Empress of the World', had finally fallen after about eight centuries to foreign forces. Jerome in his cave at Bethlehem wept on receiving the tidings 'because she was a captive: that city which enthralled the world'. Multitudes felt the same. After a year, Alaric died on his way to invade Africa, and his successor, instead of ruling in his own name, accepted office nominally under Honorius, emperor of the West. But henceforth the power of the emperors was but a shadow of that formerly enjoyed.

The Vandals, crossing over from Spain, in 429 ravaged the fertile province of Africa, which they wanted as their granary. However, the army of Rome and the nations of Gaul were successful against Attila and his hordes of Huns at Châlons-sur-Marne in 451. Genseric and his Vandals crossed from Africa to Italy in 455 and plundered Rome. Finally, in 476 the 'eternal city', which had proudly ruled the nations for twelve centuries, fell before Odoacer, the Herulean, thus marking the end of an epoch.

The last of the Roman legions had left Britain in 410 to defend Gaul and Italy. The Jutes, Angles and Saxons, fierce pagans, poured across the North Sea from northern Germany, and destroyed the Christian church in eastern England and south-eastern Scotland. The Celtic church lived on in western Britain and Ireland and showed great vitality. Being separated from the churches in Europe by the pagan belt established in the east of the country, it was preserved from much of the decline in spiritual fervour and culture that characterized continental Christianity during this period.

The Roman Empire of the West was now under barbarian dominion and broken up into various states. There ensued a period of great uncertainty in these different countries as victors and vanquished, Catholics, Arians and pagans, all tried to settle down side by side. The old Roman culture had received a shattering blow, but the strong Teutons brought with them a new vigour and a new vision to replace a civilization that had become ineffective. It was a difficult time for Christianity, and although the barbarians gradually became Catholic Christians (for example, in 496 Clovis, king of the Franks, was baptized with 3,000 of his warriors), these accessions were by no means all gain to the church. Sadly, the spiritual tone was lowered and many barbarian errors and superstitions found entry.

Contrary to what we might expect, the fall of the Roman Empire increased the personal prestige of the Bishop of Rome. When Alaric entered the city, most of the great patrician families fled. Some, for example, had been welcomed in Palestine by Jerome. This left the bishop pre-eminent in the social life of the city, and his moral authority increased enormously as a result.

6

The beginning of the Middle Ages

At the end of the sixth century, a new order of things was emerging in Europe. The influence of the Graeco-Roman culture was lessening, and at the same time new forms of thought were becoming predominant because of the intermingling of Teutonic and Roman ideas. The Middle Ages may well be taken as beginning in 590 when Gregory I ascended the papal throne. War and famine had decimated a great part of Italy. The Lombards, who had captured northern Italy in 568, were a menace to the Roman See. Outside Italy the prestige of the Catholic Church had not been regained since the fall of the empire in 476. The regions of the Rhine and Danube had been lost to the church. Arianism and other heresies were rampant in the states formed by the barbarians. The influence of the Roman pontiff had become very weak in Spain, Gaul and Illyria, and had almost vanished in Africa.

The conversion in 496 of Clovis, the pagan king of the Franks, had not yet led to any great increase in the power of the pope, although that nation was destined to become the great bulwark of the See of Rome in the eighth and ninth centuries. The conversion of Recared, the Visigoth king of Spain, from Arianism to the Catholic faith in 587 was very encouraging to the pope, but there were still innumerable difficulties confronting the pontiff. It was a time when spiritual fires were burning low.

Pope Gregory the Great (590–604)

This was the state of affairs when Gregory became Bishop of Rome. His brilliant rule set a standard for those who came after him, and he is really the first 'pope' who can, with perfect accuracy, be given this title. Along with Leo I (440–61), Gregory VII (1073–85) and Innocent III (1198–1216), he stands out as one of the chief architects of the papal system that has influenced so greatly the history of the world.

Gregory was born about 540 into a rich, senatorial family in Rome, and early entered the imperial service, becoming, through sheer ability, prefect of the city of Rome in 573. The governor of Ravenna (representing the Eastern emperor in Italy) either could not, or would not, help in the defence of the city against the Lombards. In the emergency Gregory assumed the highest powers, and justified his management of affairs by success in the political and military spheres as well as in the civic.

Hearing the call of God, he devoted himself to a religious life and sold his vast estates in 574, dedicating the proceeds to the welfare of the poor and to the building of six monasteries in Sicily. He became a monk of the Benedictine order. In 579 Pope Pelagius II sent him on a deputation to Constantinople, where he gained invaluable experience in diplomacy. In 586 he became abbot of his monastery in Rome, and in 590 was elected pope. In character he was an ascetic monk, proud and ambitious, yet devout in his religious life. His former experience in government service and diplomacy served him in good stead in negotiations with the Lombard rulers, and he became the most potent political force in Italy. He showed the same consummate ability in managing the vast papal estates near Rome, in Calabria, Sicily, Corsica, Dalmatia, Gaul and Africa, thus helping to lay the foundations for the temporal power of the pope that became so important in international relationships at a later period.

Gregory bent his ceaseless energies towards increasing the prestige of his archdiocese in lands where it had fallen low, and his efforts were not in vain. He saw clearly the need for missions, for more than two-thirds of Europe was still pagan, and it was he who conceived the idea of sending a Roman mission to the Anglo-Saxons of England. He sought to turn the 'otherworldliness' of the monks to practical account and sent them forth to evangelize.

Gregory, on the same grounds, renewed the claim to universal supremacy in the church, first made by Leo I. When in 588 John, the

Patriarch of Constantinople, assumed the title of 'Universal Bishop', Gregory protested strongly to the emperor and to the patriarch himself that this act was 'proud, profane, wicked, blasphemous', and suggested that the patriarch was 'the forerunner of Anti-Christ'. Gregory himself assumed the title of 'Servant of servants' that is still borne by the popes. His attitude seems somewhat ludicrous considering that he made for himself the stupendous claim of being the 'Successor of Peter' and the 'Vicar of Christ on earth', which clearly implied supremacy over all the church. He made this claim specifically. It was recognized almost everywhere in the West, the Celtic church being again a notable exception. Even the East granted him a certain 'primacy of honour', although not of episcopal authority. Like Augustine, he taught that there was no salvation for anyone outside the one Catholic Church, and claimed to be the head of it.

He was a man of deeply devotional spirit who regarded the holy Scriptures with profound respect and looked for the speedy coming of the Lord to judge a wicked world. He was long remembered as a powerful preacher and an able theological writer. The doctrine of purgatory that others had adumbrated since the days of Origen was now officially promulgated by Gregory. The Gregorian chant seems to have been developed later, and his influence on music and ritual was not so great as was at one time supposed. However, he encouraged the use of pictures and images in church on condition that they would not be worshipped. Gregory strengthened the Roman church remarkably in a difficult period, and helped to secure for his successors that predominance for which he himself strove with all his might.

The Christianization of Britain

The fact that in 596 Pope Gregory sent his friend and brother monk Augustine from Rome to Christianize the Anglo-Saxons in England is well known. It is not so well known that in Roman times, by the end of the third century in fact, the gospel had made a strong impact upon England. Tertullian, at the very beginning of the third century, makes reference to this, as does Origen about forty-five years later, and British representatives attended the Councils of Arles (314), Sardica (343) and Ariminum (359). The invaders who began to come across from Germany in 449 were still pagan and destroyed Christianity on the eastern seaboard. In the west the inhabitants remained Christian, and there the Celtic church developed in association with Ireland and Scotland.

In 597 Augustine and forty followers landed at Ebbsfleet in the Isle of Thanet (the most easterly point of Kent). It was the same year in which Columba died in Iona after leading a life of vigorous evangelism in Scotland as well as in his native Ireland. Ethelbert, King of Kent, whose wife, Bertha, was a Christian princess from Paris, made generous provision for the Roman missionaries, but asked for time to study the new faith before accepting it. Within about nine months Ethelbert and 10,000 of his people professed conversion. Augustine established his headquarters in Canterbury in the church of St Martin. There grew up the great cathedral that has been so closely bound up with the religious life of England. In 604 Mellitus founded the church of St Paul's and became the first Bishop of London. Justus became Bishop of Rochester about the same time.

The efforts of Augustine to bring the leaders of the Celtic church into the Roman communion that he represented failed completely, for they clung passionately to their independence. He died in 604, having barely succeeded in extending the Roman church beyond Kent. His importance lies in his having established Canterbury Cathedral, the influence of which spread later throughout all the land.

Paulinus went from Canterbury to the kingdom of Northumbria in 625, and King Edwin and members of his court were converted. But after a few years, the work was entirely destroyed when the pagan king of Mercia killed Edwin, and Paulinus had to flee. The next attempt to bring about the conversion of Northumbria was to come from the Celtic church of Iona in 635, and this move was not to the liking of Paulinus because of the differences between their respective communions.

Ever since the arrival of Patrick in Ireland in 432 the gospel had flourished in that land. There is no evidence that he recognized in any way the authority of the archdiocese of Rome. In Scotland the first historical missionary figure was Ninian, who built his church and monastery at Whithorn on the Solway Firth in 397, and carried the gospel to the Picts, influencing even the far north. There followed a long succession of saints and preachers, but all were overshadowed historically by Columba, who came from Ireland to Iona in 563. He was a great statesman, abbot and evangelist. In 635 Aidan and his friends went from Iona to Lindisfarne, the little island off the coast of Northumberland. Within thirty years, they had not only evangelized Northumbria (from the Forth to the Humber) but had also reached south almost to the Thames. Rarely has a finer piece of missionary work been done, and yet it has seldom been adequately acknowledged.

From Bangor, in Northern Ireland, missionaries were sent out far and near. One of the greatest of these was the zealous and fearless Columbanus, who went to Burgundy about twenty years after Columba went to Iona. He founded the famous monasteries of Luxeuil, Annegray and Fontaine in the region of the Vosges mountains. He had differences from time to time with Pope Gregory I, whom he treated with respect, but whose primacy he repudiated.

To this day in the Vosges, on the Rhine, in Italy and in distant Hungary there are many monuments that testify to the intrepid work of the Celtic missionaries. For three centuries, they were incomparable in learning, piety and missionary activity, and for a time it looked as if they would evangelize all Europe. In Wales and Cornwall, as well as in Brittany, the Celtic church also played a great part in evangelization. At the Synod of Whitby in 664, where representatives of the Roman and Celtic communions discussed their differences, King Oswy of Northumbria was won over to the side of the church of Rome. From then onwards, the influence of the Celtic church gradually waned throughout Britain, but many traces of its great work remained for centuries.

The changing face of the church

Pope Gregory the Great died in 604 and as his reign marked a great step forward in papal power and in the development of the Roman church, it is convenient to glance at some changes in the church that had occurred by the beginning of the seventh century. The contrast with the first century is startling.

1. *Papal claims.* The first great claim concerned the power now exercised by the pope, and the tremendous declarations he made concerning his office. Instead of being a humble pastor, as were the early presbyters who ministered to the flock of God, he was now able to hold his own with kings and beat them at the diplomatic game. His proud claim was that he was supreme over all the churches and all other bishops.

2. *The Lord's Supper.* Although the Communion was still mainly regarded as a memorial of the death of Christ, the idea was growing fast that it was itself a sacrifice. The doctrine of the 'real presence' was widely accepted, although there was no clear understanding as to what that presence meant. Some vaguely held the idea of a bodily presence, but it was not till 831 that Paschasius Radbertus published a treatise openly advocating the doctrine of transubstantiation. This doctrine affirms that the bread and wine in the Eucharist are changed into the very body and blood of Christ when consecrated by the priest. It was practically another 400 years before it was officially formulated and promulgated as a doctrine of the Roman church at the Lateran Council in 1215.

3. *Purgatory.* This doctrine had gone on gaining ground ever since Augustine had expressed his belief in its probability as a means of purging souls of their sins by fire. In pagan religions the belief in purgatory was common. It was thought of as a place under the earth where the souls of humans were purged through suffering severe torments. The doctrine was favoured by Gregory the Great and was widely accepted, but did not become an article of faith in the Roman church till the Council of Florence in 1439.

4. *Prayer for the dead and prayers to saints.* These, with their associated beliefs of indulgences and masses for the departed,

naturally grew up as the belief in purgatory increased. Saints and martyrs were greatly venerated, and at the anniversary celebrations at their tombs the impression grew up that prayers were being offered to them, or for them. Thus, in time, prayers to the departed saints came to be regarded as normal. The church at the Second Council of Nicea officially recognized such prayers in 787.

5. *Adoration of Mary.* Since the Council of Ephesus had declared in 431 that Mary was *Theotokos*, 'Mother of God', the cult of Mary had gone on increasing, though not without great opposition. Festivals (such as that of the Annunciation on 25 March) were held in her honour, and then came her worship. By the end of the sixth century, adoration of Mary increased in prominence and prayers were addressed to her. Already there was much superstition as to her intervention on behalf of her devoted worshippers. The term 'Mother of God' suggests borrowing from paganism, where we find such a conception in expressions used with regard to Demeter, Cybele and others.

6. *Auricular confession.* From an early period, confession of sin was essential for restoration to church standing after a grievous fall. At first, it was made publicly in church. But since this seemed to foment scandals, it tended from the days of Leo I (440–61) to become a private confession before a priest. At that time, confession was permitted but was not compulsory. According to Roman Catholic sources, it was commanded for the first time by a Bishop of Metz in 763.

Strangely enough, the Celtic missionaries on the Continent were largely instrumental in popularizing confession. They had found moral life so low among the Franks that they encouraged people to come privately to confess their sins and receive instruction.

7. *Places of worship.* With increase of wealth among Christians, and the favour shown to them by the great, their meeting places became more and more ornate. Examples are the Church of St Sophia in Constantinople, and the 'seven churches' of Rome in the time of Gregory I. Against the dangers of this sumptuousness, Jerome and Chrysostom had given solemn warning about 200 years earlier, the former declaring, 'that alone is the true temple which is adorned with the indwelling of a true, a holy life'.

By 814, the worship of images in churches had become such a scandal that the emperor Michael wrote in alarm to Louis the Pious, the son of Charlemagne. Long before this, the Muslims had begun to taunt the Christians with being idolaters because of their image worship.

8. *The priesthood.* As sacerdotalism increased, the altar, which formerly had no place in the Christian church, became of greater and greater importance. This led to drastic alterations that extended even to the architectural design of churches. The priesthood of all believers was well-nigh forgotten. The priest was now regarded as of a different order from the laity and as having a special grace and divine authority by reason of his ordination. He became indispensable in the church's approach to God. He handled divine mysteries, and his work was regarded as a species of magic, like the work of the non-Christian priests. The altar at which he officiated, and upon which he offered again the sacrifice of the body and blood of Christ, came to be regarded as the most sacred place in the building and was railed off from the nave of the church. Thus, there grew up a priestly caste separated from the people.

In keeping with this sacerdotalism, vestments that seem to have been first introduced in the reign of Constantine had come to be regarded as an essential part of the priest's equipment by the end of the sixth century. Both Theodoret and the ecclesiastical historian Socrates tell us that by the end of the fourth century bishops were discussing the propriety of different colours for their robes. When Mass came to be celebrated, the custom grew up of using special clothes known as Mass vestments, some for High Mass and some for Low. For centuries prior to this, the clergy had worn no distinctive clerical dress.

9. *Incense.* The burning of incense was used at first only for the fumigation of Christian buildings. It had no connection with worship for four centuries. As late as the reign of Theodosius I (378–95), enactments ordered the confiscation of houses where it had been used. Both Tertullian and Lactantius (325) refer to the burning of incense as 'pagan', and not practised by Christians.

7

The record of monasticism

The growth of monastic communities

The monastic system, which became so important in the Middle Ages, arose from an unnatural asceticism that was manifesting itself even in the days of the apostle Paul and was condemned by him (see Col. 2:23; 1 Tim. 4:1). It was present in the East long before the Christian era, and was strongly developed within Buddhism. Christian asceticism took its rise from Anthony, who was born in Egypt in AD 251. He forsook wealth and social position, and retired to mountain caves in order to dedicate himself to lonely contemplation. Later he gathered round him a small group of disciples whom he organized into a community in the desert. Members of such communities were known as 'cenobites', meaning 'having life in common' (Greek, *koinos bios*), a more accurate term than 'monk', which really means 'a solitary'.

The first great organizer of monastic communities was Pachomius (292–346), who established a monastery at Tabenisi on an island in the Nile in Upper Egypt. The rule for this community is extant in a Latin version. Entrants had to hand over their wealth, which was then placed in a common fund. When Athanasius visited this community soon after its foundation, 3,000 monks welcomed him by chanting hymns and litanies. This shows the sudden popularity of the movement. By the end of the century, very many similar communities had been established in Egypt and the movement had begun to spread elsewhere. Pachomius set a pattern for monastic life, including encouraging monasteries to be self-supporting by various activities, especially the growing of fruit and vegetables.

In the West monasticism grew up more slowly, in spite of the support of Athanasius, Jerome, Ambrose and Augustine. One of the very earliest and best leaders in the West was Martin of Tours, in Gaul, in the fourth century. Even before the system was practised in Italy, he had introduced it to Gaul directly from the East. He had been in military service before becoming a hermit, and very reluctantly accepted appointment as Bishop of Tours in 372. He greatly influenced Ninian, who established his church and monastery at Whithorn in 397, on the Solway Firth in Scotland, and took Martin's work as his model. This was the first Christian advance north of Hadrian's Wall, in an area where there was doubtless a partly Romanized population who might have had previous Christian contact. There Ninian built Scotland's first church building, which was called Candida Casa, the 'white house' or 'hut'. This settlement had powerful effects, not only upon Scotland but upon Ireland as well (Northern Ireland being near Whithorn), and was one of the decisive factors in making the Celtic church so intensely monastic.

The Irish connection with Scottish Christianity depends largely on the work of two later monks. Patrick (c.389–461) stimulated the Celtic church to mission, and in the seventh and eighth centuries it provided a large number of monks who evangelized in Europe. In 563 Columba (521–97) left Ireland and, with twelve companions, sailed to the island of Iona on the west coast of Scotland. There he established a monastery that served as a base for evangelizing the people who were under the influence of the Druids, strong opponents of the Christian faith. It is uncertain whether Columba and his fellow-monks were able to evangelize parts of Scotland beyond the western seaboard. Our knowledge of much of Columba's ministry comes from a biography written by Adamnan, the ninth abbot of the Iona community.

The Celtic monasteries were also noted for their scholarly activity. This may have been stimulated by migration to Ireland of monks who fled the barbarian invasions in Europe in the fifth century. The most notable manuscript (held in Trinity College, Dublin) is the Book of Kells, an illuminated manuscript of the four Gospels in

Latin. It may have originated from Iona, but was taken to Kells in Ireland when monks fled a Viking invasion. Several scribes and artists clearly worked on the manuscript, and it displays magnificently the varied gifts scholarly monks possessed.

The varieties of monasticism

Some of the monastic orders may be noted.

1. *The Benedictine order.* It was founded by Benedict of Nursia at Mount Cassino in Italy in 529. The discipline was very strict and the order became immensely popular and very rich. With prosperity and success came degeneracy and abuses.

2. *The Cluniac movement.* It was started by Bernon in 910 at Cluny in France to counteract the corruption and lack of zeal that had manifested themselves in the Benedictine order. It stood for the freedom of the church from all secular interference by princes or patrons, and the free election of bishops and abbots by the chapter or the monks. It also stood up fanatically for clerical celibacy. The influence of Cluny spread far and wide because of its exacting discipline.

3. *The Cistercian order.* It was founded at Cîteaux in Burgundy by monks who wanted to keep strictly the original Benedictine rules. They aimed at simple living. Bernard founded the famous monastery of Clairvaux in 1115 in a wild and remote valley. His influence was immense, and stories regarding the force of his eloquence became legendary. He was, however, very intolerant. The Cistercian order grew to include 700 monastic houses. The church has greatly treasured several of Bernard's hymns such as 'Jesu, the very thought of Thee'.

4. *The Mendicant orders: the Franciscans and Dominicans.* The members of these orders were recruited from humble life and their democratic spirit made a wide appeal. The term 'mendicant' refers to the fact that they originally begged for their keep (Latin, *mendicus*, 'beggar'). They soon completely eclipsed the older orders, a fact that caused grave jealousies.

The founder of the *Franciscans* was the saintly Francis of Assisi in Italy. Their aim was to live a life of poverty in imitation of our Lord.

They came to have a dominant position in the church, counting among their great men Bonaventura, Duns Scotus and William of Occam. In time they set aside the ideals of Francis as to poverty, and entered the same vicious circle as other orders with regard to wealth and worldliness.

Dominic, a Spanish nobleman, founded *the Dominican order* in 1215, at the time of the bloody campaign against the Albigenses (see p. 77). He insisted on a simple life to impress the common man, an aim in which he succeeded. The pope committed to the Dominicans the iniquitous institution of the Inquisition that was to bathe so many lands in blood. It was first established by a council at Toulouse in 1229 and was supposed to be operated by the bishops (see p. 77).

At their best, the monasteries of the various orders did a great work in forwarding agriculture, providing schools of learning, caring for the poor and giving hospitality to the sick and needy. After their founders had died, however, and the first enthusiasm had waned with the growth of wealth and power, it generally happened that these orders fell into spiritual decadence and in time moved far from their early ideals.

5. *The Military orders.* These were (1) the Knights of St John of Jerusalem (founded 1048), (2) the Knights Templars (founded 1119) and (3) the Teutonic Knights (founded 1121). They were all composed of soldier-monks. The orders began in Palestine with the object of caring for and protecting pilgrims. They soon, however, became very militant, and made it their chief object to fight the Saracens: the Arabs and Muslims who had captured Jerusalem. These knights all became very wealthy and influential and spread to various lands.

8

From Gregory I to Charlemagne

The rise of Islam

The rise of Islam presented a grave challenge to Christianity and profoundly affected the history of the world. Muhammad was born in Mecca, in Arabia, about 570, and at an early age lost his parents. When he grew to manhood, he prayed much in the solitudes of the desert, fell into trances and claimed that he heard voices. He had met Jews and heretical Christians who had only apocryphal gospels. While they gave him the idea that there was but one God, he was not at all impressed by their lives, and this might have prevented him from becoming a Christian. He resolved to replace the degraded polytheism of Arabia with the one, true religion of Allah, whose prophet he claimed to be.

Owing to the intense opposition to his preaching, he had to flee from Mecca in 622 and went with some 200 of his followers to Medina. This 'Hegira', as his flight was called, was the turning point in his career and from it the Islamic era is dated. Nine years later, after a somewhat chequered career, he re-entered Mecca in triumph, and by the time of his death in 632 had won over all Arabia.

In the Qur'an, which Muhammad began writing when he was about 40, and which later became the sacred book of Islam, he recorded what purported to be divine revelations made to him by the angel Gabriel. His character was full of contradictions. He could be friendly and generous, resolute and shrewd, but could also be cruel to his enemies, and was undeniably sensual. Only ninety years after his flight from Mecca in 622, his religion, called by its followers 'Islam' (meaning 'submission'), stretched all the way from India to the Atlantic. Soon it penetrated into Central Asia and China, and later stretched through all southern Asia to Malaya.

The Muslim conquests brought disasters for the church. In the great patriarchates of Antioch, Jerusalem and Alexandria, which extended over vast areas, only remnants of the Christian church remained. Thus, in Syria alone, 10,000 churches were destroyed or became mosques. The church of North Africa, with its memories of Tertullian, Cyprian and Augustine, was practically obliterated. Only small Christian communities survived here and there. This destruction of the ancient and illustrious church east and south of the Mediterranean was nothing less than the fulfilment of the warning 'Repent, and do the works you did at first. If not, I will come to you and remove your lampstand from its place, unless you repent' (Rev. 2:5).

After conquering Spain, the Muslim armies pushed across the Pyrenees in 732, and reached the heart of France. All Europe seemed open to them. Then Charles Martel, who was mayor to the palace of the Frankish king, marshalled the Christian forces, and inflicted a crushing defeat on the invading armies at Tours. It was one of the most important battles in history. As a result of it, Europe remained Christian and the Islamic forces were driven back thoroughly defeated.

The conversion of the Germanic tribes

At the very time when such terrible calamities were falling upon so many of the ancient centres of church life, the faith was being carried to the Germanic tribes in the neighbourhood of the Rhine. In this work missionaries from Britain played a remarkable part. The great work done by Columbanus (see p. 50) was energetically extended by crowds of zealous monks from the Celtic church in Britain, who flocked to evangelize the Continent, especially after the Synod of Whitby (see p. 50) in 664. From that date, the Roman church began little by little to absorb the Celtic church at home, and the Celtic Christians sought an independent field abroad.

Two great Englishmen did a vast work in building up the Roman church among the Germanic tribes. The first was Willibrord, a native of York, who went as a missionary to Frisia in 690. At first, he met considerable opposition from the pagan inhabitants. In spite of this, however, he made very many converts, and lived to see the whole region of Frankish Frisia professing Roman Catholicism. In 695 he became Archbishop of Utrecht.

Boniface (or Winfrith), another English monk, is often called 'the apostle of Germany'. A native of Crediton in Devon, he was an able scholar and a born administrator who proved himself invaluable to the Roman church in founding dioceses, and in building churches and monasteries. His activities in Thuringia, Bavaria and Hesse were conspicuously successful. In 732 he was made an archbishop, and further increased his influence. He was most subservient to the pope, to whom he swore complete obedience, and as papal legate (personal representative) himself enjoyed vast prestige. In certain districts he reaped where the Celtic church had sown, and brought their churches and monasteries under the Roman See. He died as a martyr in North Frisia in 753.

In Saxony, towards the end of the eighth century, the freedom-loving Saxons were compelled by the sword to profess Christianity. This brutal action is a blot on the name of Charlemagne, who nevertheless had the hearty support of the pope in the action he took. Again and again the Saxons had revolted and devastated the Frankish countryside, slaying priests and burning monasteries. They hated Christianity because it came to them from their enemies, the Franks. As a punishment, Charlemagne had 4,500 Saxons beheaded in one day. When, after thirty years of constant fighting (772–803), peace was established, missionaries were sent among them and Germany became, at least nominally, Christian as far as the Elbe. These missionaries found a better way of spreading the gospel than Charlemagne's plan for 'converting the Saxons by the Word and the sword', and soon these courageous people were brought to know Christ.

The Frankish rulers and the Holy Roman Empire

In the eighth century an alliance took place between the papacy and the Frankish rulers that was to have far-reaching effects for the church and the world in general. The pope found the support of the powerful Frankish kings Pepin and Charlemagne essential, because of Lombard hostility and the presence of enemies even in the city of Rome itself. The Frankish kings, for their part, valued the moral support of the papacy when taking over the throne from the Merovingian line (a Frankish dynasty based mainly in Gaul). Hence, Pepin was ostentatiously crowned by the papal legate in 752. The pope received from Pepin the lands taken from the Exarchate of Ravenna (the official name of Italian territory that remained under the rule of Roman emperors at Constantinople until the middle of the eighth century). This became part of 'the patrimony of St Peter', and was land belonging to the papacy whose revenues were used for various ecclesiastical purposes. This was the beginning of the 'temporal sovereignty' of the popes that was to embroil them in many quarrels. Charlemagne not only saved the pontiff from the Lombards, who were enemies of the Roman See, but in 799 delivered him from the wrath of the Roman populace, who had accused the pope of glaring faults.

On Christmas Day 800, in St Peter's Church, the pope suddenly advanced and crowned Charlemagne as emperor of the Holy Roman Empire of the West. The latter professed to be much surprised, but the indications are that it was all carefully planned beforehand. It was an epoch-making event that affected Europe and the church for centuries. In the formation of this new empire there was present the idea of one state and one church with the emperor and pope working hand-in-hand for the glory of God and the welfare of the people. In the days of Charlemagne the alliance worked well, but he was always careful to maintain his position as emperor over the pope as well as over everyone else.

The popes claimed that by crowning Charlemagne they had transferred to him the rights of the Eastern emperor, and revived the glories of the ancient Roman Empire. The claim was vigorously resisted on the grounds that the crowning was only an acknowledgment of monarchical power that was as effective before the coronation as after, and depended in no way on the See of Rome. The Roman pontiff, however, continued to press his claims for many centuries. It was a sore question and productive of much strife and bitterness. Henceforth, the pontiff was found intervening in all kinds of affairs throughout Christian Europe. With a quiet assurance, he assumed that he had to be obeyed on the grounds of his being the successor of Peter. The famous 'capitularies', or laws, of Charlemagne had to do with the church as much as with secular affairs. He significantly regulated the lives of all the clergy, forbidding them to have wives or concubines, to frequent taverns or go out hunting or occupy themselves with worldly business. He also ordained that bishops and abbots should set up their own schools, and wished every parish priest to do the same. This, however, proved difficult to put into effect, but Charlemagne's insistence on the value of learning had a profound influence throughout the empire and prepared the way for the great scholastic movement of the Middle Ages.

The worship of images

Gregory the Great, at the beginning of the seventh century, had allowed the use of pictures and images in churches, but insisted that they must not be worshipped. During the eighth century, the question sprang into renewed prominence. Prayers were by now addressed to them and they were surrounded by an atmosphere of ignorant superstition, so much so that the Muslims taunted the Christians with being idolaters. It was a sad commentary on the argument of those who had introduced the images because of their beauty and for the instruction of the illiterate.

In 726 the eastern emperor, Leo III, interfered to remedy the abuses in his dominion, asking merely that the images and pictures be placed so high that worshippers could not kiss them. The Patriarch of Constantinople and his supporters were furious, and before long insurrections broke out there and in Greece and Syria. The emperor and his council then ordered the complete removal of all images. A bitter fight ensued. Both sides fought on an unspiritual plane. Leo's cause was injured because of the brutality with which his orders were executed. Pope Gregory III denounced the emperor and strongly advocated the use of images. This great controversy is known as the 'iconoclastic' dispute, an adjective that signifies the breaking of images. In 754 the emperor Constantine V called a great synod that met at Constantinople. It prohibited image worship as 'contrary to Scripture', a pagan and anti-Christian practice that led Christians into temptation. The question was a serious one for the church, since images had become objects of idolatry and incense was burnt before them. Unfortunately, both sides of the dispute encouraged violence and abuse throughout the Christian world.

Through the influence of the empress-mother Irene, the widow of Leo IV, who succeeded Constantine V as emperor, the Second Council of Nicea in 787 completely reversed the policy of Leo III, and decided that images of Christ, the Virgin, saints and angels could be set up. The council recommended 'the offering to the images of salutation and honorific worship', and the giving of 'offerings of incense and lights in their honour'. This was a retrograde policy.

Nevertheless, in the West, in spite of the pope's strong support for the use of images, Charlemagne and the Frankish clergy remained resolutely opposed to them, and emphatically pronounced against them at the Council of Frankfurt in 794. Charlemagne in his *Carolingian Books* declared, 'God alone is to be worshipped and adored. Saints are only to be reverenced. Images are by no means to be worshipped.'

9

Disorder and intrigue

The false decretals

Of all the strange chapters in church history none is more amazing than the story of the forged decretals and the supposed Donation of Constantine. 'Decretals' is a general term for papal decrees, judicial decisions, mandates, edicts and similar official pronouncements. The fabricated decretals were put in circulation about 850 by some unscrupulous Frankish ecclesiastic, and the collection was ascribed to the renowned Isidore of Seville, a great prelate and writer of the early seventh century. The real decretals of the popes went back only to Siricius (384–99), but in this collection there were now embodied letters, decisions and laws of the Bishop of Rome supposedly going back to the first century, together with various other spurious ecclesiastical and state documents. The forger was a most skilful worker, and obviously well educated.

The aim was to support the stupendous claims then being made by the pope for dominance in church and state, and at the same time to bolster the unscriptural pretensions of the clergy. On such a false foundation, the mighty power of the Roman church was very largely built. Since the Renaissance in the fifteenth century, scholars have realized that the documents were spurious, but this realization did not affect in the slightest degree the imposing edifice erected on these false foundations.

The Donation of Constantine

This was another forged document in which it was alleged that when Constantine was baptized by Pope Sylvester in 324, he presented him with the Lateran Palace and all the insignia of the Western empire, with the whole of Italy, and other provinces of the Roman Empire. The falsity of this appears at once, for Constantine was not baptized by Sylvester at all, but by Eusebius of Nicomedia, an Arian bishop, and in 337, not 324. The aim of the forgery was to antedate by about 500 years the pope's temporal power that, as already noted, was actually granted by Pepin and Charlemagne. Neither Constantine nor any of his successors ever dreamt of giving away to the Bishop of Rome their temporal power in the West. It is not necessary to believe that any pope actually took part in the production of these forgeries, but popes acted upon them, perhaps innocently, in later generations, and without question this strengthened their claims to almost limitless authority. The first to base his claims upon these false documents was Pope Nicholas I (858–67). He proudly proclaimed, 'that which the pope has decided is to be observed by all', and showed his authority by compelling Hincmar (died 882), the powerful Archbishop of Rheims, to reinstate Rothad, the Bishop of Soissons, whom he had deposed. He also obliged the emperor Lothair II to take back his queen whom he had divorced, and, in spite of many threats, deposed two archbishops who had aided the monarch in his evil designs.

Disorder in the church

Nicholas succeeded against Hincmar and Lothair because they were morally in the wrong. His two successors, Popes Hadrian II (867–72) and John VIII (872–82), claimed the right to interfere in political disputes and even to dispose of the imperial crown, but fared badly, the latter coming to a violent end in 882. Then ensued a period of incredible disorder when the popes were constantly embroiled in the political quarrels of the age and many of them perished ignominiously. The descendants of Charlemagne had fallen into disrepute because of their incapacity and debauchery. The last emperor of this dynasty was Charles the Fat, who was deposed in 887. Thus ended the great empire founded by Charlemagne.

In this time of misgovernment, the Norse pirates threatened to submerge Europe once more in barbarism. They attacked the coasts of Germany and France, destroying great seaports, and carried fire and sword right along the Rhine valley. They accepted Christianity at last and settled down in Normandy, from which they conquered England in 1066. The Muslim armies crossed over from Africa in the ninth century and took possession of Sicily and southern Italy, bringing havoc in their train, while the Hungarian Magyars were threatening Europe from the east. All this had a very evil effect on both civil and religious life. Abuses started with the kings and nobles, who fought among themselves, and oppressed the general population. They gave their favourites bishoprics and abbeys, while they themselves pocketed income from them. Within the church the various officials – archbishops, bishops and priests – oppressed those under them.

After the deposition of Charles the Fat, the Italian nobles became very powerful and fought one another for pre-eminence. The church suffered severely in the prevailing disorder, and the papacy was in disarray. Pope succeeded pope in rapid succession, and rather than ending their lives by natural deaths, many of them were imprisoned or murdered. The powerful counts who ruled Tuscany and Tusculum were in control of both Rome and the papacy for fifty years.

During this time, three strong-minded women of high rank, but of very low morals, dominated the papacy. Theodora the elder and her two daughters, Marozia and Theodora, filled the papal chair with their lovers and illegitimate children. They were beautiful but utterly unscrupulous women, and the story of their immoralities with popes and nobles is shocking. Meanwhile the old idea of a Holy Roman Empire still influenced many hearts. Various attempts were made to revive it but failed. In 960 Pope John XII, one of the worst of the pontiffs, appealed to Otto I, King of Germany, to protect him against Berengar II of Italy. Otto came to the help of the papacy as Pepin and Charlemagne had previously done. The new empire formed by him was smaller than that of Charlemagne. Often it is called the Holy Germanic Empire because the Teutonic influence was dominant.

When Pope John turned against Otto, the latter retaliated by getting a Synod of St Peter's Church to depose the pontiff on charges of murder, blasphemy and gross sensuality. Otto was a strong monarch and, in spite of insurrections, helped to save the papacy morally, but at the loss of its independence.

Early in the eleventh century, matters again went from bad to worse with the papacy. At one stage, from 1044 to 1046, there were three very unworthy priests each claiming to be pontiff. They were Benedict IX, Sylvester III and Gregory VI. The emperor Henry III was asked by a Synod in 1046 to nominate future popes, and this saved the church from chaos at that time. Then arose a reforming party at Rome aiming to expand papal power at everyone's expense. Among them was an able and astute young monk, Hildebrand, who earnestly supported the edict promulgated by Nicholas II in 1059 to place the election of the pope in the hands of the College of Cardinals alone, without the intervention of either emperor or Diet. Hildebrand quickly became the adviser and, indeed, master of successive popes. His methods were brutal, involving the free use of military force.

The spread of Christianity in Europe (800–1073)

Early in the ninth century, Ansgar carried the gospel to Denmark and Norway, but all Scandinavia did not become Christian till late in the eleventh century. In 846 Rastiz slaughtered his subjects in Moravia until he succeeded in making his domain ostensibly Christian. Fourteen Bohemian princes were baptized in 848, but the people fought stoutly against Christianity because it came to them from German sources. In 860 Boris, king of Bulgaria, followed the dreadful policy of Rastiz and massacred many. In 968 Poland became nominally Christian. The Magyars fell under Christian influences from 973 onwards through the work of Piligrim. The Russians received the gospel from Constantinople in 988, through emissaries of the Greek Orthodox Church, sent at the request of King Vladimir. Russia became one of the great bulwarks of the

Greek Orthodox Church and made up somewhat for the terrible losses sustained elsewhere through the conquests of Islam. By the end of the thirteenth century, at least nominal Christianity covered all Europe except Finland and Lapland.

10

Gregory VII to Boniface VIII
(AD 1073–1294)

The papacy at its height

When Hildebrand became pope in 1073, taking the name of Gregory VII, he carried through a revolution in the position of the church. He held that, as vicar of Christ and representative of Peter, he could give or take away 'empires, kingdoms, duchies, marquisates, and the possessions of all men'. Everyone on earth, from the emperor down to the humblest peasant, must acknowledge the pope.

He began his campaign with a scathing attack on the theory that had allowed some priests to marry. Henceforth, the priests of the Roman church were a class apart, cut off from the most sacred and elevating experiences of family life. His next attack was on simony, the sin of buying or selling ecclesiastical office (named after Simon in Acts 8:18–24). There was need for action here, for unscrupulous princes and others not infrequently sold sacred offices to the highest bidder irrespective of spiritual qualifications. Hildebrand's greatest fight, however, was over the question of lay investiture. Under feudal law a vassal had to do homage to his lord on taking possession of lands. He was then presented with a symbol in recognition of his legal rights. The same applied when certain offices were taken up. This ceremony was called 'investiture'. As the great churchmen held lands and domains, they had to be invested like others. Hildebrand, following the Cluniac teaching, objected strongly to all interference of the secular power in church affairs, and held that ecclesiastics should take up office without any sanction from the civil ruler. The secular powers, however, were not without solid grounds for their attitude. In some countries virtually half the property belonged to the church. To have dispensed with homage and transferred vast territories to the pope would have meant chaos in civil government.

In 1075 Hildebrand boldly prohibited lay investiture and summoned the emperor Henry IV to Rome as if he were a feudal vassal. When Henry refused, and persuaded a German council that met at Worms in 1076 to depose the pope, the latter placed him under an interdict (a formal prohibition). The emperor found himself abandoned by all. No one would have any dealings with him, or give him food or shelter, for fear of eternal torments, so great was the terror inspired then by a papal interdict. Within a year, Henry hurried across the Alps in the depth of winter with his wife and child to make his peace with the pontiff. He went to the palace of Canossa where the pope then was. Barefoot, and dressed as a humble penitent, he was compelled to stand for three days in the courtyard in the snow. On the fourth day, the pontiff deigned to receive him. He pleaded for clemency, confessed his fault and, making his humble submission at the feet of the pope, received absolution. The triumph of the papacy seemed complete.

In the end, however, after a war with his rival Rudolf of Swabia, Henry emerged triumphant. In spite of powerful support from the army of Robert Guiscard of Sicily, Hildebrand was driven out, and Henry, whose victory was overwhelming, appointed an anti-pope, Clement III, in his place. In 1085 Hildebrand, the Napoleon of the eleventh century, died in exile at Salerno, declaring, 'I have loved righteousness and hated iniquity, therefore I die in exile.'

Although he ended his life in eclipse, his principles were accepted and cherished by his successors. The fact that even the secular head of the Holy Roman Empire had had to fall prostrate at the feet of the pontiff could never be forgotten. The Hildebrandine party appointed as pope Urban II, a very adroit and skilful leader of men. Like his successor, Paschal II, he encouraged the sons of Henry IV to revolt. His influence grew enormously, especially after he started the crusades, while that of the anti-pope dwindled away. In 1122, in the Concordat of Worms, an agreement was reached with Henry V on the vexed question of lay investiture. The emperor agreed to substitute the touch of the monarch's sceptre for investiture by ring and crozier, the election to be in his presence but without his interference. Thus ended one of the most difficult questions of the Middle Ages.

By the beginning of the twelfth century, the strong and prosperous cities of Lombardy became republican in outlook. Among their leaders arose Arnold of Brescia (1100–53), a pupil of the famous Abelard. He urged a return to the simplicity of life in New Testament times, and manifested some of the spirit of the Reformation. One of his great opponents was Bernard of Clairvaux. In 1143 he was received with wild enthusiasm in Rome, where a republic had been proclaimed. In the fighting that ensued, one pope was slain and the next had to flee to France.

The young emperor, Frederick Barbarossa, marched into Italy and overcame temporarily the Lombard League. To ingratiate himself with the pope, he handed over the fearless Arnold of Brescia, who was put to death.

The friendship of Frederick with the pope was, however, short-lived. When, in 1176 at Legnano, Frederick was thoroughly beaten by the Lombard cities, the outcome was astonishing. On 24 July 1177, outside St Mark's Church in Venice, the great Frederick Barbarossa spread his cloak upon the pavement, knelt before Pope Alexander, and kissed his feet. Then he behaved like a menial, holding the pope's stirrup and leading his horse by the bridle along the street. It was an even greater triumph for Pope Alexander than was Canossa for Hildebrand a century earlier.

The crusades (1095–1270)

The idea of a crusade, espoused by Hildebrand, was carried out by his successors. The fanaticism of the rough Turkish Muslims who captured Jerusalem from the Arabs had become a menace to Christendom, and they were interfering seriously with pilgrims. Pope Urban II threw all his strength into preparing for the First Crusade. He was quick to see the moral prestige that would accrue to himself and the papal system through his leadership of the movement. He was not mistaken. He deeply moved his audiences by his lurid descriptions of Saracen barbarities against pilgrims. 'Saracen' was a term used by medieval Christians to embrace both Arab and Muslim. To persuade the people to take part, many kinds of inducements were held out – absolution from all kinds of sin, eternal blessedness for the fallen, miracles to help, cancellation of debts, pardon for criminals. The crusades did more to popularize indulgences than any other single influence.

Peter the Hermit, an uncouth and unkempt preacher, worked the multitudes into a frenzy of enthusiasm. It was soon regarded as a disgrace not to join the crusade. Many thousands of men, women and children, in various unofficial expeditions, set out in 1096 without any preparation, expecting that miraculous provision would be made for them. Of 275,000 who joined these groups, all either perished of cold or disease, or were scattered. Peter himself fled at the first approach of danger.

The first official crusade, with 600,000 men, set out in August 1096, going via Constantinople. Tens of thousands perished in the cold uplands of Asia Minor. Sadly, rivalries and jealousies also weakened the expedition, but the bravery of many was unbounded. They reached Jerusalem in 1099. Of those who left Europe, only one-tenth completed the journey. Legend told for centuries of the miracles supposed to have taken place in the siege. It is a strange reflection on the spirit of the crusade that when they entered the Holy City, their first action was to massacre the Saracens.

This was the only one of the eight crusades that can really claim to have achieved what it set out to do. The Second Crusade was an unmitigated failure, although sponsored by the most powerful men in Europe. It was organized when the Turks captured Edessa from the Christians in 1144. The recapture of Jerusalem in 1187 by Saladin, the Saracen leader, was a sore blow to Christian sentiment and led to the Third Crusade. The emperor Frederick Barbarossa, Philip of France and Richard Coeur de Lion of England all set out for Palestine with strong armies. Barbarossa was drowned in 1190 while crossing the river Self in Seleucia. Philip and Richard, in spite of unsurpassable heroism, virtually failed in their mission. The Fourth and Sixth Crusades were successful in a way, but their achievements were not fully recognized by the pope. The Fifth, Seventh and Eighth were all lamentable failures. Nearly all Europe, apart from the pope, heaved a sigh of relief when, in 1270, the crusades were abandoned.

Those who participated in the crusades did so for very mixed motives. The immorality, pillage and massacre that so often disgraced the movement show that, in spite of great zeal in pursuance of an ideal, no true spiritual power had taken possession of these people. The effects were mainly political and social rather than religious.

Pope Innocent III

In the time of Pope Innocent III (1198–1216) the papacy reached the height of its power. In policy he followed Hildebrand but was more successful in carrying it out. Circumstances favoured him. The humiliation of Henry IV at Canossa and of Barbarossa at Venice had led the people to believe that the pope was all-powerful and that every ruler was under his authority. Moreover, the enthusiasm engendered by the crusades had greatly strengthened papal prestige. The success of Innocent III was dramatic. Both King John of England and the powerful Philip of France were humiliated and brought to their knees. It is not too much to say that Pope Innocent's political power extended in one way or another over almost all Christian lands. In Italy itself he moulded everything to his will, ruling most effectively over the papal dominions. The pontiff had, once more, real temporal power.

In the more religious domain, he instituted the Fourth Crusade, which, however, violated all his orders. He launched a full-scale war against what he regarded as heresy, and his persecution of the Albigenses (see also p. 77), a heroic sect in southern France, will always stand out as a lamentable scandal. His magnificence reached its culminating point in the splendour of the Lateran Council in 1215, one of the greatest ecumenical councils of all time.

Thomas Aquinas

Amid all the developments concerning the crusades and the intrigues of the papacy in this period, one name stands out. It is of the great philosopher and theologian Thomas Aquinas (1224–74). He was a profound thinker whose work not only influenced scholars at the time of the Reformation but also continues to influence both Catholicism and Protestantism to the present day. Born in Italy and educated in Paris and Cologne, Aquinas wrote profusely, but it is his *Summa contra Gentiles*, a manual of apologetics for missionaries, and his *Summa Theologica*, a systematic theology, that especially make his reputation as that of a great thinker.

The main question that Aquinas was attempting to answer was 'How can God be known?' He believed that God's existence could be proved philosophically, and that divine revelation in Scripture could be expressed in propositions, through using philosophical concepts. His dependence on Aristotle is clear. For Aquinas, God can only be spoken of imperfectly, by means of analogy and negation. Trust in matters divinely revealed was a product of God's grace.

Thomism was given official standing in the thinking of the Roman Catholic Church by the encyclical *Aeterni Patris* by Pope Leo XIII in 1879.

Pope Boniface VIII

The mighty power of the papacy, which reached its height under Innocent III, continued in unabated strength until the days of Boniface VIII (1294–1303), when it began to decline. Boniface insisted most strongly that all temporal rulers were subject to him, and in his bull (an official papal document) *Unam Sanctam* he wrote, 'we declare, state, define and pronounce that for every human creature to be subject to the Roman pope is altogether necessary for salvation'. Further than this, the claims of the papacy could not go. The very arrogance of the papal claims, however, irritated many rulers and provoked violent reactions. This is clearly demonstrated in the conflicts waged by Edward I of England and Philip the Fair of France against the pope. Finally, Philip sent a servant, Nogaret, to Italy, and Boniface was arrested at Anagni. So roughly was Boniface treated, that he died within a month. This was symptomatic of a great change in the attitude of nations towards the papacy. Not only had the pride and power of the popes sown the seeds of spiritual decay, but the growing nationalist spirit in the various countries heralded the opening of an era of hostility to the papal claims. It was not so easy to manage a number of national rulers as it had been to control a single emperor.

The Avignon popes

The next step in the weakening of the papacy was the removal of the popes to Avignon, on the Rhône. Pope Clement V (1305–13) was so much under the power of Philip of France that he could not face the indignation of the Italian people. He resided first at Bordeaux and then Poitiers, but in 1309 removed to Avignon. The popes resided outside Italy for more than seventy years, a period that some ardent Roman Catholics have designated 'the Babylonish Captivity' of the church, for it was a time of miserable servitude to the French monarchy. The situation in Rome, in the long absence of the popes, became dangerous for the church politically and religiously. Great efforts were made by Roman citizens and other influential people to get the pope back, and in 1377 Gregory XI returned from the long exile.

The Great Schism (1378–1417)

Scarcely had one scandal ended when a greater began. On the death of Pope Gregory in 1378, Urban VI, an Italian, was elected. The French cardinals elected a fellow countryman, Clement VII, who returned to Avignon. Some nations supported the pope at Avignon; some, the pope at Rome. So serious was this schism that the power of Rome was weakened for several centuries. Catholics had believed that their salvation depended on acknowledging the successor of Peter. Here were two popes for nearly forty years, each anathematizing the other, and each claiming to be the only true occupant of Peter's chair. No wonder the Catholic world was perplexed.

11

Rising opposition to the Catholic Church

Anti-Catholic sects

About the middle of the seventh century, in the region of the Euphrates, appeared a Christian sect called the Paulicians. They spread to Armenia, Asia Minor and Thrace. Somewhat akin to them were the Bogomils (Friends of God) in Bulgaria and Bosnia, in the tenth century. Later still, under the name of Cathari (The Pure), various groups of ascetically minded Christians, characterized by a marked reverence for the Scriptures, spread from the Balkans westwards. From the end of the twelfth century, the Beghards, a praying people, flourished in the Netherlands and along the Rhine. In the twelfth and thirteenth centuries, the Albigenses became very numerous in southern France, and the Waldenses in northern Italy.

In all these sects, and in others besides, there was a strong testimony against the errors prevailing in the Catholic Church. They attracted numerous passionate followers. Their doctrines were not identical and, in some cases at least, heresy existed among them. The favourite accusation of the Catholic Church was that they were Manichaeans; that is, that they followed the ascetical practices and doctrines of Mani, who tried to reconcile Christianity with Zoroastrianism, the ancient faith of Persia, which believed in an eternal dualism of light and darkness. But whatever else these numerous sects stood for, they represented a common trend to organize life and worship independently of the Roman Catholic clergy and on the basis of the Bible in the vernacular. They pleaded for a simple, devout life. Not all the popes condemned them.

The best known were the Albigenses. They regarded the clergy of their time as corrupt, and counted their rites as worthless because they were not men of God. Their persecution began under the Bishop of Cîteaux and Simon de Montfort. It lasted for twenty years and in the end almost exterminated them. Since the bishops, in dealing with opposition of this kind, had made little use of the Inquisition (see p. 57), in 1231 Pope Gregory IX put this iniquitous practice into the hands of the Dominican order, giving its leaders vast powers to coerce bishops and nobles, whose help they wanted, in their nefarious work. They were only too successful, so much so that by the middle of the fourteenth century probably few Albigenses existed. It is certain that, although outwardly suppressed, the spirit of these persecuted sects continued to live in the hearts of the people till the Reformation. Much historical research is still needed in order to bring out the true story and theological position of these numerous groups. There are complicated questions involved, and historians have depended too much on the statements of the enemies of the dissenting groups for their assessment of their doctrine and morals.

Opposition from within the Catholic Church

Other individuals and groups were from within the Catholic Church. They contended against its policy and practice from their unique position as part of the church. One of the most remarkable was Marsilius of Padua (1270–1342), a physician by profession. In his *Defensor Pacis* (Defender of Peace), written in Paris in 1324, he maintained that the supreme standard is the Bible. The supreme authority is a general council made up of representative clergy and laymen. The clergy are equal, he declares, and such offices as those of popes and bishops are of human origin. The clergy should be appointed by the civil authorities, on behalf of the people. Excommunication by a priest is nothing unless it coincides with the judgment of God. Such declarations seem remarkable for that epoch, but were merely a development of ideas current for some time among both papist and anti-papist thinkers.

A far greater man, an Englishman, William of Occam (1280–1347), the renowned nominalist philosopher at the University of Paris, and a leading Franciscan, expressed views not unlike those of Marsilius. Such men represented the strong, rising individualism of the epoch, and the determination not to accept blindly all that emanated from the high ecclesiastical authorities.

John Wyclif (1320–84)

John Wyclif was in his day the ablest scholar at the University of Oxford, with which he had a lifelong connection. Although a priest of the Roman church to his dying day, he declared that 'the only head of the Church is Christ. The pope, unless he be one of the predestinate who rule in the spirit of the gospel, is the vicar of Antichrist.' He further wrote that 'the power-grasping hierarchy, and the monks and friars, who claim special religious sanctity are without Scriptural warrant'. He rejected transubstantiation (see pp. 29–30 and 51) as utterly contrary to both Scripture and reason. He denied the infallibility of the Roman church in matters of faith, rejected auricular confession and criticized belief in purgatory, pilgrimages, worship of saints and veneration of relics, as all being unscriptural. No wonder he has been acclaimed as 'the morning star of the English Reformation'.

He organized bands of preachers who lived very simply, and went throughout the land preaching the Word of God at a time when the priests seldom preached and the people were left uninstructed. The importance of the translation of the Latin Vulgate into English made by his followers – the first Bible in English – cannot be exaggerated. Its effects were far-reaching, for it brought home the truth to prince and peasant alike.

The reception given by the laity to Wyclif's writings reveals how widespread was the desire for reform of the church. Hundreds of monks and nuns also welcomed these writings, but there was, naturally enough, much opposition. His enemies would gladly have burnt him, but, in the providence of God, he was protected by the Court, especially by John of Gaunt. The motive was, perhaps, political rather than religious. It expressed their hostility to the pope, then living at Avignon, and a puppet of the French king with whom the English were at enmity.

John Hus (1360–1415)

This man, born a poor peasant, became by sheer ability Rector of Prague University, then the most important university in Europe after Paris and Oxford. He had a genuine experience of conversion, and became a powerful preacher in the Bohemian language, proclaiming the gospel with fiery zeal and rebuking fearlessly the common vices. The clergy turned on him only when he attacked their own covetousness, sloth and luxury. In those days there were close links between the universities of Oxford and Prague, and the teachings of Wyclif made a deep impression on Hus and others in Bohemia. As he was a zealous patriot, the Germans, who opposed the Bohemians, avenged themselves by charging him with heresy. His books were publicly burnt at Prague and the archbishop tried to stop him preaching.

Eventually Hus was summoned before the Council of Constance (1414–18). Relying on a safe conduct granted him by Sigismund, the German king and emperor elect, he went. He was thrown into prison and barbarously treated. The emperor gave an order for his release but was terrified by the pope and cardinals into cancelling it. After seven months of cruel suffering, Hus faced what purported to be a trial. His defence was drowned with shouts of 'Recant, Recant!' He declared he would retract nothing unless it was contrary to God's Word. In 1415, after the most shameful degradation by the council, he was burnt by the civil authorities outside Constance at the request of the church.

It is ironic that Pope John XIII, who, with the council, was responsible for the death of this righteous man, was himself steeped in wickedness. He has been called 'a clerical brigand', and before this same Council of Constance was over, was compelled to resign as he did not wish to face an enquiry into the very serious offences of which he was accused.

12

Attempted reformation and the Renaissance

The reforming councils

The development of a new attitude to the papacy is clearly seen in the three reforming councils that took place during the years 1409 to 1449. To find a solution to the Great Schism (see p. 75), men such as John Gerson, Chancellor of the University of Paris, and Cardinal d'Ailly of the same university, were driven to propose a general council. They held that such a gathering, representative of the whole body of the church, was superior to the pope, and could judge and remove him, and reform the church. Thus it was that the Council of Pisa (1409) deposed the two rival popes, Gregory XII and Benedict XIII, declaring them to be notorious schismatics, heretics and perjurers, and elected Pope Alexander V. When, however, the council proceeded to the work of reformation, they were thwarted by the new pope, who wanted no curbing of his powers, and at the earliest opportunity dissolved the gathering.

The second council was held at Constance from 1414 to 1418. It was this gathering that condemned John Hus to death, an act that cost the Roman church much support. As already noted, it also compelled the pope to resign because of his 'detestable and unseemly life and manners', and appointed Cardinal Colonna to succeed him, who then took the name Martin V. It also again deposed the rival popes Gregory XII (who died during the time of the council) and Benedict XIII (who refused to acknowledge its sentence and maintained his claim to be the lawful pope until his death in 1424). Although the council had little or no success in effecting any lasting reform, it is important since it declared that its authority was derived 'immediately from Christ' and was effective over the pope as well as over other members of the church. This was, in effect, the denial of any claim that the pope had authority over the universal church.

The third council met at Basel in 1431 to deal with the Hussite revolt in Bohemia and generally to seek the reform of the church. The pope tried to dissolve it but its members refused to obey his orders, again maintaining that a general council was superior to the pope. With the passing of the years, however, it lost credit and was finally dissolved by the Emperor Frederick III in 1449.

Although these councils failed to secure even moderate reform, it was good that they had raised this serious question of the need for it. The disease was deadlier than they knew. Others after them were to tinker with the matter of reform, for everywhere its necessity was realized. Only a man such as Martin Luther could bring it to pass, and in the only way it could be done – by laying an axe to the roots of the whole papal system.

The Renaissance

Of all the factors, other than religious ones, that prepared for the Reformation, the great movement called the Renaissance was the chief. It was not a religious movement, but prepared the way for the reformers by opening human minds and breaking the shackles imposed for centuries by the hierarchy. The word 'Renaissance' means 'a rebirth', and is used to designate the revival of Latin and Greek literature and art that took place at the end of the medieval period and the beginning of the modern age.

The watchword of the Renaissance was the Latin phrase *ad fontes* (to the sources), as the whole movement was a return to original manuscripts and ideas. While a reformation might have developed without the Renaissance, the form it took was governed by the preceding renewal of scholarly activity. A new spirit was abroad – a spirit of adventure, enterprise, geographical discovery and intellectual quickening. Arabic translations of Greek authors, especially Aristotle, had helped to counteract the sad neglect of Greek culture in Europe in the Middle Ages. In the fourteenth century Dante, Petrarch and Boccaccio had helped to revive interest in the classical writers. The use of the printing press spread knowledge among the masses as never before. The sterile word-spinning of Scholasticism was replaced by the methods of genuine science with its new and precious discoveries, while philosophy too was entering a new era. Scholasticism had been the dominant theology and philosophy in the medieval schools from the eleventh to the fourteenth century. It was an application of the philosophy of Aristotle to Christian teaching, attempting to reconcile reason and faith.

When in 1453 Constantinople fell to the Turks, many great scholars fled to the West, bringing not only knowledge, but treasures of Greek literature that had been carefully preserved throughout the years. A flood of manuscripts from the East ended up in the Vatican Library in Rome and elsewhere. Several of the popes were most enthusiastic supporters of the New Learning and the Arts, not realizing that the new spirit of independent enquiry would deal a deadly blow to the authoritarian system the papacy represented.

Nicolas V, the illustrious founder of the Vatican Library, was the first pope to interest himself in the Renaissance. Artists and scholars were greatly helped by him, and he ordered many Greek classics to be translated into Latin. Some of the greatest architects, artists and sculptors the world has ever known flourished during this era. Among them were Donato Bramante, Raphael, Michelangelo and Leonardo da Vinci. They were employed in the great work of building and decorating St Peter's in Rome, and the beauty of their work astonishes all visitors.

The devotees of the New Learning were called humanists. In the Netherlands and Germany, they were definitely more Christian in their outlook than in Italy, chiefly because of the excellent influence of the schools of the Brethren of the Common Life, begun at Deventer in 1376. These stressed the importance of religion in education, and produced many brilliant scholars such as Erasmus, Mutianus Rufus and John Wessel of Groningen, scholars who prepared the way for the Reformation. Little by little, the New Learning entered the universities, schools and leading social circles.

Some of its exponents were cruelly persecuted; for example, the great scholar Johann Reuchlin.

Among outstanding Christian humanists, we notice the following.

1. *Girolamo Savonarola (1452–98)*. Although he still accepted the medieval theology, he profoundly affected the lives of many scholars in days when the Renaissance had led a great number of them into the sensualism of paganism in his native Italy. His saintliness and earnest preaching profoundly affected the masses, transformed the lives of intellectuals and caused fashionable women to make 'a bonfire of vanities' (cards, dice, jewellery, cosmetics, lewd books) in the public square. He aimed at making Florence a theocratic republic. He was unjustly charged with heresy, and was strangled and burnt in 1498. Thus, the Roman church had one of her noblest sons executed, and showed that purification of the Roman system as it was then constituted was impossible.

2. *John Colet (1466–1519)*. He was one of a group of brilliant humanists at Oxford and fell under the influence of the ideas spread by Savonarola. He broke away from the methods of Scholasticism, and his lectures on Paul's letters caused a sensation, because he made the apostle's message live again. Becoming Dean of St Paul's in London, he preached, in 1512, a startling sermon before Convocation in which he declared that the vicious and depraved lives of the clergy were the worst heresy of the times. First reform the bishops, he declared, and it will spread to all and sundry. The laws of the church would never be enforced until the bishops became new men. He taught his students that the important matter was to keep the Bible and the Apostles' Creed. He believed in no priesthood and denied transubstantiation.

Among his famous students was Erasmus, whom he persuaded to produce his Greek version of the New Testament, and William Tyndale, to whom we owe so much for his English translation of the Bible, although it cost him his life at the stake.

3. *Desiderius Erasmus (1467–1536)*. Born at Rotterdam, he became easily the greatest of the humanists. For a short time, he was Professor of Divinity and Greek at Cambridge. His literary labours were constant. His *Enchiridion*, *In Praise of Folly* and *Colloquies* abounded

in good-humoured ridicule against the medieval church, its ceremonies and clergy. His aim was to reform the church of Rome from within, and when, during the Reformation, many were leaving her, he refused to do so. He was scathingly attacked by both Roman Catholics and Protestants, and accused of lack of courage. His Greek edition of the New Testament was invaluable. He wanted to make it understood not only by 'women', but by 'Scots and Irish, and by Turks and Saracens'.

Losses and gains from the Renaissance

The study of the great classics of Greece and Rome and the enthusiasm for Greek art reintroduced pagan ideals, with the result that a great degeneration of morals ensued. On the one hand, beautiful works of art were being produced for St Peter's and the Vatican, and for churches throughout Italy. On the other hand, many indulged to excess their love of pleasure, and became treacherous in their dealings with one another. Poison, the dagger and the gun were freely used to secure the aims of the ambitious. It was the period of Cesare and Lucretia Borgia (children of Pope Alexander VI), and they represented 'all the elegance, all the vices, and all the crimes of that epoch', in spite of being outstanding supporters of the Renaissance movement. The popes themselves were far from being models of correct living. Obviously, something more than the New Learning and a love of art, however beautiful, was required to make saints. The greatest gain from the Renaissance was that it broke the shackles the medieval church had placed upon thought and investigation.

Although many of the greatest Christian humanists died while still members of the Roman church, it would be impossible to exaggerate their importance as precursors of the Reformation. The effect of Renaissance scholarship in general was to lead scholars back to the original Greek and Hebrew documents, past the Vulgate and imperfect translations of patristic texts. Thus, it was possible once again to return to the teachings of the early church on important matters, and to rediscover truths that had long been obscured by incorrect renderings of Scripture.

13

The Reformation in Germany

Martin Luther

The humanists, although they had prepared the way, had produced no reformation in the church. A person of intense spiritual conviction was required to do this, someone on fire with zeal for the gospel, and possessing in addition great ability and courage. Such a man was Martin Luther, the originator and leader of the Reformation in Germany.

Born on 10 November 1483, the son of a poor miner, he knew the struggles and outlook of the working classes. Having obtained a free education at Eisenach School, he entered Erfurt University in 1501. There the influence of the Christian humanist John Wessel had left a decided impression on the young Luther, who was a brilliant law student, fond of music and philosophy. Suddenly, however, after being caught in a thunderstorm, and to the surprise of all his friends, he entered the convent of the Augustinian Eremites. From boyhood, he had had a keen sense of the reality of the spiritual world. His Pelagian (see p. 42) teachers now taught him to save himself through prayers, fasting and penance. The Scriptures were withheld from him, but he wearied his superiors with his constant confessions and penance. And still he found no rest. Then, when he was 20, he discovered a Latin Bible. John Staupitz, his Vicar-General, encouraged him to read it, and pointed him to Christ Jesus, who alone takes away sin and gives us fellowship with God. While reading Romans, the peace of God came into Luther's heart. Through studying Augustine's works, he came to see even more clearly that people are saved by God through Jesus Christ and not by their own good works, and that this salvation depends on God's grace alone. The monastic life and external observances in religion became of less importance to him. He began to study carefully the Hebrew and Greek Scriptures, especially the Psalms and Paul's letters.

Tetzel and the indulgences

Pope Leo X (1513–21) needed great sums of money to continue the building of St Peter's Church, and to gratify his own extravagant tastes. To secure the money, he resolved to extend the sale of indulgences. Such sales had produced grave abuses in the past, and the new drive for money brought matters to a climax. A famous seller of indulgences, a Dominican monk named Johann Tetzel, shamefully offered his wares near Wittenberg, declaring that 'no sooner will the money chink in the box, than the soul of the departed will be free' from purgatory. The spirit of Martin Luther was stirred to the depths. On All Saints' Day, 1517, he nailed his Ninety-five Theses to the church door at Wittenberg, where vast crowds congregated. In this famous document, it was emphatically laid down, among other things, (1) that an indulgence can never remit guilt; God has kept that in his own hand; (2) it cannot remit divine punishment for sin; that also is in God's hand alone; (3) it has no efficacy for souls in purgatory; and (4) the Christian who has truly repented has already received pardon from God, and needs no indulgence. Copies were made in German of the Latin theses and printed off by friends for circulation in tens of thousands all over Germany. The conflict had begun that was to usher in the Reformation.

The issues raised were far greater than even Luther himself knew. The pope thought it was merely 'a squabble of monks', but soon realized his mistake and summoned Luther to Rome in July 1518. To go would have meant certain death, and he therefore refused. Then the pope asked his legate in Germany, Cardinal Cajetan, to deal with the question. On meeting Luther at Augsburg, Cajetan objected to statements in the theses, such as that the merits of Christ free the sinner without papal intervention. Luther, however, refused to recant, appealed 'from the pope ill-informed to the pope better-informed', and returned to Wittenberg. Up till then, Luther had accepted the pope's supremacy; but when he began to examine the arguments for it, was filled with indignation to find that the claims were based on the forged decretals (see p. 64).

Discussion at Leipzig (1519)

In 1519 a disputation was arranged at Leipzig between Carlstadt, an enthusiastic but not always wise supporter of Luther, and Eck, the papal champion. In the course of this discussion, Luther caused an immense sensation by roundly declaring that the supremacy of the pope was unknown in the Scriptures, that it had grown up only in the previous 400 years and that general councils had erred in giving their support to it.

The die was now cast. The reformer himself saw the full implications of his position. He freed himself for ever from the authority of popes, fathers and councils, and henceforth took the Word of God as the only rule of faith. He stood before the world as a free Christian man, no longer subject to papal usurpation. The younger humanists now rallied around Luther. The people of the German cities realized that not only true religion, but also the freedom of their country, depended on his campaign. He seemed now to have immeasurable strength, and poured forth a constant stream of sermons and pamphlets through the printing presses.

When Luther went to Leipzig, he was accompanied by a bodyguard of 200 students and by Melanchthon, the young professor of Greek at Wittenberg. Melanchthon became the fervent follower and lifelong friend of Luther. They were complementary to one another – the calm learning and gentleness of Melanchthon standing over against the fiery passion and rugged boldness of Luther. As an expounder and systematizer of Protestant theology, Melanchthon became immensely popular, and when the great Reformer died the brilliant Melanchthon succeeded him as leader of the Lutheran movement.

In 1520 Luther sent forth his three most famous pamphlets: *To the Nobility of the German Nation*, *Concerning Christian Liberty* and *On the Babylonish Captivity of the Church*. They were nothing if not forcible in expression, and could hold the attention of even the most casual reader.

On 15 June 1520 came the pope's bull (a papal edict) excommunicating Luther and ordering his works to be burnt. The reformer gave an appropriate reply. Having arranged a bonfire outside Wittenberg, he went arrayed in the robes of his order, amid a crowd of sympathizers from the university and town, and publicly flung the bull, the canon law and the forged decretals into the fire. No gesture could have given a more emphatic message of defiance.

The emperor Charles V and the Diet of Worms

The young emperor, Charles V, King of Spain, was at that time the most powerful monarch on earth, with vast territories throughout Europe and in the Americas. He was a fervent Roman Catholic and aimed at one big united empire and one big united church from which no one could dissent. He would willingly have wiped out the Protestants, but refrained for two reasons. His constant wars with his enemy Francis I of France and the invasion of the Danube valley by the Turks meant that he needed the help of his Protestant subjects in his fight against these deadly foes.

In 1521 he called the imposing Diet of Worms, to which princes, dukes, prelates and other high-ranking nobles were invited. His principal aim was to put down Luther, to whom, however, he gave a safe conduct. The reformer's friends urged him not to go, for they remembered the fate of John Hus. The reply has never been forgotten: 'Though there were as many devils in Worms as tiles on its roofs, I would go.' The Diet, presided over by the emperor in person, was hostile. Luther was questioned roughly about his books and ordered to retract. Like Hus a century earlier, he declared he would retract nothing unless it was proved to be contrary to Scripture. His noble declaration 'Here I stand. I can do no other. So help me God. Amen' has thrilled freedom-loving people through the centuries.

Owing to his having a safe conduct, he was dismissed but was condemned and placed under the ban of the empire. To save his life, the Elector of Saxony secretly sent a troop of horsemen to arrest him on the way home. He was carried off to the castle of the Wartburg, and his enemies thought he had perished. In his confinement of nearly a year, he translated the New Testament from the original

Greek into German – a work of supreme importance for the Reformation.

On his return to Wittenberg from the Wartburg in March 1522, Luther found the community in a frenzy of excitement because of the attacks of Carlstadt upon the ordinances of the church and the preaching of Claus Storch and other fanatics from Zwickau. The situation appeared to be very serious but, in eight days, Luther calmed the excited minds and restored order, thus keeping his movement on the paths of moderation.

The Revolt of the Nobles in 1523 and the Revolt of the Peasants in 1525 caused great distress to Luther and hampered his work. The revolts were due to hard social and economic causes, but the reformer was blamed. Luther foolishly urged the authorities to crush the Peasants' Revolt unmercifully, and many of his followers were alienated and a good number became Anabaptists.

The Diet of Speier (1526 and 1529)

Having defeated his enemy Francis I, and having secured a promise of help in putting down Luther's followers, the emperor Charles V called the first Diet of Speier and ordered action to be taken against the reformer's views. Strangely enough, he quarrelled seriously with the pope at the same time. The Diet, instead of condemning Luther, gave the famous Edict of Speier in favour of toleration – that each state in Germany was allowed to hold the religion of its ruling prince. This principle of *cuius regio, ejus religio* (Latin, 'whose realm, his religion') was finally accepted at the Peace of Augsburg in 1555.

The second Diet of Speier in 1529 decided that the districts that had become Lutheran after the decisions of 1526 should remain so, but that the other districts should remain Roman Catholic in perpetuity with no opportunity to introduce Reformed teaching. The evangelical minority in the diet protested against the finding, because no diet had the right to bind consciences in matters of religion. Because of their protest they were called 'Protestants', and the origin of the term is worth noting. The Roman Catholics formed a league to further the interests of their religion. Knowing that the intention of the emperor was to destroy Protestantism, the Elector of Saxony, the Landgrave of Hesse and other princes formed a Protestant league, known as the League of Schmalkald, to resist aggression. It was most unfortunate that just at that time, when the enemies of the Reformed cause were banding together in Germany to destroy the cause, a bitter conflict should have arisen between the Lutheran and Swiss theologians as to the meaning of the Lord's Supper. Philip of Hesse arranged a conference in 1529 at Marburg with a view to settling the dispute. Complete agreement was secured on fourteen points. On the fifteenth point there was serious disunity. While all rejected the Roman Catholic doctrine of transubstantiation as unscriptural, Luther believed in a related doctrine called consubstantiation; that is, that while the bread and wine remain what they are, yet in a miraculous way Christ is present bodily in, under and along with the bread and wine. Ulrich Zwingli, the Swiss leader, held that the bread and wine were only signs that reminded worshippers of the sacrifice of Christ, and that they fed on him by faith, but Luther was immovable and bitter. His intransigence caused incalculable loss to the Protestant cause.

Luther was initially so successful as a reformer because he represented the spirit of the German people in their resistance to the abuses of the Roman church, such as the scandals over indulgences and the saying of masses for the dead. The conviction was general that ecclesiastical reform was necessary and that there had to be a return to the simple faith of New Testament times. After the second Diet of Speier, however, and the formation of the Catholic League, Germany was irrevocably divided into Protestant and Catholic sections bitterly opposed to one another.

While Luther's work as a reformer was of surpassing importance, he has been criticized for being too conservative in holding a doctrine of the Lord's Supper halfway between the Roman and the Zwinglian view, and at the same time retaining the crucifix, candles, Mass vestments and other elements characteristic of the Roman Catholic system. With regard to organization, he placed church power in the hands of the civil authorities as representing the Christian community. The ruling princes in the large states, and the local councils in the free cities, appointed committees to manage ecclesiastical affairs and exercise church discipline. These committees were called consistories. The dominance of the civil power established in this way in the German church proved a source of spiritual weakness for generations.

The Anabaptists

This is the name given to certain groups of Christians who came into prominence from about 1523 onwards, soon after the start of the Reformation. They objected to infant baptism and rebaptized those who joined their communion. Hence the term 'anabaptist' (Greek, *ana-*, 'again' or 're-', and *baptismos*, 'baptism').

Reference has already been made to the excitement caused in Wittenberg in 1522 by Storch and other 'prophets' from Zwickau. In that town, a certain Thomas Müntzer was closely associated with Storch and the 'prophets'. They preached a wild millenarianism and insisted that God's day of wrath was about to break, and that the saints would dominate the governments of the world. They appealed strongly to the power of the sword to impose their views, and during their brief control of the city there were many excesses. While most historians have represented these wild fanatics as being the founders of the Anabaptist movement, research has shown that this view is undoubtedly erroneous. The real Anabaptists arose in Zurich in 1523 among honourable men who called themselves 'Brethren', and were led by Conrad Grebel and Felix Manz. They laid great stress on Bible study, objected strongly to such a state church as was countenanced by Luther and Zwingli, and asked for the removal of pictures and images from churches. They were men of sincere piety, who insisted that the sword of the Spirit, the Word of truth, was their only weapon. They refused to recognize infant baptism.

During 1525 these views spread widely in the region around Zurich, and the council of that city passed cruel and unjust laws against the Anabaptists. Unhappily, Zwingli was a party to these proceedings, and most of the Anabaptist leaders suffered the penalty of death. From 1525 to 1528, the movement became very strong in Germany, especially in Strasburg and Augsburg. Its members were often accused of being revolutionary and of plotting treasonable activities against the state, and were unjustly maligned in many ways. The Diet of Speier in 1529 approved an imperial mandate of the previous year that both rebaptizers and rebaptized should be put to death even without proper forms of trial. It is reckoned that in a few years no fewer than 2,000 perished. At first, Luther strongly opposed persecuting methods but, as the Anabaptist movement spread, he became alarmed and in 1530 urged 'the use of the sword against them by right of law'. The movement continued to spread, however. In the Netherlands, Menno Simons exercised much influence, and Jacob Hutter, a Tyrolese, did the same in Austria, Moravia and Poland, until his martyrdom in 1536. The Mennonite and Hutterite movements, which have done notable work in many countries, including Russia, the USA and Canada, took their designations from these men. They have always been pacific, earnest and industrious Christians, and have often lived in communal settlements.

In view of the variations in teaching and practice that existed among the different Anabaptist groups, it is difficult to give a description of them that would cover all. Some of them, at least, inherited the traditions of certain of the anti-papal sects that abounded from the thirteenth century onwards. Generally speaking, they expected the speedy return of Christ, rejected completely the idea of a state church and possessed boundless enthusiasm that sometimes carried them to extremes. The worst persecutions came from the Roman Catholics, but the Protestants were far from guiltless. Even John Calvin, though he did not persecute them, could see little good in them. The Anabaptists stood for religious liberty at a time when neither Protestants nor Catholics fully appreciated the importance of freedom of conscience. While the Baptists, Quakers and Brethren have affinities with them, none of these movements claim to have originated from the Anabaptists. Over the years, this whole movement has often been judged by the excesses of a few. Those who suffered for their convictions, including Hubmaier and Denck, should not be placed in the same category as the more radical leaders, such as Müntzer and Carlstadt.

14

The Reformation in Switzerland

Ulrich Zwingli

While Lutheranism spread from Germany into Denmark, Norway and Sweden, and was eventually recognized as the state religion in these countries, there grew up in Switzerland a somewhat different type of Protestantism. Although the Reformation here lacked the dramatic incidents of the German movement, it was in reality more important. The Swiss type of the Reformed religion was more easily transplanted, and spread to France, Scotland, Hungary, the Netherlands, a great part of Germany itself, to the English Puritans, to America and to the British dominions. The Swiss took their stand strongly on the Word of God as the only rule of faith and practice, and were not bound by as many medieval traditions as the early Lutherans. They swept away images, relics, pictures, pilgrimages and the use of the organ in public worship. Generally speaking, it may be said that the Reformation in Switzerland was far more radical than in Germany.

Ulrich Zwingli (1484–1531), the leader of the Swiss Reformation, was a saint, scholar and patriot. He developed his ideas quite independently of Luther. On finishing a brilliant career at the Universities of Vienna and Basel, he was appointed priest of Glarus, and was later called to the great cathedral church of Zurich. He preached strongly against the corruption engendered among his countrymen through enlistment in foreign mercenary armies, including that of the pope, and also denounced the prevalent superstitions in the Roman church and the sale of indulgences. Taking his stand on the Word of God, he fearlessly attacked in public disputation the distinctive doctrines of the Roman church, and was supported strongly by the city council of Zurich that set up an independent church in 1522.

In 1528 the Reformation triumphed in Berne and St Gall, and in 1529 at Basel, Mühlhausen and Schaffhausen. All these became Protestant and republican, and carried out the political and religious reforms advocated by Zwingli. Very soon, he saw the impending danger from the five Forest Cantons that remained Roman Catholic and had entered a league with Ferdinand of Austria to destroy the Reformation. In spite of all his warnings to the Swiss and German Protestants as to the perils that threatened from this source, they failed to prepare. When the Catholic Cantons attacked Zurich, Zwingli died heroically with his people on the field of Cappel. He was a great reformer but more radical in outlook than John Calvin, who was soon to appear as the outstanding leader of the Reformed church.

John Calvin

Few people have suffered more from ignorant detraction than John Calvin. There was a time when many wanted to comment on Calvin's views without a detailed knowledge of his writings. For the English-speaking world things started to change with John McNeil's fresh translation of Calvin's *Institutes*. Then came the Torrance New Testament commentaries, followed by the influence of men such as Lloyd-Jones, James Packer and John Stott. More recently Alister McGrath and Professor Anthony Lane have been prominent in Calvin studies. In North America there are the New Calvinists, represented by men such as Ligon Duncan, Albert Mohler, John Piper and Mark Dever. More of Calvin is available in English now than ever before, with some of his French commentaries being translated by Douglas Kelly and Robert White. Some of those who condemn Calvin out of hand seem to have spent little time studying his works. There is general agreement among serious scholars that Calvin was the greatest man of the Reformation era.

Born at Noyon, in Picardy, France, on 10 July 1509, he had good family connections and was educated among the nobility. He aroused remarkable affections in others so different from himself such as Luther, Melanchthon, Bucer and John Knox, even when they disagreed violently with him. His father first of all destined him for the priesthood, and then sent him to Orleans to study law. There, as formerly at Paris, he proved himself a most brilliant student. Under humanist teachers, his mind became steeped in classical learning. His legal training, coupled with logical precision and clarity of mind, made him one of the most lucid and systematic theologians ever known.

When his father died in 1532, Calvin returned from Orleans and joined a group of Protestants in Paris for the study of the Scriptures and for prayer. The following year, he had to flee from Paris because of his evangelical views and the oration on 'Christian Philosophy' that he had written for his friend, Nicolas Cop, the Rector of Paris University. Passing through Strasburg, he was kindly received by Martin Bucer, one of the greatest scholars of the Reformation period, who was Professor of Theology in the university of that city. In 1535 Calvin settled in Basel as a refugee and continued his studies. In 1536 he published there his great work *The Institutes of the Christian Religion*. It was the first really systematic exposition of Reformed theology. Although much smaller than subsequent editions, it was the ablest theological work ever written by a young man of 26. As a presentation of Christian doctrine, it has never been surpassed. It is readily available from several publishers, and its circulation has increased in recent decades.

The work was based upon the Apostles' Creed, and the aim was to show that Protestants were thoroughly loyal to this creed and could not be regarded as heretics. Reformers such as Luther and Calvin were giving no new creed to the church but were, instead, leading it back to the beliefs and practices of the apostolic age. Calvin more than any other person insisted that the church must return again to the principles of the first three centuries in its simplicity.

When passing through Geneva in 1536, Calvin was visited by the local pastor, William Farel, who implored him in God's name to come to his help. In the previous year, the city had become formally Protestant. Political factors played a large part in this transformation, for the people wanted to be independent of the Duke of Savoy and the bishop, who had formerly ruled them jointly. No moral or spiritual change had come over the community, which for long had been notorious for its licentiousness. Immoral doctrines were now entering under the guise of liberty. In despair, Farel appealed to Calvin to settle there. The latter was bent on devoting his life to literary work, but this seemed a call from God and he consented. Thus began the historic connection of Geneva with Calvinism.

Calvin immediately prepared articles of faith for the church, a form of church government and a catechism for the children. He proceeded to attack at the roots the licentiousness that was a disgrace to Geneva. Long before his arrival, the rulers of the city had made laws against gaming, drunkenness, masquerades, dances and extravagance in dress. As there was no change of heart, these laws proved unavailing. It is entirely erroneous to charge Calvin with the drawing up of such laws, and with vexatious interference in trivial matters affecting the private lives of the citizens. Every medieval town had such laws.

What Calvin rightly insisted on was that church members should live in accordance with the demands of the New Testament. To secure this end, he asked that the church should exercise its own discipline and debar from Communion unworthy members – what is now done in most Christian communities. Although he asked only for this small measure of spiritual independence, and the right to excommunicate flagrant and unrepentant sinners, the government of Geneva (supposed to be Protestant) rose in arms and expelled both Calvin and Farel. He went again to Strasburg, where for three years he was pastor to the French refugees. He ministered in a church where his name is still honoured and his tradition maintained. It was at this time that he became acquainted with both Luther and Melanchthon, and his near neighbour was Martin Bucer, who afterwards became Professor of Theology at Cambridge.

In Calvin's absence, matters deteriorated in Geneva. Some of its citizens now realized that he was right in seeking a church in which Christian law would rule. They saw, as he did, that infidelity was the root cause of their troubles. After various political conflicts, and when their freedom seemed in danger, the people of Geneva implored Calvin to return. He was very reluctant to do so as he had found a fruitful field of work at Strasburg. Only when he was pressed by his friends, and urged by Berne, Zurich and Basel, did he decide to go. He felt it was the will of God.

For twenty-four years, he laboured in the city of his adoption. One feels amazed at the extent of his work – several sermons a week, a lecture every day, and a vast amount of correspondence with people all over Europe. He was the undoubted leader of the Protestant cause. No man had a more realistic conception of the needs of Europe in that day than Calvin. In the face of the growing opposition of the Roman church, he longed for a general council of all Protestant churches, but this he was unable to obtain owing to racial and theological prejudices.

Calvin stood up strongly for the principle that the church members should elect office-bearers to carry on the government of the church and that, in spiritual matters, the church had to be independent of the state. He maintained, however, that the civil government was also a divine institution, and that church and state should cooperate while respecting one another's separate spheres.

In 1541 the Ecclesiastical Ordinances set forth the laws by which the magistrates of Geneva dealt with church affairs. Pastors were to be elected by ministers already in office, and were to be appointed by the magistrates by consent of the people (who had only the right of veto). The elders were appointed by the city council on the advice of the pastors. The pastors and elders together formed the consistory that dealt with ecclesiastical affairs, and asked the civil authorities to impose penalties where necessary. There is much in these ordinances contrary to what Calvin had earlier taught in the *Institutes* about the freedom of Christian people to elect their own church office-bearers. It is obvious that in many things Calvin did not get his own way in Geneva, and was not responsible for much that was done by the city council and the consistory. It was only in the French Protestant church, and in Scotland, that Calvin's ideals as to Presbyterian church government found a free field, with most beneficial results. In this system, nothing was to be introduced into the church but what was positively sanctioned by the Word of God; the church must conform to the New Testament pattern; its office-bearers (ministers and elders) must be elected by the church members; and these are to rule the church in presbyteries, synods and general assemblies. Above all, Christ must be recognized as the only head of the church.

While it has often been claimed that Calvin's theology did not encourage missionary effort, the evidence points in a different direction. Calvin's Geneva was a centre that attracted religious refugees from other countries. In Geneva, they were educated and instructed in the faith, and often returned home to minister, many in dangerous situations that claimed numerous lives. It must be remembered that often there was a political aspect to the work of these returnees, as they were seeking religious freedom so that they could propagate the truths they had come to hold. This fact helps to explain the formation of the revolutionary parties such as the Huguenot forces in Spain, the Lords of the Congregation in Scotland and the Sea Beggars in the Netherlands. While the early attempts to evangelize produced good results in regions such as Poitou in south-west France, from 1555 onwards the Company of Pastors in Geneva had an organized scheme to produce a network of Protestant work throughout France. Though the records are incomplete, they show that between 1555 and 1563 eighty-eight missionaries were sent from Geneva. Many French-speaking churches in Switzerland were deprived of pastors in order that Huguenot churches in France could have settled ministries. By 1562, more than 2,100 Huguenot congregations existed, with about three million members.

Two other aspects of Genevan missionary influence need a mention. One of these is the importance of the French seaports as places where the Protestant Reformation made strong progress. It appears that Calvin himself originated the work at La Rochelle in the 1530s, though Scots carried it on. Certainly, this is what happened at Dieppe, where Knox and fellow-countrymen saw many converts, especially among the nobility. Another important consideration is the amount of Protestant literature that emanated from Geneva, both in French and English. Pamphlets helped both to explain and disseminate the gospel, while the most important publication, the Geneva Bible (published in 1560), was widely used. Its annotations were very effective means of promoting Calvinistic theology, and strengthened the Puritan movement in England. It remained in use for decades after the publication of the Authorized Version in 1611. Even at the opening of the General Assembly of the Church of Scotland in Glasgow in 1638, Alexander Henderson preached from the Geneva Version. The fact that the Genevan Bible went through 140 editions between 1540 and 1644 testifies to its widespread distribution and use. Every Puritan household in England and Scotland is thought to have possessed a copy.

The central thought in Calvin's theology was the sovereignty of God. All things, therefore, that have to do with our salvation are founded on the will of God. We are saved only through the grace of God ministered to us by the Holy Spirit. God alone saves, not we ourselves. Hence, Calvin taught the doctrine of predestination and election. These are profound mysteries and were treated as such by Calvin himself. They are very perplexing but are undoubtedly taught in the Bible. All the other reformers, including Luther, believed these doctrines, but it was Calvin who gave them logical consistency. It is easy to criticize them. It is not so easy to solve the tremendous questions involved. Calvin always realized the vast importance of sound education and founded the College of Geneva with the illustrious Theodore Beza as head. Eight hundred students flocked to its classes in the first year. Pastors from there passed to many lands and exercised a mighty influence in making known the Reformed faith throughout Europe.

Geneva became a crowded city, with many refugees from Italy, France and Scotland taking up residence there. For the Protestants in Europe, Geneva became 'a second Rome'. Another aspect of Calvin's ministry was the vast correspondence in which he engaged. English reformers, French Huguenots, Scots and leaders of the Reformation in Germany all asked for and received advice from him. Worn out by his abundant labours, Calvin preached his last sermon on 6 February 1564, and died on 27 May that same year. By his own instruction, nothing marked his grave, and its location remains unknown.

Calvin's legacy of biblical exposition and profound theology has at times been diminished by reference to his involvement in the execution in Geneva of Michael Servetus, a Roman Catholic who denied the Trinity. However, Calvin was not the prosecutor in the case, and he has to be judged by the standards of his time. As Alister McGrath expresses it, 'Servetus was the *only* individual put to death for his religious opinions in Geneva during Calvin's lifetime, at a time when executions of this nature were a commonplace elsewhere' (*A Life of John Calvin: A Study in the Shaping of Western Culture*, p. 116). The death of Servetus was the fault of the culture and the age, not of one individual in sixteenth-century Europe.

The Reformed church in other countries

Some brief reference needs to be made to the Reformation in France, the Netherlands, Hungary, Spain and Italy. While information about Luther's views and works became widely disseminated, the major influence on several countries was Calvin's theology and vision for the church.

In France, Lefevre may be taken as the founder of the Protestant movement. Later, Calvin's influence became powerful and his views were adopted. For political reasons, Francis I persecuted the Protestants at home and helped them abroad. Four thousand Waldenses (see p. 76), belonging to that heroic body of evangelical Christians in northern Italy and southern France that dated back at least to 1170, were massacred in Provence in 1545. In spite of persecution, the Protestants had 2,000 places of worship by 1558. On the night of 24 August 1572 came the dreadful St Bartholomew's Day massacre, when, under the direction of the Queen Mother, Catherine de Medici, and the Guises, 2,000 were murdered in Paris, and 20,000 in the rest of France. Among them were the wise and noble Admiral Coligny and other great French leaders who were Protestants. It was not until 1598 that the French Protestants were granted religious freedom through the Edict of Nantes. The Netherlands early gave a ready welcome to Calvinism, and the Reformed church became strong. Philip II of Spain introduced the Inquisition in 1555, and it became an offence even to read the Bible. Beheading and burning became very common under this reign of terror until William the Silent, Prince of Orange, took up the fight for religious and civil freedom. In spite of the numerous executions carried on under the Duke of Alva, the gallant Netherlanders in 1572 formed the Union of Utrecht, comprising the seven northern provinces, which were Protestant, and laid the foundations of the Dutch nation. William was assassinated in 1584 by a Roman Catholic fanatic, but his work lived on.

In Hungary, Calvinism became the prevalent form of Prot-estantism. In spite of the hostility of the emperor Charles V in the sixteenth century, and severe persecutions by the Hapsburgs in the seventeenth, the movement could not be destroyed. In 1781 it was granted toleration, and by the nineteenth century had grown into the second largest Presbyterian church in the world.

In spite of the Inquisition, Lutheran doctrines passed early into Spain and Italy and were accepted by a wide circle of the cultured communities. There were no finer Protestants than those of Spain. The movement, however, was completely stamped out by the Inquisition in 1559 and 1560. Much the same happened in Italy, but there the Inquisition was less cruel although used freely by Pope Paul IV. Even bishops were suspected of harbouring Lutheran views in both Italy and Spain, and the situation seemed favourable for the Reformed cause. Nevertheless, torture, imprisonment and death almost destroyed Protestantism in these countries.

In the mountains and valleys of northern Italy, the Waldenses had survived since the twelfth century in spite of much bitter persecu-tion. In 1532 they became a definite branch of the Reformed church, with a Presbyterian policy. They have struggled nobly for centuries, and since 1848 have enjoyed religious freedom.

15

The Reformation in England

The break from Rome

The Reformation in England took a form very different from that on the Continent and in Scotland. It was carried out directly under Henry VIII, who looked neither to Luther nor to Calvin for a model. There is no reason to doubt that in his early days Henry was a sincere Roman Catholic who loved his church. He entered the controversy against Luther and wrote his treatise *On the Seven Sacraments*, which from a grateful pope brought him the title 'Defender of the Faith'. The fact that he broke with the Vatican in order to secure a divorce from Catherine of Aragon, to whom he had been married twenty-four years, has led at times to misrepresentation of the English Reformation. Catherine was the widow of Henry's deceased brother, Arthur, and it was clearly against Scripture and canon law for the pope to grant in the first place a dispensation permitting the marriage. This was the emphatic opinion of Warham, Archbishop of Canterbury, and of every bishop in England except two. Many of the universities of Europe held the same view. For political reasons, Ferdinand of Spain and Henry VII of England eagerly wanted the marriage, and brought pressure to bear upon Prince Henry and Catherine, and even upon Pope Julius II, as, from the outset, all of them had scruples against it. The pressure from such powerful monarchs secured consent and the pope signed the dispensation allowing the marriage to take place. As all the children, except Mary, were stillborn, and there was no son to carry on the Tudor line, Henry VII and others regarded it as a judgment for Henry VIII's marrying his brother's widow.

By 1526, Henry VIII had fallen in love with Anne Boleyn, and with Cardinal Wolsey's help had applied to the pope for an annulment of his marriage with Catherine. To her credit, Anne courageously told the king she could not be his wife and would never be his mistress. Although the pope used his dispensing power freely when it suited him, he refused Henry's claim, not so much on moral grounds as for fear of Catherine's nephew, the emperor Charles V.

With the connivance of Parliament, Henry took steps in 1531 to dominate the situation. He boldly charged the English clergy with treason under the old statute of *Praemunire* that forbade receiving orders from a foreign power. In the province of Canterbury alone, they were fined £100,000. The following year, with the help of Parliament, the king secured the abject 'submission' of the clergy. Henceforth, the Church of England was under his control.

In spite of being unpopular at the Vatican, Thomas Cranmer was made Archbishop of Canterbury in 1532 when Henry threatened to stop the dispatch of 'annates' to Rome. The annates represented a year's income claimed by the pope on the death of a bishop, abbot or parish priest, and paid by his successor. In 1533 Parliament passed the famous Act of Restraint of Appeals to stop all appeals to the Holy See. Henry secretly married Anne Boleyn. Later, Archbishop Cranmer tried the question of the divorce before his own court, and declared the marriage with Catherine null and void. The pope fulminated and ordered the faithful to resist Henry, but in vain. This led to the definite break with the church of Rome in 1534. Of many acts passed then, the most important was the Supremacy Act by which the king was declared to be the 'Supreme Head of the Church of England'. It became treason to call the king a heretic. The two Houses of Convocation made the declaration that 'the Roman Pontiff has no greater jurisdiction bestowed on him by God in the holy Scriptures than any other foreign bishop'. (The Houses of Convocation are provincial assemblies of the clergy of Canterbury and York; they antedate Parliament.)

At first, the change in England could scarcely be called a reformation. Matters remained virtually as before, except that now the king, not the pope, was head of the church. At the same time, there were some very hopeful factors. There was a strong desire for reform latent in the hearts of the English people. Without this, not even the ruthless and despotic Henry could have brought about the separation from Rome. For centuries, many had strongly resented the intervention of the pope, whom they regarded as a foreign potentate in the affairs of England, and this was reflected in the legislation of the country. From the days of Wyclif, many had read the Scriptures in their own language and were openly critical of the Roman church. Many objected to paying tithes to the priests, and in particular to paying annates and 'Peter's pence' to the pope. The latter originated in Saxon times and were donations or payments made directly to the Roman See.

There was much private piety of an evangelical kind in the land even before Luther's day. Men such as Thomas Cranmer, Thomas Cromwell and Hugh Latimer came to have strong Protestant leanings. But most bishops, while wishing for a reform in conduct, still wanted to retain the theology and practice of the Roman church. In 1536 the king himself prepared Ten Articles of Religion. They claimed to be based on the Bible and the ancient creeds, but still retained Roman Catholic elements regarding baptism and the real presence in the Lord's Supper.

'Injunctions' were issued in 1536 and 1538, warning against unnecessary holy days and against the abuse of images, relics and supposed priestly miracles. It was a great step forward when it was ordered that a large Bible should be placed in each church and that the people be encouraged to read it. What was not taught in Scripture was to be avoided, such as 'pilgrimages, offering money or candles to images . . . and saying prayers over beads' (Bettenson, *Documents of the Christian Church*, p. 327). The church was obviously moving in the right direction; but there were setbacks, such as when the bishops prepared a manual called *The Bishop's Book*, which was reactionary and recognized seven sacraments. The greatest gain was the place given to the Scriptures. The church owes an unspeakable debt to the scholarly William Tyndale in this connection. His translation of the Bible was epoch-making. When condemned and persecuted at home, he carried on his work on the Continent, and, in spite of bitter opposition, sent his translations in great quantities into England and Scotland. He was burnt in Brabant in 1536 at the request of Henry VIII.

The dissolution of the monasteries in 1536 and 1539 and the sale of the lands cheaply to his courtiers brought Henry large revenues and established an upper middle class that ever since then has had a great influence in English life. When the king realized that the Reformation was moving too fast for public sentiment, he became violently reactionary. To deny transubstantiation, or to say that a priest or nun might marry, meant burning. Thomas Cromwell was executed and Bishop Latimer was sent to prison. Both Protestants and Romanists who differed from Henry were hurried to execution. When he died in 1547, England was in ferment, some wanting the new ideas, others wishing to adhere to the medieval system.

The Reformation under Edward VI (1547–53)

This young king, the son of Henry VIII, was only 10 when he ascended the throne after his father had died in 1547. He was a youth of genuine piety and a frank and avowed friend of the Reformation, due in no small measure to Archbishop Cranmer's training. The cruel Six Articles of Henry VIII, and other repressive legislation, were swept away and the people became free to form their own views on doctrine. The Lord's Supper was now observed in Protestant fashion, and the clergy were allowed to marry. The publication of the First Prayer Book of Edward VI in 1549 was a great step forward. The whole service was in English for the first time, and the new prayer book had to be used in every church.

Because of the change of attitude, refugees returned from the Continent. They included those such as Nicholas Ridley and John Hooper, who had been under the influence of such Continental Reformers as Ulrich Zwingli and Heinrich Bullinger. They were helped by Cranmer, who was by that time a thoroughgoing Protestant, and others of the type of Hooper, Ridley, Miles Coverdale, John Ponet and John Scory were made bishops.

In 1547 Charles V had gained a great victory over the German Protestants at Mühlberg, and as a result the position of many Reformed church leaders on the Continent became perilous. Among those who fled to England were Martin Bucer of Strasburg, the friend of Calvin, who became Professor of Theology at Cambridge, Paul Buchlin, a brilliant Hebrew scholar, and the great Italians Peter Martyr and Bernardino Ochino. One of the most interesting was John à Lasco (or Łaski), a Polish nobleman, who had become a great theologian and fervent supporter of the Reformed church. He was destined to exercise a profound influence upon the religious life of England.

The British people are, indeed, debtors to all these refugees, who greatly strengthened the hands of those who maintained that the Reformation in England was incomplete and that too much of the discipline, ritual and ceremonial of the Roman church still remained. They wanted to model the Anglican Church on the pattern of Continental Protestantism, especially on that of Geneva. Those who took this attitude were known as Puritans. In later years, the name was applied specially to those of their number who practised austerity and strictness in religious matters. Since the Continental refugees, for political reasons, were allowed to have a congregation of their own in London, free from governmental interference, their church became a rallying ground for the Puritans in times of opposition.

When Edward VI ascended to the throne, the government was in the hands of the Privy Council, under the control of Edward Seymour, who was created Duke of Somerset. There was great need for the ecclesiastical changes brought about by the Protectorate. Shortly before the death of Henry VIII, Bishop Hooper had written, 'The impious Mass, the most shameful celibacy of the clergy, the invocation of saints, auricular confession, superstitious abstinence from meats and purgatory, were never before held by the people in greater esteem' (*Zurich Letters*, p. 36). A new set of 'Injunctions' was sent out for the guidance of the clergy (see Bettenson, *Documents of the Christian Church*, pp. 325–328). They are illuminating as to the condition of the church. Ministers were not to 'extol or set forth any images, relics, or miracles'. They were instructed to preach 'four times a year', which shows how preaching had lapsed in the Roman church. On every holy day, the clergy were to recite 'openly and plainly' from the pulpit the Lord's Prayer, the Creed and the Ten Commandments in English 'to the intent the people may learn the same by heart'. They were enjoined 'not to frequent taverns or ale houses, not to give themselves to drinking or riot, or spend their time idly at dice, cards, tables or gaming', a sad reflection on the people's spiritual condition.

In 1552 came the Second Prayer Book of Edward VI, the aim of which was to make the worship of England more like that of the Continental Reformed churches and less like the church of Rome. The Communion service was made Protestant. It is highly significant that the word 'table' is used instead of 'altar'. The terms 'minister' and 'priest' are interchangeable, and officiating clergy are forbidden to use 'Alb, Vestment, or Cope'. The preparation of the Prayer Book was principally the work of Cranmer. In it we see a manifestation of his deeply devotional spirit and his mastery of the English language. He made succeeding generations his debtors. In the words of Bishop J. C. Ryle:

> People were taught that justification was by faith without the deeds of law, and that every heavy-laden sinner on earth had a right to go straight to the Lord Jesus Christ for remission of sins, without waiting for pope or priest, confession or absolution, masses or extreme unction.

This Second Prayer Book is important because it has influenced all successive liturgical formulations in the Church of England and other episcopal churches.

In spite of the lack of political acumen in the Protector, Somerset, and glaring weaknesses in other members of the council, a most salutary change came over the religious condition of the people during the short reign of Edward. The response of the people, in the cities at least, showed that they were wearied to death of the cruel Romanism that under his own headship Henry VIII had favoured.

The Roman church re-established under Mary (1553–8)

The Reformation was perhaps beginning to move too fast for some when the pious young monarch died on 6 July 1553. He was succeeded by his half-sister, Mary Tudor, daughter of Catherine of Aragon, who, like her Spanish mother, was a fanatical Romanist. Her great aim was to bring England back to the Catholic fold. The misgovernment of Somerset and Northumberland in the previous reign made this easier because of the discontent it had aroused.

One of Mary's first acts (18 August 1553) was to prohibit all preaching and printing without her licence, thus striking a blow at all Protestant work. Soon the great Protestant bishops, such as Cranmer, Ridley, Coverdale, Hooper and Latimer, were lodged in prison, and bishops loyal to Rome took their place. In 1554 the queen married her cousin, Philip II of Spain, son of the emperor Charles V. It was part of the scheme to bring all Christendom within the orbit of Spanish power and under the ecclesiastical guidance of the papacy. The marriage was most unpopular in England and proved very unhappy for Mary and Philip themselves.

On 30 November 1554 the Lords and Commons, on royal instigation, presented a supplication 'that they might receive absolution, and be received into the body of the Holy Catholic Church, under the pope, the Supreme Head thereof'. Cardinal Pole, the new legate in England, was graciously pleased to grant this absolution, the Queen, Philip, the Lords and Commons receiving it on bended knees. It was a humiliating spectacle. The pope, and not the sovereign, was now once more head of the church in England.

The former laws against heretics were revived, and the old Roman Catholic ceremonies brought back. Terrible persecution began. Bishops Edmund Bonner and Stephen Gardiner stand out as cruel and insatiable in their lust for blood. The first to perish was John Rogers, Prebendary of St Paul's, to whom Tyndale had entrusted the great work of completing his translation of the Bible. His fate evoked great sympathy and vast crowds cheered him as he went to execution. Within five days, Bishop Hooper, the great Puritan bishop, who had protested against the use of vestments, was burnt in his cathedral town of Gloucester on 9 February 1555. God had blessed his work, and his devoted people were deeply moved by his death.

The British people have never forgotten the martyrdom of Bishops Ridley and Latimer, who were burnt at Oxford in front of Balliol College on 16 October 1555 for denying transubstantiation and the sacrifice of the Mass. The words of Latimer to Ridley as they faced the flames were prophetic. As recorded by Foxe in his *Book of Martyrs*, Latimer said, 'Be of good cheer, Master Ridley, and play the man; we shall this day, by God's grace, light such a torch in England as will never be put out.' Archbishop Cranmer was not burnt at Oxford until 21 March 1556. In a moment of weakness and under terrible pressure that momentarily broke him down, he had signed a recantation of his views. He made ample amends for his weakness. In the church, on the morning of his martyrdom, he bore an unflinching testimony before his enemies. At the stake, he showed the world his sorrow for signing the document. He threw it in the flames, pleading for God's pardon and the forgiveness of the people, and urging them to maintain the doctrines he had taught. He then held the offending hand and arm in the flames until they were burnt to a cinder.

Mary Tudor deposed at least 1,200 clergymen for being married men. In her short reign, no fewer than 286 were burnt for being Protestants, besides 'those that dyed of famyne in sondry prisons'. A multitude suffered imprisonment and the spoiling of their goods. It was no wonder the people called the Queen 'Bloody Mary'. Her life was indeed one of tragedy. Forgetting the brightness of her youth, she became ever more embittered, and ended her life as one of the most disappointed and miserable of women – hated even by her husband and at variance with the pope, whose cause she had served with unbounded devotion.

Queen Elizabeth and the Puritans

The accession of Queen Elizabeth in 1558 brought immense joy to multitudes, for persecution now ceased. Protestant exiles returned from abroad and congratulated the new queen. Even the returning Puritan leaders (see the later discussion on the Puritans, pp. 127–9) were given a place in the reconstituted church. Elizabeth, however, disliked the theology of Geneva, and this was soon shown in her treatment of the Puritans. She missed a great opportunity of making the Church of England a national and united church, for a few concessions would probably have retained the Puritans in the national church.

In the eyes of the Vatican, Queen Elizabeth was illegitimate, for the pope had never recognized the divorce of her father from Catherine of Aragon. In the opinion of the Roman church, her cousin, Mary, Queen of Scots, was the legal heir to the English throne. In spite of Elizabeth's love of Romish pomp and ceremony, she was compelled to fall back upon Protestants for her bishops. She could not look to France or Spain for help, because both strongly favoured Mary of Scotland on religious grounds. In France, Mary's uncles, the Duke of Guise and the Cardinal of Lorraine, were very powerful. Elizabeth was thus compelled to maintain an Anglican Church. She was careful to exercise her full power as supreme governor of the church, and kept the church's management in her own hands.

The Acts against heretics under which so many Protestants were burnt in Mary's time were repealed. A commission recommended that the Second Prayer Book of Edward VI be adopted once more. It was rather too Protestant for Queen Elizabeth, and from the proceedings in Convocation it is clear that the clergy were prepared to go much further in the matter of reform than she was. She insisted that the law concerning vestments and ornaments should be as in the Prayer Book of 1549. This was much less Protestant than that of King Edward's Second Prayer Book in 1552. She also insisted on certain alterations being made in the proposed Articles as to the Lord's Supper, in order to bring it somewhat nearer the Lutheran position. The queen was imperious and had her way, but fortunately the changes made in the proposed Articles were not considerable. Taking them all in all, the Thirty-nine Articles agreed to in 1562 are a magnificent statement of Reformed doctrine and made for stability in the religious life of England. The degree to which the doctrine of the Church of England (as established in the reign of Elizabeth) was Calvinist is remarkable. Even on the matter of the Communion there was practical agreement with Geneva as shown by the revised Articles XXVIII and XXIX.

The Act of Supremacy of 1559 made the queen Supreme Governor of the Church of England, and the Act of Uniformity of the same year made it obligatory for all to join in one public worship according to the rules laid down. This produced dissensions afterwards, as did the Ornaments Rubric introduced by Elizabeth into the Prayer Book, whereby rites and ceremonies could be increased.

The queen was blessed with very wise counsellors, of whom William Cecil was chief. These urged the importance of helping the Dutch and the Huguenots, as well as the Protestant party in Scotland. It was difficult for her to give support to these, for she disliked the Genevan doctrine, and in particular hated John Knox. Finally, however, help was given. On her attitude to the Puritans, Professor A. F. Mitchell writes:

> What Froude has said of Knox may be said in a measure of his Puritan brethren in England: that they saved Elizabeth's throne and secured the triumph of Protestantism in Britain, in spite of herself, and all her caprice and cruelty towards them. (*Westminster Assembly*, p. 44).

These were the men who could be relied upon, not the Marian clergy, who could change from one religion to another so easily. Ignoring this fact, Queen Elizabeth set herself sternly to repress what were called 'prophesyings'. These were gatherings of ministers and godly people to study the Scriptures, who had already been greatly blessed. They were cordially supported by the good Archbishop Grindal. He refused to carry out the queen's command to suppress them, and as a result was suspended and imprisoned in his own house.

At that time, Thomas Cartwright, the great Puritan and Presbyterian divine, came into prominence. A distinguished Fellow of St John's College, Cambridge, he was appointed Lady Margaret

Professor of Divinity in Cambridge, in succession to Archbishop Whitgift, who became an enemy of the Puritans. Puritanism was exceedingly strong in Cambridge, a fact that greatly displeased the queen. Cartwright was very popular, and his lectures caused ferment in the university. In spite of the support of the great minister Cecil, and the favourite Leicester, Whitgift persuaded the queen to remove Cartwright from his chair in 1570. According to Cartwright, the church was entitled to regulate its doctrine, polity and worship by the Word of God without restriction by the state. He asserted that the head of the Commonwealth was only a member of the church, not its governor, and episcopacy, as then known in England, was of human origin. These were the principles afterwards adopted in the Westminster Assembly in the seventeenth century. Indeed, Cartwright's *Directory for Church Government* was carefully studied in that Assembly. In spite of being one of the most learned men in Europe, and one of the most pious, he was cruelly treated, and twice had to flee from his native land. In his old age he died almost in obscurity at Warwick, in 1603. Nevertheless, his influence on the Puritan movement was very far-reaching.

While Queen Elizabeth could control the church, she found a majority of the House of Commons against her. They were led by two strong Christian men, Strickland and Wentworth, who favoured the Puritans. The conflict was severe and was the beginning of that contest between Crown and Parliament that was to issue in the civil war of the seventeenth century and the overthrow of the Stuart dynasty.

In 1571 an act was passed acknowledging the validity of ordination by presbyters, without a bishop. While it demanded acceptance by the clergy of the doctrinal part of the Thirty-nine Articles, it did not bind clergy to the constitution or ritual. This is how the Presbyterians were able to remain inside the national church until driven out at the Restoration in 1660.

Queen Elizabeth carried out her arbitrary will through the bishops, the inquisitorial Star Chambers and the Court of High Commission. When Archbishop Grindal would not proceed against the 'prophesyings' (religious training exercises), she did it herself.

Cases such as the proceedings against the writers of the Marprelate Tracts that had attacked prelacy, roused intense feeling in the land, and the cruel sentences on Penry and Udall, Puritan propagandists who were hanged, turned many against the sovereign. The very name of the Star Chamber became an abomination in the eyes of the people, and Elizabeth became very unpopular. The feeling grew up in the hearts of many that civil and religious liberty must be fought for, and this finally blazed up against Charles I in the civil war of the next century.

Elizabeth regained the love of her subjects to an eminent degree during the dangerous time of the invasion by the Spanish Armada in 1588. In those perilous days, she seemed to embody all that was best in the nation. In her faith and strength and courage, she stands forth as a noble figure. For years, the pope and the kings of Spain and France had done everything possible to overturn her regime. She was excommunicated, and her Catholic subjects were encouraged to revolt. On Mary, Queen of Scots centred innumerable intrigues aiming at the removal of Elizabeth with foreign help. English priests were specially trained at Douay in the Low Countries and other places on the Continent with the express intention of leading England and Scotland once more into allegiance to the papacy. Elizabeth was compelled for her own defence to send help openly to the Netherland Protestants in their gallant fight against Philip II of Spain. Meanwhile, Sir Francis Drake harried Philip's ships on the Caribbean Sea (the route of the Spanish treasure ships) in exploits that have become legendary.

In 1588 Philip resolved to carry out the invasion of England of which he had dreamt for years. The Spaniards proudly named the great Armada 'The Invincible'. It numbered 160 ships with some 30,000 marines and sailors and was far more powerful than the English fleet. At Calais was a strong army with everything ready to cross to England. The superb seamanship of the English admirals and their novel tactics, coupled with the boundless heroism of their men, won a great victory in the Channel. Storms did the rest, and the Armada was scattered through the North Sea and wrecked on the coasts of England, Norway and Scotland. Many felt it was the doing of the Lord. It was a great deliverance for Protestantism, and a shattering blow for Spain. Henceforth her power was on the wane.

In spite of her Tudor obstinacy and autocracy, Elizabeth was a great queen. The foundations of England's civil and religious greatness were solidly laid in her reign. To the religious and political leaders of that age, we owe much. Their work meant that England was no longer dependent on an Italian pope, and from that time onwards laymen and ecclesiastics were both subject to civil law. No longer did monks have control over much of English life, and doctrines such as purgatory and priestly and saintly mediators were abolished in the Church of England. The doctrine of purgatory, the source of much clerical wealth, was also discarded. The English Reformers taught the centrality and supremacy of Christ in salvation.

16

The Reformation in Scotland

In no other country in the world was the Reformation so complete or thorough as in Scotland. It is also remarkable that in this small country, with its turbulent history, the Reformation was carried through with virtually no loss of life to the Roman Catholics and with very few imprisonments. This was due to such historical factors as (1) the precious spiritual legacy left by the old Celtic church; (2) the influence of Lollardy brought back from Oxford by Scottish students; (3) the teachings of John Hus, Peter Dubois and William of Occam brought home by many Scottish travellers and students on the Continent; (4) the steady percolation of Lutheran ideas; and (5) the well-known depravity of the Catholic clergy that had become a byword and had revealed the need for reform.

The first martyrs

Scotland was profoundly moved by the martyrdom of the high-born and saintly Patrick Hamilton in 1528. Returning home at the end of 1527, he fearlessly preached the gospel of God's grace. Under the guise of friendship, he was invited by Cardinal David Beaton to a conference, and was then charged with heresy and burnt in front of St Salvator College, St Andrews, on 29 February 1528. His death produced a mighty impression throughout the land. 'The reek [smoke] of Master Patrick Hamilton infected as many as it blew upon' (Knox, *History of the Reformation*, vol. 1, p. 18). Eighteen years later George Wishart was betrayed into the hands of Cardinal Beaton and, after a mock trial, was put to death in the same city on the latter's own responsibility, contrary to the Regent's orders. The spirit of the nation was deeply stirred by this shameless proceeding. Many felt the time for resistance had come.

On 29 May 1546 Norman Leslie (Master of Rothes), Kirkcaldy of Grange, and others, forced their way into the Castle of St Andrews, early in the morning, slew the cardinal and hanged his body out of the window. These men never came to be closely associated with the Reformation, and their action was chiefly due to political motives and personal bitterness. After the death of Patrick Hamilton, enquiries had constantly been made for those who had New Testaments or who professed Reformed doctrines. Some were burnt, others sentenced to severe punishment and many fled. In spite of the burnings the Reformed views spread more and more. The clergy, both secular and regular, were held up to ridicule all over the land in plays and satires condemning their vicious lives, as in the writings of Sir David Lyndsay of the Mount, and George Buchanan, a great classical scholar. It was not until John Knox arose, however, that the widespread Protestant sentiment was brought into focus. As soon as he preached his first sermon in the Castle of St Andrews, which was then in Protestant hands, people said, 'Others sned [sawed] the branches of the Papistry, but he strikes at the root, to destroy the whole' (Knox, *History of the Reformation in Scotland*, vol. 1, p. 86). It was true.

Scotland was sadly in a disjointed state, virtually ruled by the French under Mary of Guise, who had a French army in Edinburgh and Leith. The young queen, married to the Dauphin and living in France, was under the influence of her Guise uncles, whose fanaticism went beyond all bounds. The European political situation was very tense. Scotland's relationships with England, France and Spain were all dangerous, and served to affect further the rising Protestant cause. If only the Roman Catholics could retain Scotland, they could use it as a base for the destruction of Protestant England. For a time, the little kingdom of Scotland was politically the most important spot in Europe.

The leadership of Knox

No other man could have guided the church in Scotland as Knox did in that stormy and critical period, when the most violent passions were wildly warring in church and state, and when the Council of Trent had aroused intense fanaticism. It is all very well to criticize the Scottish Reformer for his sternness and alleged roughness. Only a man of unyielding mould could have grappled with the situation, for he was surrounded by all the elements of war, intrigue, deception and murder. In spite of his sternness, there are many evidences of a kinder and even loving disposition. Above all, he was a man who feared God, which cast out the fear of man. He was always at his best in a great emergency when the hearts of other men were failing them. Then his strong qualities shone out.

The training this great man received for his tremendous task suggests a divine providence. After receiving a good university education at Glasgow under teachers such as the famous John Major, he trained as a priest and papal notary. Then he spent nineteen months as a slave in the French galleys after the capture by the French fleet of St Andrews Castle. Next he laboured for five years in England in the reign of Edward VI, when Scotland was still groaning under subjection to Rome. During this period, he met many out-standing church leaders, such as Latimer, Ridley, Hooper and Miles Coverdale, men who wholeheartedly accepted the Reformed point of view as presented by Geneva. Cranmer was his friend, and Knox became one of the king's preachers. His association with these good and true men in England moulded his own outlook. He was offered the bishopric of Rochester, but declined it because of his views on church polity.

When, on the accession of Mary Tudor, he had to flee from England, this too worked out for good. In Frankfurt, as minister of the English-speaking congregation, he learned to appreciate good men and 'to deal with unreasonable and tricky ones'. At Geneva, he was the intimate friend of John Calvin and Theodore Beza. He had the benefit of seeing the Reformed church in action within a thoroughly Protestant community. Above all, he saw at work the master mind of Calvin, who took the Bible as the Word of God and systematized its truths in a doctrinal framework such as had never been seen before. Thus it was that when Knox returned to Scotland in 1559, he was well equipped in every way for his tremendous task. By 1560, the Roman church had virtually vanished out of the land. On the political side, the cause of the Reformation was enormously strengthened by the alliance between England and Scotland, which was made in the Treaty of Berwick (May 1560). By the Treaty of Cateau-Cambrésis (April 1559), the kings of France and Spain had bound themselves to crush Protestantism in Europe. The danger was very real. Urged on by Throckmorton, the English ambassador at Paris, who saw the peril looming ahead, William Cecil, with extreme difficulty, finally succeeded in persuading Queen Elizabeth to enter an alliance with the Protestants of Scotland. An English fleet sailed into the Forth, the French troops were surrounded in the fort at Leith, and soon France had lost her hold on Scotland. For the first time in history, an English army was cheered as it marched through the streets of Edinburgh.

The documents
of the Scottish Reformation

At the request of Parliament, John Knox and five friends drew up a statement of the Reformed doctrine. Although it constituted a fair-sized book, they drew up this Scots Confession in four days, a truly astonishing performance. It was approved by the Scottish Parliament with very great enthusiasm and remained in force as the symbol of Scottish religion until 1647, when it was replaced by the Westminster Confession of Faith. Knox and his friends were also asked to draw up a statement as to how the church should be governed. The result was the First Book of Discipline, which expounded the Presbyterian method of church polity, a system that makes for balance and good order. Knox also set forth at this time a magnificent scheme for the education of the people, his ideal being to have 'a kirk and a school in every parish'. The Book of Discipline laid down that the properties and vast revenues of the old church should be reserved for the maintenance of religion, education and the poor. Because of this, Parliament refused to ratify it, for the greedy nobles grasped as much as they could of the patrimony of the church, to the great loss of the people of Scotland. Knox's ideal, however, was never forgotten.

The return of Queen Mary

A year before Mary, Queen of Scots returned from France (on 19 August 1561), the Reformation had been thoroughly established. John Knox and the nobles, who were aware of the atmosphere in which Mary had been reared at the court of France, knew what to expect. Her aim was to gain time at first, so as to strengthen her position. Then she would strike a blow for the elimination of Protestantism. On the very first Sunday after her return, she had Mass said by a French priest at the palace of Holyrood House. Her personality fascinated one after another of the nobles, but she could never move John Knox. Queen Mary stood for an alliance with autocratic France and Romanism; John Knox stood for Presbyterianism, democracy and alliance with England. The two ideals were utterly incompatible and a clash was inevitable.

Knox knew clearly the issues at stake. Let it be remembered in relation to their disputes that he never visited the palace except when summoned by the queen; that he was deferential as a subject, and that, before the end of her reign, Mary showed him no small sign of friendship when she invited him to visit her at Falkland Palace. This last meeting was pleasant to both. The truth is that this young and charming queen, who could dissemble so easily, was held from childhood in the grip of an evil system. She was a martyr to what she had been taught, and her own impulsiveness in throwing herself away on worthless husbands brought about her downfall, and surrounded her with a pathos that will never be forgotten.

Continuing struggles after Knox's death

After the death of Knox, first the Regents and then the young king, James VI, did their best to undermine Presbyterianism and establish episcopacy. James followed a very tortuous policy, at one time extolling the Presbyterian Church as the finest church in Christendom, and at another endeavouring to shackle it and turn it into a church ruled by bishops and archbishops, and a tool of the court, as political exigencies seemed to demand. His great aim was to secure at all costs the throne of England on the death of Elizabeth. Andrew Melville, Principal first of Glasgow University and then of St Andrews, arose as the great defender of the Presbyterian Church system. King James was a most shifty and unsatisfactory man, and Melville had the temerity to tell him to his face that there were two kings and two kingdoms in Scotland – the kingdom of the Lord Jesus Christ, where James was only a subject, and the civil kingdom where James was the sovereign. In 1592 Melville gained a very great victory for the Presbyterian system, when both Parliament and king recognized amply the claims of the Church of Scotland. An Act was passed guaranteeing all the Church's rights and privileges and its Presbyterian polity. Yet, by 1597, King James, through his duplicity, had put an end to free assemblies. The next development was the restoration of episcopacy, and the Church of Scotland was brought into bondage to the court until 1638.

17

The Counter-Reformation

For at least a century it had been felt everywhere in Europe, outside the Roman Curia (court of Rome), that a reform of abuses in the Catholic Church was a clamant necessity. Both Jiménez (1436–1517), Archbishop of Toledo, and Savonarola (1452–98), prior of San Marco, had instituted reforms, seeking to remove corruption and aid the poor. The Protestant Reformation was not, therefore, the cause of the reforming movement in Catholicism in the sixteenth and seventeenth centuries, but served as a catalyst to quicken desire for change and for a new emphasis in missionary expansion. It was an attempt, in areas that had become Protestant, to regain lost ground, while in Roman Catholic lands the term 'Counter-Reformation' denotes reform from within. It took several different forms. Monastic orders were renewed or reformed, and the time-honoured approach by way of a general council was utilized in the appointment of the Council of Trent. The revival of Catholic power in countries that had become Protestant was another manifestation of counter-reformation.

Reform of the monastic orders

The Capuchins, recognized by the pope in 1528, attempted to recover the ideals of Francis of Assisi, as they devoted themselves to charitable works. Their name came from the coarse habit they wore with its four-pointed hood, called a *capuccio*. New orders, such as the Ursulines (1535) and the Oratorians (1575), attempted to show how practicable were the old ideals relating to celibacy, chastity and compassionate service. The Ursulines were a significant association of women, who first lived in their own homes and worshipped in their local churches. Later it became a full order, that spread from the north of Italy into France and even into French Canada. No order was as significant, though, for the future mission of the Church as the Jesuits.

The Jesuits

The Society of Jesus, initiated by Ignatius Loyola in 1534, was the most important of all the Roman orders. In 1511 this dashing and very heroic young Spanish officer, was badly wounded. In hospital, he passed through a great spiritual change, whereupon he adopted a hermit's life of extreme asceticism involving sufferings so severe that they changed his appearance. He believed he had visions of the devil, and of Christ and his saints battling against the prince of darkness. In his broodings, he decided 'some entirely new foundation pillars' must be found unless the whole Roman church were to perish. He resolved to fight against the teachings of the Reformers. Resuming again the polished life of an aristocrat, he founded at Paris the Society of Jesus with six friends. They bound themselves by solemn oaths to be 'true spiritual knights' and to extend 'the true faith among believers'. It was felt by the pope that here was an order that could help the Roman church to recover from its losses in the Reformation. In lands such as Spain and Italy, where the Catholics were in a big majority, the Inquisition could wipe out the Protestants. Where, however, these latter were numerous, it was better for the Jesuits to infiltrate and, by suavity of manners, ingratiate themselves with the influential classes and lead the people back to the Roman fold. According to Nicolini, the Jesuit was 'despotic in Spain, constitutional in England, republican in Paraguay, bigot in Rome, idolater in India'.

The discipline of the order was rigorous. The *Spiritual Exercises*, a book binding on every member, laid down, 'That we may be entirely of the same mind with the Church, if she have defined anything black which may appear to our minds to be white, we ought to believe it to be as she has pronounced it.' The acceptance of this teaching put men into spiritual bondage in relation to their ecclesiastical superiors.

To further the interests of the Roman church, Loyola taught the order that 'it is permissible to do evil that good may come', a principle that led to unspeakable wickedness. In dealing with ethical questions, the Jesuits developed a system of casuistry and sophistry that brought them into disrepute in many quarters. The Parliament of Paris in 1762 declared that their doctrines 'tended to sever all the bonds of civil society by the authorization of falsehood, perjury, the most culpable impurity, and in a word, each passion and each crime of human weakness'.

The Jesuits became the life and soul of the Counter-Reformation, their influence being very powerful in the Council of Trent in its last years. They specialized in education and established flourishing schools all over Europe, where young people were turned into eager instruments for promoting the designs of the Vatican. Everywhere the Jesuits were active among outcasts in the cities, in preaching, in personal dealing. Their schemes sometimes included plans for the assassination of their opponents, including the highest in the land. Meanwhile the bloody engine of the Inquisition was set in motion wherever it would work. In one way or another, the Roman church won back much territory lost in southern Germany, Austria and Bohemia. The plots of the Jesuits were numerous in many countries. We find them intriguing in England in Queen Elizabeth's time and in Scotland in the days of Queen Mary and James VI. At times, they were protected in Scotland by local magnates, especially in the north-east and south-west parts of the country. The Catholic Church in Scotland lacked leadership, and Reformed Protestantism triumphed in most of the country.

In connection with the Counter-Reformation, Francis Xavier (1506–52) and other Roman Catholic missionaries displayed great zeal and self-sacrifice. Xavier, a Jesuit and friend of Loyola, claimed that in his ten years' work in Goa (India), Malacca, the Moluccas and other East Indian islands, and in Japan, he baptized no fewer than 700,000 converts. There are indications that the work was somewhat superficial and the Jesuits were afterwards severely censured by other Roman Catholic orders for accommodating themselves too much to non-Christian customs and practices. This led to the breakup of the Jesuit missions.

So glaring became the intrigues of the Jesuits in later years that they were banished or suppressed in nearly every Roman Catholic country, including Spain and Portugal with their vast territories in the Americas, France, Naples and Parma. To crown it all, in 1773 Pope Clement XIV abolished the order. He referred to the vexations suffered at their hands by some of his predecessors in the papal chair, and called attention to 'the complaints and cries' raised against them, and 'the dangerous results, rebellions and scandals' that followed on their doings. And further, he tells how the faithful Catholic kings of Spain, France, Portugal and the Scillies were constrained to banish the order 'to prevent Christ being seized and torn out of the lap of the Holy Mother Church'. For forty years, the Jesuits lay low, and then in 1814 Pope Pius VII annulled the decrees of his infallible predecessor and restored the Jesuits to their former position.

The Council of Trent

In 1545 the emperor Charles V, constantly disturbed by the religious difficulties in Germany, persuaded Pope Paul III to call the Council of Trent. It met at intervals from 1545 to 1563 at Trent, or Trento, in northern Italy. The emperor looked for reforms and a reconciliation with the German Lutherans, but the council was predominantly Italian and under the control of the pope, and the emperor failed to influence it.

The reactionary party under Caraffa (afterwards Pope Paul IV) gained a complete victory, and guided the Church skilfully into a fanatical path that led to fresh vitality and prestige after the shattering blows received during the Reformation. The papal legate was horrified at the request of the Protestants that all the decisions of the council be tested by their agreement with Scripture. The council declared the Latin Vulgate to be the only authoritative version of the Bible, and received 'with an equal feeling of piety and reverence the traditions' – although no one seemed very clear where these traditions were lodged. It was further enacted that every Catholic had to accept the interpretation of Scripture given by the Church.

The dogmas set forth left no doubt as to the position of the Roman church in regard to doctrine, and strongly reiterated the views held before the Reformation. The view of the Curia prevailed as to the pope's position of authority in the Church. It was enacted that all clergy had to swear as follows:

> I acknowledge the Holy Catholic Apostolic Roman Church for the mother and mistress of all Churches; and I promise and swear true obedience to the Bishop of Rome, successor to St. Peter, Prince of Apostles, and Vicar of Jesus Christ.

At Trent, a number of abuses were remedied and the education of priests was improved. Discipline was tightened, and in these ways the Roman church became a more compact and effective instrument for the fight with Protestantism.

Political activities

There was also a very real sense in which the Counter-Reformation involved politics, as European Catholic states regrouped both to defend the Church and destroy the Protestant faith. Militant Calvinism was competing for territory with a revived Catholicism. From about 1560, the Reformed faith met much stronger resistance than it had until that time, and it was especially Philip II of Spain who led the Catholic forces. With the reluctant cooperation of the papacy following the Council of Trent, Philip set out to get rid of the Protestants in his territories and in France. The defeat of the Spanish Armada meant that England escaped Spanish and Catholic tyranny, though countries such as Poland and Bohemia in Europe succumbed. The foreign attempts against Scotland were directed to controlling the young James VI, but his departure for London in 1603 meant this political scheming failed. Religion and politics could not be separated in that era, and it is scarcely surprising that Catholic efforts to win back lost ground in Europe blended them in a manner that led to some success, but also that saw much bloodshed.

18

The church in the Stuart period

The Puritans

When James VI of Scotland became James I of England in 1603, the Puritans hoped that, coming from Presbyterian Scotland, he would show them more consideration than had Queen Elizabeth (see pp. 109–14). They did not know of his unsatisfactory character. In his early youth, he had learned from his cousin, Esme Stewart, Duke d'Aubigny, the fatal doctrine of the divine right of kings that was to prove so disastrous to his dynasty. His absolutism could not take kindly to the democratic spirit of Presbyterianism, and his watchword became 'No bishop, no king'. 'Presbytery', he said, 'agrees as well with monarchy as God and the devil.'

The Puritans stood for the Reformed faith as known in Switzerland and France. They objected to the sign of the cross in baptism and to kneeling at the Communion (for fear of adoring the elements). They opposed the use of surplices and albs, and the introduction of certain rites and ceremonies, largely because of their sacerdotal implications. They insisted strongly that everything had to be according to the model of the New Testament. They objected to games and sports on the Lord's Day, and their enemies charged them with austerity. In England, many of the most learned men of the time were among them, as is seen from the high places they occupied in the universities of Oxford and Cambridge. Their culture is exemplified in the works of Edmund Spenser, Sir Philip Sidney, John Milton and Andrew Marvell, all of whom were Puritans and loved music and poetry. When such men objected to ceremonial and to gorgeous furnishings in churches, they did so not from lack of aesthetic taste, but on theological grounds. They believed not only that there was beauty in chaste simplicity, but also maintained that this characterized the early church, and that the gradual departure from this simplicity after the third century indicated spiritual deterioration. They called attention to the prohibition of 'graven images' in the Second Commandment, and urged that the glory of the deity could never be properly depicted on coloured windows or in sculpture, and that to attempt to do so led to error. They would have agreed heartily with Bernard Lord Manning:

> To call on the name of God, if men truly know and mean what they are doing, is in itself an act so tremendous and so full of comfort that any sensuous or artistic heightening of the effect is not so much a painting of the lily as a varnishing of sunlight.
> (*Christian Worship*, p. 163)

While some Puritans of more extreme views disparaged music, this was far from being the general attitude. Elaborate church music was objected to because it did not edify the people, and because it prevented worshippers from joining in the praises of the house of God. While the cultured Puritans stood for simplicity in worship, strictly in accordance with New Testament teaching, they highly valued beauty in other spheres, as may be seen, for example, in the lives of Oliver Cromwell and Colonel Hutchinson (see Horton Davies, *Worship of the English Puritans*, pp. 268–277). The remarkable strength of the Puritans lay in their constant appeal to Scripture to settle all questions of faith and morals. It was the 'touchstone of God's Word' that counted with them, not human opinion. Their earnestness was very impressive, and although many mocked them, they increased rapidly in numbers and influence.

At the Hampton Court Conference, called by James I in January 1604, the Puritan leaders were treated with great disrespect by their sovereign. Canon Perry in his *Students' English Church History* says, they were 'insulted, ridiculed, and laughed to scorn without either wit or good manners'. At the end, the king, addressing the learned and courteous Puritan leader Dr Reynolds of Oxford, testily declared that he would 'make them conform, or harry them out of the land or worse'. Almost the only good result of this conference was the production of the Authorized Version of the Bible (AV) that was completed in 1611. The king eagerly caught on to a suggestion made by Dr Reynolds that a new version of the English Bible ought to be made, based on the best Hebrew and Greek texts and compared with former translations. Earlier, in 1601, the General Assembly of the Church of Scotland, meeting in Burntisland, Fife, had come to a decision that a new translation was desirable. The AV is still in wide use and the beauty of its English diction, its idiomatic vigour and harmonious rhythm have never been excelled.

When a royal proclamation demanded complete conformity to the settled order of the Church of England on the part of all, and acknowledgment of the king's supremacy, 1,500 clergymen refused to sign the new canons. Many were shielded by sympathetic bishops, but 300 ministers in England were ousted and silenced, while others were imprisoned. This was the first great rift in the English church. Richard Bancroft was now archbishop and, as a strong High Churchman, believed in 'the divine right of Prelacy' in the church. According to Bishop Kennet, he 'proceeded with rigour, severity and wrath' against the Puritans. It was at this time that ornaments and ceremonies that had been discarded for many years were brought back into the Anglican Church.

The next archbishop, George Abbot, was more learned and tolerant than Bancroft. He eased the position of Puritans in various ways, and secured appointments for some of them in Ireland, to the enrichment of the Irish church. He influenced King James to authorize the Irish Articles in 1615, thus virtually giving the Puritans in Ireland what was refused them in England, and secured the appointment of Bishop James Ussher (the Chronologer) as Primate of the Irish church. This greatly strengthened evangelicalism in Ireland and provided a place of refuge for persecuted Puritans, and Covenanters. Abbot also persuaded the king to send deputies to the Calvinistic Synod of Dort in 1618, which gave help and recognition to the Reformed churches struggling against Romanism on the Continent.

The Pilgrim Fathers

Despairing of ever finding liberty of conscience in their own land, a group of men with their wives and families sailed in 1620 from Plymouth to New England in the *Mayflower* to seek liberty in the New World. Because of the theological disturbances caused by their religious views, something must be said about the origin and development of them.

There had grown up at Scrooby, in Nottinghamshire, a congregation of Independents under the fostering care of William Brewster (in whose home they met) and of John Robinson, who was their pastor. The latter, more than any other, was responsible for organizing and developing the system of church government, first known as 'Independency' and later as 'Congregationalism', because each congregation was autonomous and governed by its own members.

The members of these churches belonged to the separatists from the Church of England, who rejected completely the principle of a national church. In this respect, they differed from the Presbyterians. For a long time, they were often called Brownists, because Robert Browne had taught their tenets in the reign of Queen Elizabeth. He was imprisoned but escaped in 1582 to Middleburg in the Netherlands, where he formed a congregation, although he soon afterwards re-entered the Anglican Church. In 1583 two pastors in England were put to death because they refused to acknowledge the queen's supremacy in ecclesiastical matters. In 1593 Henry Barrowe and John Greenwood, like Brewster and Robinson graduates of Cambridge, were executed by order of the High Commission Court because of their religious views. Barrowe asserted before the court that each church should govern itself, and also objected to liturgies. The fate of these good men gives us a glimpse of the intolerance that drove so many Independents into exile.

The members of the independent church at Scrooby were being similarly sorely harassed by the authorities because of their religious beliefs. As a result, they all resolved to emigrate, and in

1608 settled in the Netherlands. They were unhappy there, however, so in 1620 returned to England and then embarked in the *Mayflower* for New England, landing at Plymouth in December. Their sufferings were indescribable in that first winter, and about half of them died. Through faith and indomitable courage, however, the little colony prospered and grew. The tide of Puritan emigration to New England continued and by 1640 20,000 had arrived, bent on forming communities where their views of Scripture could find expression. The world then had little idea how much humanity was to owe to the 'Pilgrim Fathers', as they came to be called, and to those other emigrants who founded a great home of liberty in the West.

The growth of independence

Early in the seventeenth century the Baptists emerged as a distinct body. They maintained that baptism ought to be by immersion and that children should not be baptized at all. Only those adults who professed faith in Christ and gave signs of being regenerate should receive this sacrament. In 1611 a group that had separated from an independent church at Amsterdam came to London under their leader Helwys, and a few years later formed a Baptist church in London. From then onwards, their denomination has had continuity. They have often been confused with the Anabaptists (see pp. 91–2), some of whom suffered in England in the sixteenth century. But as early as 1620, when Helwys's group presented a petition to Parliament, they were recognized by the civil power as being distinct from the Anabaptists. Like the Independents, they adopted the congregational form of church government, and took up a separatist attitude to the national church. This brought on them many sufferings. Under the Commonwealth, they enjoyed freedom and flourished, but at the Restoration in 1660, they again had to endure much persecution. An example of this is shown in the twelve years' imprisonment of John Bunyan, one of the greatest Baptists of all time. Soon the denomination began to grow apace in Britain, America and many other lands, and today numbers around a hundred million. Of these, almost half belong to the Baptist World Alliance, but some large churches, such as the Southern Baptist Convention in the USA, have stayed outside it.

Socinus and Arminius

These two theologians are of considerable importance because of their effect upon the history of doctrine from the end of the sixteenth century onwards. Faustus Socinus (1539–1604), an Italian, denied the divinity of the Lord Jesus and his atonement for sin. He also rejected the doctrines of original sin and human depravity, and his teachings led to the formation of many 'Unitarian' churches.

Jacobus Arminius (1560–1609), a professor at Leyden, originated the theological system that now bears his name, but it was much developed by his followers, who became known as Remonstrants because they presented a Remonstrance to the Estates of the Netherlands against the Calvinistic views held in the Dutch Reformed Church. They affirmed conditional election on the ground of foreseen faith, as against absolute predestination, and declared that the atonement was made for all people, although only believers benefit. They insisted that, while regeneration by the Holy Spirit is necessary, the work of the Holy Spirit can be resisted and rejected, and maintained that the final perseverance of the saints in the way of life is doubtful and that they may relapse from grace and be lost. These views were discussed and condemned by the Synod of Dort, which met in 1618, and at which deputies from the English church were present. Arminianism, however, became the accepted view of the Laudians and the Latitudinarians in the Anglican Church. Later, in the eighteenth century, it became the official doctrine of Methodism, and was also adopted by sections of the Baptist and Congregational churches. The questions involved are far from being as simple as may appear from a first glance. The Calvinists maintained that while the Arminian system was attractive to the popular mind, it was lacking in logical and biblical consistency.

The policy of Charles I and Archbishop Laud

King Charles and his archbishop stood for the divine right of kings in the state, and the divine right of episcopacy in the church. The Puritans were 'more than ever discountenanced and persecuted'. Charles was 'so bent on being an absolute, uncontrollable sovereign, that he was resolved to be such a king or none'. He was 'habitually faithless to his pledges'. Such were the comments of an aristocratic lady who knew King Charles well. Laud turned the Communion table into an altar, and began the practice of bowing to it. There had been no reference to an 'altar' since the abolition of the sacrifice of the Mass. Parliament manfully sought to defend the Puritans and objected to High Church ceremonies and the erection of altars. When, on 10 March 1629, the Speaker of the House of Commons, acting on royal instructions, tried to adjourn the House, he was held in the chair. Sir John Eliot, the leader of the Protestant faction, moved resolutions against innovations in religion and against levying taxes without consent of Parliament, which were passed. As a result, nine members were imprisoned and, for eleven years, Charles ruled despotically without a Parliament, Laud being his friend and helper. On the slightest provocation, Puritans were handed over to the Court of High Commission, to suffer crushing fines, life imprisonment, the pillory or to have their ears cut off or noses slit.

When the famous Long Parliament met in 1640, it refused to vote any money until political and religious grievances were redressed. Fifteen thousand Londoners presented the 'Root and Branch Petition', demanding that episcopal church government should be abolished and the faithful preachers should no longer be silenced. It also objected to such practices as bowing to the altar, and the use of images, crucifixes and candles. The king, on receiving from Parliament the Grand Remonstrance that set out his many acts of misgovernment, went in person to arrest the five members chiefly responsible, but failed. By 22 August 1642, the English Civil War had begun.

At first, the war went against the parliamentary party. They were depressed by the early loss of leaders such as John Hampden and

Lord Brooke. Eventually they appealed to the Scottish people, who were already greatly incensed by the king's interference in their own affairs, for help in the fight against royal absolutism.

Events in Scotland

The Scots had suffered much from Charles's despotic rule. No general assemblies of the church had been permitted and the bishops were tools in the hands of Laud, who quite misunderstood the Scottish people. When the king and he visited Scotland in 1633, they were amazed at the resistance in Parliament. Laud treated meetings of presbyteries as irregular conventicles, and ordered that the new liturgy and Book of Canons for Scotland should be used by the Presbyterian ministers. Neither the king nor the archbishop would listen to objections.

By the end of 1637, Scotland was in ferment from end to end. On 28 February 1638, there was signed in Greyfriars Church, Edinburgh, the National Covenant that bound its signatories by an oath to maintain the freedom of the church. Lords, burghers and peasants all rallied with enthusiasm to the Presbyterian cause, and copies of the covenant were signed all over the land, some signing in their own blood. In November 1638, the General Assembly met in Glasgow, the first free Assembly since 1596. The Moderator was Alexander Henderson, a calm, courageous and wise leader. In spite of a peremptory order from the king to dissolve, they deposed the prelates, abolished the Articles that enslaved the church and re-established Presbyterianism. The episcopal Primate declared truly, 'Our work of thirty years is overthrown at a single stroke.'

King Charles prepared for war, and the Scots put their forces under General Alexander Leslie and his relative General David Leslie, superb soldiers who had learnt the art of war under Gustavus Adolphus, the Swedish Protestant king, a truly great military leader. They had notable successes against the king. In 1643 the Scots and the English Parliamentary party entered the Solemn League and Covenant, binding themselves to seek the reformation of religion according to the example of the best Reformed churches – what many excellent people had long sought for, although overborne by royal autocracy. The Westminster Assembly of Divines met from 1 July 1643 until 22 February 1649, with the object of finding a basis for a united church for the whole of Britain. Its members were mostly outstanding graduates of Oxford and Cambridge, scholars whose piety and learning would have graced any gathering, and the six Scottish representatives were in no way inferior to the rest. These men gave the clearest and most orderly presentation of divine truth ever set forth in a Confession of Faith. The Westminster Confession was adopted in Scotland in 1647, and has remained the symbol of orthodox Presbyterian churches throughout the English-speaking world. It is the finest fruit of Reformed theology.

The bloody battles of the great Civil War were fought between 1642 and 1646, the Scots fighting with the English parliamentary forces against the royalist party. In time Oliver Cromwell, in his 'New Model' army, forged an instrument by which the parliamentary party gained a crushing victory. The Independents and sectaries, who featured so prominently in Cromwell's forces, were determined to bring the king to execution. The Presbyterians did not wish to go to this extreme, and were therefore 'purged' from the House of Commons by the military dictatorship. Charles I was condemned to death, and beheaded at Whitehall on 30 January 1649.

The Restoration

The Scottish leaders had Charles II crowned at Scone on 1 January 1651. He went hypocritically through the mockery of swearing to support the Solemn League and Covenant, although his sympathies were Roman Catholic. Loyalty to an unworthy dynasty led the Scots to fight and die for an unprincipled profligate, and to break with Oliver Cromwell, one of the greatest Englishmen of all time, with whom they had much in common.

The great ideal of religious liberty cherished by Cromwell was wrecked through the wild intransigence of many of the sectaries that surrounded him. On his death in 1658, the Presbyterians, then very numerous in England, took a leading part in bringing back

Charles II. They met, however, with nothing but hostility from the new regime. Because of the Act of Uniformity of 1662, which demanded complete acceptance of the Anglican Prayer Book in every jot and tittle, no fewer than 2,000 Presbyterian, Independent and Baptist ministers heroically resigned their livings. The Corporation Act (1661), Five Mile Act (1665) and Test Act (1673) placed under further serious disability every Englishman who was not an Anglican churchman.

Charles II made a secret treaty with Louis XIV that, when the time should be opportune, he would declare himself openly a Roman Catholic. Then, with Louis's help, he would establish absolute government and the Roman Catholic faith in Britain. The policy of his Parliament, however, was unbending: there was to be no concession of any kind either to Roman Catholics or to Nonconformists. As a result, there was much suffering for conscience' sake. For example, John Bunyan was imprisoned for twelve years in Bedford jail and there wrote *The Pilgrim's Progress*, now recognized as one of the world's greatest religious books. Of a somewhat different type was George Fox, who, in the same period, founded the Society of Friends, known as the Quakers. He too suffered much for his convictions. During these years of persecution, many emigrated to North America. Among them was the young aristocrat William Penn, who introduced Quakerism into the colony of Pennsylvania, which he founded in 1682, and so gave the Society of Friends a notable place in the New World.

The folly of the Scottish people in espousing the cause of Charles II brought untold suffering to the land. The 'Drunken Parliament' in Edinburgh carried out the behests of Charles and once more imposed episcopacy upon the church. There followed the disastrous defeats of the Covenanters at Bothwell Bridge and Rullion Green. Then the staunchest Presbyterians organized their societies and, when forbidden to worship God in public, met in secret amid the moorland mists and deep ravines of the southern uplands of Scotland – constantly hunted down by men such as Graham of Claverhouse and Grieson of Lag with their dragoons. No fewer than 17,000 suffered for conscience' sake during their heroic Covenanting struggle, many being executed at the Mercat Cross and in the Grassmarket of Edinburgh.

Under the Roman Catholic James II the doings of the atrocious Judge Jeffreys in England filled people in every denomination with horror. Now not only the Scottish Covenanters but also English bishops refused to bend the knee before Stuart tyranny. Before the popular uprising, James II fled, and in 1688 William of Orange was invited to occupy the throne.

It was the beginning of a new epoch and made for lasting stability in church and state. In England, the Anglican Church was approved as the established church. The Toleration Acts of 1689 alleviated the position of the Nonconformists but inequalities continued for many years. In a short period, the Nonconformists grew so rapidly in numbers that a thousand new places of worship were built. By this time, several parties were distinguishable in the Anglican Church, including High, evangelical and Broad.

In Scotland, the Revolution Settlement (1689–90) brought great joy to an overwhelming majority of the people. The Presbyterian Church was once again established, and the sovereign came under obligations to recognize it. The Westminster Confession of Faith was taken as expressing the creed of the Scottish church, and these measures were solemnly recognized by statute. It was a day of wonderful deliverance after all the horrors of the 'Killing Times'.

Summary of events in Europe

On the Continent during the first half of the seventeenth century, the feud between Protestants and Roman Catholics culminated in the Thirty Years' War (1618–48). The intervention of Gustavus Adolphus, the Christian King of Sweden, whose territories were then very extensive, greatly helped the flagging Protestants. Many parts of Germany were devastated in this great conflict, which was ended by the Peace of Westphalia in 1648. Protestantism was then given a recognition on the Continent such as it had never received before, the Lutheran and Calvinistic forms being equally recognized. Formerly, Calvinism had been scarcely tolerated by the Holy Roman Empire.

In France Louis XIV, in order to further his own autocratic aims, supported in 1682 the claim of the French Catholics to enjoy 'the Gallican Liberties', and to be free from the intervention of the pope in the temporal concerns of the nations. They claimed a certain freedom from the Vatican, even in ecclesiastical affairs. But there was no liberty for Protestants. The king's tyrannical policy led in 1685 to the revocation of the Edict of Nantes. Under this cruel blow, Huguenots fled from their country and greatly enriched other lands, including Britain, with their industry, skill and great human worth.

19

The eighteenth century

A period of decay

This century does not stand high spiritually and yet during it there arose evangelical movements of vast importance. Wearied to death by the wars and struggles of the previous century, churchgoers were glad of a period of respite, but this inactivity bred stagnation in the church. The religious outlook of the period was profoundly affected by the rise of deism. This system of thought originated in England, and was the outcome of those philosophical and scientific ideas that had come into prominence in the seventeenth century. Men such as Francis Bacon, Thomas Hobbes, René Descartes, Johannes Kepler, Galileo Galilei and Isaac Newton based their scientific conclusions on reason and the inductive method. Observation and experiment suggested that the universe was ruled by natural law. The belief, then, became common that this law was immutable. Hence, God began to be regarded by some thinkers as an absentee deity who had set the universe in motion and then had left it to itself under inflexible natural laws. Thus, there was no place for the supernatural in this world. The incarnation, miracles, prophecy and the divine inspiration of the Scriptures were ruled out as being doctrines no longer worthy of belief.

Among the leading exponents of these deistic views were John Toland, who in 1696 published *Christianity not Mysterious*, and Matthew Tindal, the author of *Christianity as Old as Creation*, written in 1730. From England, deism spread to Germany and France. In the former country, it took shape as 'The Enlightenment' and was associated with Christian Wolff and Immanuel Kant in philosophy, and with J. W. von Goethe and G. E. Lessing in literature. In France, it profoundly influenced the Encyclopaedists, a group of brilliant scientific and literary men who contributed articles to the *Encyclopédie*, a resource of information but also a polemical publication. Among them were outstanding Roman Catholic clergymen. By their principle that everything was dominated by an inflexible natural law, they raised doubts among churchmen as to the Christian doctrines that depended on divine revelation. For them reason, not revelation, was the final arbiter. David Hume's *Treatise of Human Nature* (1739) and Voltaire's works, somewhat later, were features of the period. These strong tendencies to unbelief had their natural culmination in the French Revolution in 1789. In the Continental universities, deism developed into rationalism, and then returned with renewed force to British centres of learning.

In Germany the Pietists, who largely owed their evangelical outlook to the writings of John Bunyan and Richard Baxter, had exercised a significant influence on religious life through the universities from about 1670 onwards. This was largely due to Philip Spener (1635–1705), and August Hermann Francke (1663–1727) who, at the University of Halle, stressed the evil of sin and the need for atonement in much the same way as did the English Puritans. Their influence spread, and among those affected was Count Zinzendorf, who allowed a group of Moravian Brethren (a branch of the church of John Hus) to settle on his estate at Herrnhut in Saxony in 1722. This small group became the pioneers of modern missionary enterprise and profoundly influenced the thinking of churchmen in various lands. Unfortunately, the spread of the warmhearted faith of the Pietists was arrested by the rise of rationalism, and the development of deism. In the German church as a whole, the cold, critical teachings of the philosophy of Wolff prevailed.

J. S. Semler (1725–91) and J. G. Eichhorn (1752–1827) marked a new era in the criticism of the Bible. They rejected its divine inspiration and refused to believe in miracles and prophecy. While Christ was exalted as a teacher, the New Testament doctrine of salvation through his atoning death was not accepted. The result was the spread of unbelief until men such as F. A. G. Tholuck, I. A. Dorner, E. W. Hengstenberg and F. J. Delitzsch brought about a revival of Reformation doctrine in the following century.

In England the evil trend was seen in the growing influence of Latitudinarianism in the Anglican Church, and Unitarianism among Presbyterians and General Baptists. The full deity of our Lord was widely denied and spiritual deadness invaded congregations. In Scotland, the 'Moderates' were in the ascendancy and decried fervent evangelical preaching and all enthusiasm in religion. True, certain apologists, such as Bishop Butler, Bishop Berkeley and Waterland, had done excellent work early in the century, but it made little impression on the mass of the people. The words of Mark Pattison were substantially true: it was a period of 'decay in religion, licentiousness of morals, public corruption, and profaneness of language' (*Essays*, II, p. 42).

The evangelical revival

In the earlier part of the eighteenth century, a wonderful awakening from God came to the whole of Great Britain. In Wales, it began largely as the result of the faithful ministry of men such as Griffith Jones, Daniel Rowlands and Howell Harris. In England, it is closely linked with the names of John and Charles Wesley and George Whitefield. In 1729 the Wesleys with some other student friends founded at Oxford 'The Holy Club', their aim being to promote in themselves and others the more faithful observance of the Christian religion. In derision, their fellow-students gave them the name 'Methodists'. Few of the members of the Club, however, had then a personal experience of conversion and forgiveness of sin.

George Whitefield

It was not until 1735 that Whitefield, overwhelmed by the dreadful burden of his sins, found what he called 'inexpressible peace' through a living faith in Christ. His first sermon, preached at Gloucester on 27 June 1736, was so unusual in its treatment of sin that many were scandalized. But there were fifteen conversions. His next sermon was on the 'new birth', from the text 'if anyone is in Christ, he is a new creation' (2 Cor. 5:17). He roundly rejected the doctrine of baptismal regeneration, then widely received in the Anglican Church, and stressed the absolute necessity of being regenerated by the Holy Spirit in accordance with the teaching of Christ (see John 3:3–11). He denied that those who never fight against the world, the flesh and the devil can be real Christians simply because a few drops of water had been sprinkled on them. For him, the new birth was a mighty spiritual change, wrought in the penitent by the Spirit of God, and one that transformed the heart. This teaching caused strong opposition. Shut out from many pulpits, and severely censured in the newspapers, he yet drew immense crowds and many professed conversion. He preached to vast gatherings of miners in the open air – men who were alienated from the organized churches – and the Spirit of God worked mightily among them. Thousands of them became earnest followers of Christ.

When Whitefield visited America for the first time in 1738, he became a lifelong friend of Jonathan Edwards, under whom four years earlier a mighty revival had taken place in New England. During his long ministry, he returned frequently to North America and exerted a profound spiritual influence upon the new colonies there.

John Wesley

In spite of his enthusiasm and incessant activity as a member of the 'Holy Club' at Oxford, John Wesley was without any personal assurance of salvation, and when he went as a missionary to the American colony of Georgia in 1736 his work was a failure. On the voyage out, however, and in Georgia itself, he made contact with members of the Moravian Brethren, contacts that were momentous for himself and for the whole English-speaking world. He realized that they had a faith in Christ as their personal Saviour that he did not possess. He saw that this made their whole being radiate with a great joy. On his return to London in 1738, what he learned from his encounter with the Moravian Brethren made him realize the meaning of the saving change wrought by the new birth. After a great mental struggle during which he passed through times of darkness and terrible depression, he finally came into the light on 24 May 1738 at a meeting of an evangelical society in Aldersgate, London. Wesley wrote in his journal:

I felt my heart strangely warmed. I felt I did trust in Christ, Christ alone, for salvation; and an assurance was given me, that He had taken away *my* sins, even *mine*, and saved me from the law of sin and death.

After his conversion, Wesley embarked on that great work of evangelism with which his name will ever be associated. Because of his preaching on man's lost condition through sin, regeneration through the Holy Spirit and salvation through the cleansing power of Christ's blood, he found, like Whitefield, that many pulpits were closed to him. There was much ecclesiastical opposition, as well as attacks upon him by ungodly mobs. Nothing, however, could stop this dauntless evangelist. In fifty years, during his evangelistic tours, he travelled 250,000 miles, mostly on horseback. Remarkable scenes were constantly witnessed as he preached the gospel. Hardened sinners could be seen at open-air meetings with tears of penitence rolling down their cheeks. The roughest in the land came humbly to the foot of the cross. Wesley was an Arminian (see p. 132) in theology, but was loved by most Calvinists because of his passionate proclamation of salvation to sinners. The Methodist Church, which he founded, has today more than forty million communicant members throughout the world, beside a vast number of adherents.

George Whitefield did not establish a new denomination. He was greatly helped by the pious and wealthy Countess of Huntingdon. The Anglican Church received significant evangelical impetus through his work. In Wales, his followers founded the Calvinistic Methodist Church, now known as the Presbyterian Church of Wales. Just as God had touched the hearts of men such as Griffith Jones, Howell Harris and Daniel Rowlands, and used them mightily in Wales before the great awakening in England began under Wesley and Whitefield, so now in the Church of England the Spirit of God raised up ministers of virile evangelical faith. They had been affected only indirectly by the revival movements under Wesley and Whitefield, and were largely Calvinistic. The result, however, of all the movements was a wonderful strengthening of evangelicalism throughout the land. To this day, the heart of many a Christian warms at the mention of such names as Fletcher of Madeley, Samuel Walker of Truro, William Grimshaw of Haworth, John Berridge of Everton, William Romaine of London and Augustus Toplady, author of *Rock of Ages*. Such men were greatly blessed to their own generation and handed on in the national church a great tradition of evangelistic zeal.

Charles Simeon

Of all the English church evangelicals of that period however, Charles Simeon of Cambridge made the profoundest and most lasting impression. Coming up to King's College in 1779, he found Cambridge almost moribund, as far as religion was concerned, in spite of its great spiritual traditions inherited from Reformation times. A young man of intense sincerity, Simeon soon awakened to the need of being right with God, and made the momentous discovery, in his own words, that he could transfer his guilt to another. 'I sought', he wrote, 'to lay my sins on the sacred head of Jesus.' There were few at the university then who held his point of view, for the great evangelical revival had scarcely touched Cambridge. Ordained to the ministry in 1782, he became vicar of Holy Trinity at the age of 23. He was already a fellow of his college.

Almost at once his church became thronged with worshippers. At first, however, he had many opponents, including the majority of his parishioners, for his presentation of the gospel was something new to Cambridge at that period, and seemed unbalanced and too enthusiastic. Gradually he found staunch friends among outstanding members of the university and, in spite of continued hostility, his influence increased apace. His saintly life and sane scholarship made an abiding impression upon a vast number of students.

Few people have ever done a more remarkable work in guiding the footsteps of suitable men towards the office of the Christian ministry. But it was not just the church in the homeland in which he was interested. He did immense service in promoting foreign missionary enterprise, and through him many devoted their lives to the evangelization of the non-Christians overseas, outstanding among them being the young Cambridge scholar Henry Martyn. Simeon was remarkably effective both in preaching and teaching the great truths of the Christian faith; and when he died in 1836, all Cambridge mourned his loss and recognized that a great man had gone from their midst.

Events in Scotland

In Scotland, the dead hand of moderatism had a serious effect upon the church. In 1733 Ebenezer Erskine and three others were driven from the Church of Scotland because of their opposition to the Patronage Act of 1712, under which patrons could nominate ministers contrary to the will of the people. Their vigorous evangelicalism could not tolerate such a situation and they founded the Secession Church. In 1752 Thomas Gillespie was shamefully treated for similar reasons and founded the Relief Church. These churches flourished in the towns and burghs of Scotland, which, by the end of the century, had 500 such places of worship. Their testimony was most valuable in those days of spiritual deadness. The main part of these two bodies united later to form the United Presbyterian Church in 1847.

In 1740 occurred the great Revival of Cambuslang, near Glasgow. After the movement had begun under the minister, William MacCulloch of the Church of Scotland, they received a visit from George Whitefield, who one Sunday preached in the open air to 40,000 people. Unprecedented scenes were witnessed and the effects were widespread. The young minister Dr John Erskine of Greyfriars Church, Edinburgh, nobly led the evangelicals within the Church of Scotland for sixty years. Moderatism, however, continued in the ascendancy until well into the next century.

During the first half of the eighteenth century, there were three Jacobite risings (in 1715, 1719 and 1745) in the Scottish Highlands, all aimed at bringing back the Stuart dynasty to the British throne. They had plenty of sympathy, and even some help from English Jacobites. The defeat of these rebellions ensured that the British monarchy had to be Protestant, which made for peace and stability. The romance and heroism of these movements have blinded the eyes of many to their real meaning.

The latter part of the century saw the revolt of the American colonies, and the founding of the USA. Independence greatly affected the development of every phase of life in America, including the ecclesiastical. One great change was the establishment of the principle that all religions should enjoy complete liberty, and that there should be no state church. In 1789 came the French Revolution, with all its violence and bloodshed culminating in 1793 in the Reign of Terror when the 'goddess of reason' was set up in Paris on the altar of Notre Dame, and the wild cry went up 'There is no God!' The Roman church was identified by the people with the earlier misgovernment of France and suffered greatly. At the end of the century, Napoleon Bonaparte appeared. He led the French army that entered Rome in 1796, and compelled the pontiff to cede one third of the papal territories. In 1799 when the pope raised difficulties, he was removed to France after Napoleon had turned Rome into a republic. Napoleon, however, was very conscious of the value of an alliance with the Roman Catholic Church from a political and social point of view. Hence, he entered a concordat with the papacy in 1801. Under it, all bishops had to resign and new ones were nominated by Napoleon.

Altogether, the century was a difficult one for the Roman Catholic Church, but in Britain a more tolerant attitude was gradually being manifested. Thus, in 1737, some of the disabilities of Irish Roman Catholics were removed. In 1780 the government permitted Roman Catholics to hold land once more in England. The sympathy shown to sufferers during the French Revolution produced good feeling among English Catholics, and all this paved the way for the Catholic Emancipation Act of 1829.

Evangelical hymnology

The eighteenth century was marked in England by a great outburst of sacred song. While Joseph Addison and Bishop Thomas Ken had written hymns that found wide acceptance, it was Isaac Watts (1674–1748) who first made the period notable for its hymnology. He began by writing paraphrases of the psalms that have left an indelible impression, such as 'Jesus shall reign where'er the sun' (on Ps. 72) and 'O God, our help in ages past' (on Ps. 90). Then he proceeded to write hymns that have found a lasting place in the churches. Among these are 'Come, let us join our cheerful songs', 'I'm not ashamed to own my Lord' and 'Come, ye that love the Lord'. He did more than any other to break down, in the dissenting churches, the Puritan tradition of using the psalms only in singing God's praise in public worship. There are some who regret this aspect of his work.

Philip Doddridge (1702–51), the great dissenting divine, who wrote *The Rise and Progress of Religion in the Soul*, was also the author of many hymns. Among the best known of these are 'Hark, the glad sound, the Saviour comes' and 'O happy day that fixed my choice'. Then there were the *Olney Hymns* published by John Newton (1725–1807), the well-beloved curate of Olney in Buckinghamshire and later rector of St Mary Woolnoth in London. Many of these hymns are still widely used. For example, 'How sweet the name of Jesus sounds' comes from this collection. His friend, the poet William Cowper, contributed sixty-eight hymns to the book, and many of these have become equally well known. It was, however, Charles Wesley (1708–88), the brother of John Wesley, who produced the greatest number of hymns in that period. Like his brother, he was a preacher, but his fame now rests on his hymns rather than on his sermons. John S. Simon wrote, 'Charles Wesley's hymns convey clear and decisive teaching on the subjects of sin, righteousness, and judgment. The exceeding sinfulness of sin is set forth in uncompromising language; and the perfect righteousness of Jesus is displayed' (*Revival of Religion in the Eighteenth Century*, p. 303). A large number of Charles Wesley's hymns are now found in nearly every hymn book, such as 'Rejoice the Lord is King!', 'O for a thousand tongues to sing', 'And can it be that I should gain' and 'All praise to our redeeming Lord'.

Revival in North America

A series of revivals took place in the North American British colonies between 1725 and 1760. They are usually referred to as the Great Awakening. Beginning in New Jersey with the preaching of a Dutch pastor, T. J. Frelinghausen, they soon involved the Scots–Irish communities in New Brunswick, where many were converted under the preaching of Gilbert Tennent. Just a few years later, under the ministry of Jonathan Edwards (1703–58) at Northampton in Massachusetts, a period of revival occurred in 1734–5. Local at first, this revival became more geographically diverse in 1740–41. The enthusiasm and physical manifestations that were part of the awakening provoked opposition. Led by Charles Chauncy of Boston, opposition arose against Edwards and his associates. To counter what he saw as incipient Arminianism and Socianism among the opposition, Edwards wrote his works *Freedom of the Will* and *Original Sin*. In answer to criticism of revivalist practices and excesses, he wrote several works, but most notably *Religious Affections*.

20

Modern missionary expansion

Roman Catholic missions

Nothing can be more remarkable than the difference between the intense missionary zeal of the church in the early centuries and the slowness of the church in the modern epoch to awaken to its responsibilities in this respect. True, the Jesuits and other Roman Catholic orders began a vast work in the second quarter of the sixteenth century in India, the East Indies and Japan, a project later extended to China and other lands. It was, however, a work that was largely concerned with externals. All that seems to have been required of the 'converts' was that they should observe a few ceremonies, and be able to repeat the Lord's Prayer along with the Creed, and to cross their arms over their breasts. The French occupation of vast territories in North America, and the Spanish and Portuguese conquests throughout Central and South America, opened to the Roman church a vast mission field. While individual priests and monks showed wonderful devotion and heroism, no one would seriously claim that the Roman church showed itself full of spiritual vitality during the 350 years when it was virtually the only representative of Christianity from the Rio Grande down to Tierra del Fuego. It is, however, a remarkable fact that in North America, where it existed side by side with Protestantism, Roman Catholicism developed a zeal and energy greatly in excess of anything that existed in the South, where that religion had a free field.

European missionary endeavours

Early British missions

The first British missionary endeavours were connected with efforts to convert the Native Americans in the new British colonies across the Atlantic. Under Cromwell, Parliament formed in 1649 'the Corporation for the Propagation of the Gospel in New England', with which were associated the self-sacrificing labours of John Eliot (1604–90), and the Mayhew family, who strove for generations for the conversion of the Native Americans. Later workers were John Sergeant and Jonathan Edwards's friend David Brainerd. Although Brainerd died within three years of commencing the work, he did much to arouse the church to the needs of the Native Americans. All these were friends of Whitefield, who, through the effect of his teaching upon John Newton, Claudius Buchanan, William Wilberforce and Thomas Scott, liberated immense missionary energies that began to manifest themselves soon after his death.

Dutch and German missions

In the sixteenth and seventeenth centuries, when the Dutch extended their colonies in Malaya, India, Ceylon and other places, their missionaries did a noble work, especially when Pietism began to enter the Netherlands through contacts with the English Puritans. The German Pietists, with their evangelical fervour, had a marked effect upon the development of missions through the teaching of August Hermann Franke (1663–1727) of Halle University. The Lutheran Church had fallen upon a period of formality and spiritual deadness, but Pietism brought new life to many. In cooperation with the King of Denmark's chaplain, Franke organized the Danish-Halle Mission to India in 1705, when Ziegenbalg and Plütschau, the first Protestant missionaries to India, began a truly notable work in Tranquebar, where they translated the whole New Testament into the Tamil language, and set up a printing press. Their most bitter enemies were often European officials of the trading companies from the Protestant lands of Britain, the Netherlands and Denmark.

The Moravians

The next landmark in the history of Protestant missions is the work of the Moravian 'Unitas Fratrum' (Unity of the Brethren). In spite of almost ceaseless persecution, the followers of John Hus (martyred in 1415) lived on, often in 'caves and dens of the earth'. In 1722 a group of them fled from Austrian intolerance in Moravia, and settled on the estates of Count Zinzendorf of Herrnhut in Silesian Saxony. Zinzendorf had been profoundly moved by the Pietist teaching of Spener and Franke. He and his wife early covenanted with God to give their wealth for the proclamation of the gospel in the non-Christian world. On their land was organized the Moravian Church in 1732. The achievements of this small church, infused by God's Spirit and run on lines of apostolic simplicity and faith, fill one with wonder. There were fewer than 600 people in Herrnhut at the beginning, yet in twenty-five years they sent out eighteen missionaries to different parts of the world. In 150 years they sent out no fewer than 2,170 missionaries. But even more important was the spiritual influence they exerted on many lands, as in the conversion of John Wesley and other great Christian leaders, which in turn reacted most powerfully on the development of modern missions. Yet for more than sixty years the great churches of Europe, infected with deism, rationalism and a dead formality, looked on coldly while this mighty work of God developed.

Openings in India

The East India Company, the forerunner of the British Empire in India, professed in its earlier days much interest in the religious welfare of its employees, and of the Indian population. Chaplains were appointed in many centres and, although these were not expressly missionaries, they helped to evangelize some of the Indian people. Before the end of the eighteenth century, however, the Company had become an enemy of Christian missions, so much so that they would not allow William Carey, the first English foreign missionary of modern times, to enter their territory, and he had to settle in Serampore, although it was under the Danes.

The Baptist Missionary Society

William Carey (1761–1834) stands out as one of the greatest missionaries since apostolic days. Born in Northamptonshire, he became a cobbler, but showed a remarkable genius for natural science and languages. Falling under the powerful evangelical influence of men such as Thomas Scott and Andrew Fuller, he became a Baptist minister. He strongly advocated the sending of missionaries to proclaim the gospel throughout the world, and gave his ministerial brethren no peace. At one meeting, an old minister told him sternly, 'Sit down, young man, and respect the opinions of your seniors. If the Lord wants to convert the heathen, He can do it without your help.' His persistence led to the founding of the Baptist Missionary Society in 1792 at Kettering, with Andrew Fuller as secretary. That day twelve poor Baptist ministers subscribed £13 2s 6d – a large sum for them. It was the beginning of a mighty work for the kingdom of God. The following year, Carey set out for India. A few years later J. C. Marshman and W. Ward, who were equally enthusiastic, joined him. They supported themselves by teaching. Carey pointed the way for succeeding missionaries in India, and within half a century of his death in 1834 there were half a million Indian Protestants.

The formation of the London Missionary Society

As stirring reports of William Carey's work in Bengal began to reach home, Presbyterians, Anglicans and Congregationalists were aroused to form a missionary society for non-Baptists, and the famous London Missionary Society (LMS) was founded in 1795. In this, and in all the missionary societies formed about the end of the eighteenth century, is seen the fruits of the great evangelical awakening that had been going on for about fifty years. While the denominations as such were still apathetic to the clamant call for worldwide evangelization, good men, whose souls the Lord had touched, formed these independent missionary-sending agencies.

In 1796, stirred by the story of Captain Cook's voyages in the South Pacific, the LMS sent thirty missionaries to that region. Its vigorous work spread to India, China, Africa, Madagascar and the West Indies. Its famous missionaries included Robert Morrison (1782–1834), pioneer missionary to China, John Williams (1796–1839) of the South Pacific, martyred on Eromanga Island, Robert and Mary Moffat, and their renowned son-in-law, David Livingstone, the African missionary and explorer, and James Chalmers, a native of Argyll, Scotland, who did a great work on Rarotonga and New Guinea, where he was slain by cannibals.

The LMS existed until 1966, when it merged with the Commonwealth Missionary Society to form the Congregational Council for World Mission. Two further mergers created the Council for World Mission (CWM), which as of April 2020 has thirty-two members, situated in the Pacific, Europe, Southern Africa and the Indian Ocean, South Asia, and the Caribbean. In 2012 the secretariat was moved to Singapore in keeping with the global scope of the membership.

Influence of the Clapham Sect

What was known as the Clapham Sect provides a remarkable example of the deep spiritual devotion, missionary zeal and practical Christianity of Anglican Church evangelicals towards the end of the eighteenth century. Its members belonged mostly to the upper classes. They began to meet for prayer and Bible study because of the grave situation that presented itself at the time of the French Revolution, and held their meetings in Clapham, in the neighbourhood where most of them lived. The widespread nature of their activities and the success that attended them is astonishing.

It was largely through their help and enthusiasm that the agitation for the abolition of the slave trade was successful. Zachary Macaulay had seen its evils while managing an estate in Jamaica. From 1787 onwards, the Clapham Sect kept the matter before Parliament. William Wilberforce took up the question with untiring energy and finally persuaded William Pitt to promote a bill in Parliament in 1807 for the abolition of the slave trade. In 1833 all slaves in British territory were emancipated. Members of the group, with the object of showing how the black Africans ought to be treated, had already founded the Colony of Sierra Leone, of which Zachary Macaulay was governor for seven years.

These Christians at Clapham also demonstrated how effective an instrument Christian literature could be in disseminating ideas of the right kind. Wilberforce founded the *Christian Observer* in 1801 and exposed the evils of slavery. James Stephen followed along the same lines. The vigorous pamphlets of Hannah More with titles such as *Village Politics* led to the founding of the Religious Tract Society (RTS), which did work of priceless value throughout the years. Encouraged by Wilberforce, she was instrumental in founding schools in Somerset, and other members of the Society also did much for the promotion of education. In 1935 the RTS merged with the Christian Literature Society for India and Africa to form the United Society for Christian Literature (USCL).

Charles Grant, a rich East India merchant, wrote a pamphlet in 1792 calling for the toleration of Christian missions by the East India Company. He helped forward the building of churches in India and played a leading part in promoting missionary effort in various lands. Other members of this group took an important share in founding the British and Foreign Bible Society, of which John Thornton, a banker and merchant, in whose house at Clapham the members often met, was its first treasurer. Five years later, the National Bible Society of Scotland was founded, and the American Bible Society came into existence about the same time. The importance of these societies for Christian work at home and abroad cannot be exaggerated.

The members of the Clapham Sect also realized the importance of maintaining Sunday as the Lord's Day and as a sacred heritage. William Wilberforce founded a society for its defence called the Lord's Day Observance Society (LDOS). This position is not so vocal now, except perhaps in the north of Scotland. In recent years, the LDOS has become Day One Christian Ministries, with a strong publication programme of general Christian books.

Wilberforce and his friends were also foremost in promoting schemes for social betterment throughout the land and, in this respect, favourably influenced the legislature. In the purely spiritual field, a notable step forward was taken in establishing the Islington Clerical Conference, an annual gathering of evangelical Anglican clergy that continued until 1983. But, apart from the abolition of slavery, the most outstanding achievement of the Clapham Sect was the part taken by its members, along with others, in forming in 1799 the Church Missionary Society (CMS). The CMS was the outcome of the great evangelical movement then stirring the Church of England. In addition to members of the group such as Wilberforce and Charles Grant, men such as Charles Simeon of Cambridge, whose missionary zeal has already been noted, and Thomas Scott, the Bible commentator, were connected with its foundation. The CMS spread to India, West Africa, the Lake Victoria region, Egypt, Palestine, Persia, China and Japan. Among the outstanding men who served this Society was Henry Martyn, a Senior Wrangler (top mathematics graduate), who has been described as Cambridge's greatest missionary, and whose memory is perpetuated by the Henry Martyn Hall in that city. He took up missionary work in Calcutta in 1806, and in a short time translated the New Testament and English Church Prayer Book into Hindustani. In connection with further plans for translation work, he removed to Persia, where he died at the early age of 31, having made only one direct convert. The touching example of self-sacrifice given by this brilliant student, who was cut off before his work had well begun, stimulated many others to offer themselves for missionary service.

After the First World War, there was a struggle within the CMS between liberal elements and more conservative evangelicals. The society split, with the conservatives forming the Bible Churchmen's Missionary Society (BCMS) – now Crosslinks. The CMS changed its name in 1995 to Church Mission Society and, by the end of the twentieth century, there was a notable swing back to a strongly evangelical position. The reintegration of the Mid Africa Ministry (formerly the Ruanda Mission) assisted that change, and the CMS is now an ecumenical evangelical society. Related organizations were established in other countries, though those in Australia, New Zealand and South Africa are now independent organizations.

In the 200-plus years since its formation in 1799, the CMS has sent out more than 9,000 missionaries.

Other agencies

The General Methodist Society was founded in 1796. Its labours extended to the West Indies, South Africa, South India, China, Polynesia and other lands. In the same year, two missionary societies were formed in Scotland by individual ministers and laymen of the Church of Scotland and the Secession Church. Chief among them was Dr John Erskine of Greyfriars Church, Edinburgh. Still under Moderate dominance, the Church of Scotland was then officially opposed to foreign mission work. A famous incident took place at the General Assembly of the Church of Scotland in 1796. Two leading Moderate ministers had opposed a proposal that mission-aries should be sent to the non-Christian world on the grounds that it would be improper to propagate the gospel overseas while there was a single individual at home without religious knowledge. Erskine rose and exclaimed, 'Moderator, rax [Scottish, 'reach'] me that Bible,' and proceeded to argue from the Scriptures of the necessity of mission work. These societies did magnificent work in Sierra Leone, India, Jamaica and South Africa, and were later taken over by the Scottish churches. Among the great missionaries was Alexander Duff of India – the first missionary ever sent out by a church as distinct from a society. This was in 1829.

The China Inland Mission (CIM), founded in 1865 by Dr Hudson Taylor, was a remarkable agency for evangelization in China. Though suffering many hardships, its missionaries pioneered Christian work in many parts of China and Tibet. A large number of them suffered martyrdom in the so-called Boxer Rebellion of 1900, an event that tested even the faith of Taylor himself. The mission continued in China until 1950, when its missionaries were forced to leave, and then concentrated its activities mainly on South Asia instead. In 1964 it changed its name to Overseas Missionary Fellowship (OMF), and later to OMF International. Thousands of devoted men and women have laboured for this great interdenominational society.

It is typical of the large number of so-called 'Faith Missions', many of which have contributed in an outstanding way to the building up of the kingdom of God overseas. North American missionary organizations accomplished vast work in the nineteenth and twentieth centuries. The contribution they have made to the task of world evangelism is of the highest importance. Without the generous giving of North American churches and the devoted service of North American missionaries, the expansion of effort seen in more recent years would have been quite impossible. This contribution demonstrates the size of the North American evangelical community and its liberality as compared with the similar constituencies in European countries.

The great missionary work of the various denominational and interdenominational societies now encircles the globe. From their labours have arisen young and vigorous churches that are fast taking an important place beside the older denominations. The nineteenth century was pre-eminently the century of missionary expansion. The churches were difficult to arouse to their responsibility towards those who had never heard the gospel message; but once the work really began, it flourished and extended in an amazing way.

21

The nineteenth century

The nineteenth century was a great era in human history, and its astonishing social, economic and scientific progress was closely linked with the religious life of the period. The evangelical movement that began in the previous century grew in a remarkable way. This is true not only of the dissenting or Nonconformist churches in the UK but also of the Anglican Church, where the evangelical section became a powerful influence in the life of the country during the first half of the nineteenth century. The same can be said of the evangelical forces in North America and Scotland.

The churches in Britain

In the Anglican Church, Charles Simeon did great work at Cambridge by inspiring young men to dedicate themselves to the service of Christ at home and overseas (see pp. 144–5), and the multifarious activities of the Clapham Sect (see pp. 153–4), associated with the names of such Christian leaders as Henry Thornton, William Wilberforce and Zachary Macaulay, brought a Christian influence to many parts of society. There was also the far-reaching influence of Thomas Scott, who made the Bible live through his commentary and other writings, and who did much to arouse interest in missions.

The same spiritual vitality is seen among Nonconformists in such movements as the emancipation of the slaves, in which T. J. Buxton and John Smith of Demerara distinguished themselves. The rapid development of Sunday schools after their founding by Robert Raikes in 1782 had as their aim teaching children to read the Bible. Prison reform, which is for ever associated with the names of John Howard and Elizabeth Fry, was another sphere in which

Nonconformist involvement was strong. It has been estimated that the Nonconformists rose from about one twentieth of churchgoers to almost a half during this period.

The Industrial Revolution was raising many problems, and Christian statesmen, such as the great Lord Shaftesbury, were zealous in promoting bills in Parliament to ameliorate the hard lot of factory workers, especially women and young children, to stop the opium trade, to protect the Lord's Day and to put an end to flogging in the army. All such movements were symptomatic of the new life that had come to the churches through the evangelical revival. Increasing stress was laid on the need for education. In England, Christian statesmen could see the dangers of illiteracy, especially in the rapidly expanding urban areas. But it was felt strongly that all schools should have a religious foundation and should not be under the secular control of the state. The Anglicans founded the National Society in 1811 and this was followed by the Nonconformist British and Foreign School Society in 1814. In later years, there was, from time to time, much rivalry between these bodies. But both were motivated by a desire to relieve the ignorance and misery of the poorer classes, and it is on the foundation they laid that later state education was built. In Scotland, thanks to the emphasis laid by the reformer John Knox on his great ideal 'a Church and a school in every parish', a remarkable number of schools already existed by the beginning of the century.

The Christian Brethren

In 1827 the religious body known as the Christian Brethren came into existence. It was destined to exercise a considerable influence upon the spiritual life of Britain and North America. It began in Dublin and soon passed to England. Among its early leaders were Anthony Norris Groves, a returned missionary, J. G. Bellett, a lawyer, W. F. Hutchinson of Dublin, John V. Parnell, afterwards Lord Congleton, and Dr Edward Cronin. They were joined by John Nelson Darby, a Londoner then serving as an Anglican curate in Ireland. He not only possessed considerable intellectual gifts, but led a consecrated life and became the most outstanding leader among the Brethren. In its early days, the movement was supported largely by people of the upper middle class, but in due time it began to reach the working classes also. Norris Groves declared, 'Our aim is that men should come together in all simplicity as disciples, not waiting on any pulpit or ministry, but trusting that the Lord will edify us together by ministering to us, as He sees good, from ourselves.' This indicates what has been their purpose ever since. They dreaded clericalism, and stressed that their assemblies had to be led by the Holy Spirit, and that all true Christians were priests. To them, many of the churches seemed to be worldly and dead, while others were orthodox but too cold. They also gave a prominent place in their preaching to the doctrine of Christ's second coming, a subject that had been popularized at that time by Edward Irving, the far-famed and eloquent minister of the Church of Scotland in Regent Square, London.

At Plymouth, the movement became strong under the leadership of B. W. Newton. There the name 'Plymouth Brethren' had its origin. In 1847 Newton was accused of heresy. Having withdrawn, he set up another meeting place in Plymouth and ultimately became an independent minister in London. In Bethesda Chapel, Bristol, George Müller, the well-known founder of the homes for orphan children, and Henry Craik, were joint pastors. They took a position similar to that of the Brethren, and were joined by some of Newton's followers who had come from Plymouth. This was condemned by Darby, who represented the 'Exclusive' type of Brethrenism, while Müller and Craik became leaders of the 'Open' section that was prepared to cooperate and have fellowship with Christians from outside their own religious body. The Exclusive Brethren have had, at times, considerable divisions among themselves over doctrinal questions, and it has not been possible to bring about a fusion with the Open section, which has shown a spirit of fraternity towards other communions. Darby died in 1882 and Müller in 1898.

The Brethren became a living force with a simple faith based upon an infallible Bible. They taught that people are lost through sin and can be saved from divine judgment only by faith in Jesus Christ. Because of the surpassing importance of the life hereafter, the salvation of the soul was for them far more important than social reform or political philosophy. They were well represented in the universities and business life, and their members carried on a quiet but effective work in small groups in many parts of Britain, the Commonwealth, Europe and the USA. There was also a strong missionary interest in many of their assemblies. In recent years, many Brethren assemblies have become community churches with pastors.

Events in Scotland

Early in the nineteenth century, the evangelical party in the Church of Scotland began to show marked vitality under the brilliant leadership of Drs Andrew Thomson and Thomas Chalmers, men of deep spiritual experience and great scholarship. In 1712 the government had passed the Patronage Act, which infringed the right of the Scottish people to elect their own ministers. It was a sore question and productive of much evil (see p. 145). In 1834, under the leadership of Dr Chalmers, the General Assembly passed the Veto Act giving congregations the right to reject the patron's nominee if they considered him unsuitable. When, however, the churches implemented this decision, their rights were flagrantly interfered with by the civil courts. Presbyteries were heavily fined, and the Court of Session ordered them to induct to the ministry unacceptable presentees of the patron, even though they were opposed by nearly all the congregational members and were utterly unfitted for the post.

The government was very badly served by its advisers and the House of Commons threw out the petition presented to it by the Church by 211 votes to 76. Sir Robert Peel expressed the attitude of the government: 'I think it of the greatest importance that the spiritual authority of the Church should be restrained, as it is restrained, and made subordinate to Parliament.' He forgot that the Statutes of Scotland guaranteed the spiritual freedom of the Church. Even the General Assembly was threatened with interdicts in the discharge of its spiritual functions. In loyalty to 'the Crown Rights of the Redeemer' no fewer than 478 ministers left the Church of Scotland on 18 May 1843, carrying with them the old Confession of Faith and constitution of the Church of Scotland, and formed the

Free Church of Scotland. Their action profoundly moved the nation and they were admired throughout Christendom. They gave up the privileges of their state connection and cast themselves on God. They lost their homes and endowments but kept the faith. Within a year of the 'Disruption' (as it became known), 470 new churches had been built, and by 1847, 700. Dr Thomas Guthrie led the thrust to provide manses for the ministers, while Robert Macdonald spearheaded the campaign to build schools. More than 600 Free Church schools came into existence, educating 65,000 children. The extraordinary financial support for the Free Church came largely from the new wealth of the middle classes, who had been deeply touched by the evangelical awakening. While in English the events of 1843 are called the Disruption, the Scottish Gaelic expression *An Dealachadh*, which means 'the separation', is far more accurate. Those who left the Church of Scotland were not disrupting the church but severing the church–state connection. This meant a rejection of the advantages of establishment and endowment.

The Oxford Movement

The repeal of the obnoxious Test and Corporation Acts in 1828 and the permission to Roman Catholics and Nonconformists to sit in Parliament alarmed some of the Tory churchmen at Oxford. They were appalled at the prospect of non-Anglicans voting on questions affecting the Church. A loud cry went up that the Church was in danger. John Henry Newman, then Vicar of St Mary's, Oxford, took up the challenge on behalf of the established Church, ably assisted by Richard Hurrell Froude, Edward B. Pusey, Hugh James Rose (of Cambridge) and W. G. Ward. They put themselves forward as stalwart defenders of the Church of England and, in order to strengthen its position, sought to prove its unbroken continuity with the ancient Catholic Church, and claimed that the Anglicans were the truest representatives of the church of the Middle Ages. They believed that their church was a middle way between Roman Catholicism and Protestantism. They extolled the power and prestige of the bishops, and urged that their authority had descended to them by divine appointment from the apostles of Christ. They propagated their views by means of the publication of theses that they called *Tracts for the Times*. Thus, they were known as 'Tractarians', but are frequently referred to collectively as 'The Oxford Movement'. They glorified the past and stressed the place of tradition in the church.

The leaders of the movement exerted a considerable influence. Sir Walter Scott's colourful descriptions of life in the Middle Ages had fostered an attitude in the country favourable to their outlook. John Keble, author of *The Christian Year*, had greatly influenced the Tractarian leaders in the earlier stages. Very soon their work culminated in a revival of Roman Catholic ideas and practices that had been thrown out of the Anglican Church at the Reformation. The most important plank in their scheme was the doctrine of apostolic succession. Through the laying on of hands a special grace and authority were supposed to have descended to the bishops from the apostles. As usually conceived, the doctrine is mechanical, and has against it the fact that in the course of the ages many church dignitaries supposed to receive and transmit this grace and authority were themselves obviously devoid of the grace of God. According to Newman, 'we must necessarily consider none to be really ordained' unless ordained by those in the apostolic succession. This unchurches a vast number of devoted Christian ministers.

In one of the tracts Newman claimed that clergymen were 'entrusted with the awful and mysterious gifts of making the bread and wine, Christ's Body and Blood'. As this doctrine of transubstantiation was not officially promulgated in the Roman church until the Lateran Council of 1215, and was unknown in the early church, one marvels how the Tractarians could regard such teaching as primitive and apostolic. In 1835 Dr Pusey caused a sensation by publishing a tract on baptismal regeneration that shocked not only the evangelicals but even High Churchmen such as Bishop Davenant. The leaders of the Oxford Movement professed loyalty to the constitution of the Church of England, but were clearly drifting Romewards. Thus Oakeley, an enthusiastic follower of Newman, wrote in *The British Critic* (the mouthpiece of the movement) with regard to the Roman church, 'we are estranged from her in presence, not in heart; may we never be provoked to forget her'. W. G. Ward, another eager disciple of Newman, wrote in 1842 of English Protestantism as a 'debased, hollow, inconsistent form of Christianity'.

The spirit and aims of the Oxford Movement are best shown in Tract 90, issued by Newman in 1839. Although the formulation of the Thirty-nine Articles was an indication that England was a Protestant country, Newman in this tract tried to show that a man might sign these Articles and yet 'aim at being Catholic in heart and doctrine'. If, however, the Thirty-nine Articles could be interpreted as Newman and his friends interpreted them, they were of no value whatever as a criterion of the faith of the Church of England. The University of Oxford and the bishops were speedily roused to action. The Hebdomadal Council condemned Tract 90 outright, and charged Newman with 'evasion' for thus trying to explain away the creed of the Anglican Church. The Bishop of Oxford (who had been friendly to Newman) declared, 'I cannot reconcile myself to a system of interpretation which is so subtle, that by it the Articles may be made to mean anything or nothing.' Bishop after bishop followed in the same strain. Some were very frank and outspoken.

The Tractarians were freely accused by the public of being 'Jesuitical' and with practising 'evasion'. Their doctrine of 'reserve' and lack of frankness lent colour to the charge. In October 1845 Newman was formally received into the Roman church, where he became a cardinal. Ward, Faber, Manning and other Tractarians followed the same path. Throughout the years, many Anglo-Catholics have done likewise.

The changes wrought in a large section of the Anglican Church by the Oxford Movement have, however, been incredibly great. Bishop E. A. Knox wrote in 1933:

Probably even Newman or Pusey would be astounded, if they could visit the scenes of their old labours, and could see bishops mitred and vested in copes and chasubles, clergy and churches so ornamented as to be indistinguishable from those of Rome, images of the Virgin with lights burning before them, pyxes, monstrances, and like evidences of worship of the Host, and

could hear the Mass offered in Anglican Churches for the living and the dead.
(*The Tractarian Movement*, p. 360)

Others within the Church of England vigorously opposed Tractarianism. Considerable influence was exerted by the tracts and historical sketches of John Charles Ryle (1816–1900). A fine athlete and scholar, Ryle was converted on hearing Ephesians 2 being read in church. He served in rural parishes until, at the age of 64, he was appointed in 1880 as the first Bishop of Liverpool. Not only did he highlight the work of the Protestant reformers in England, but he also defended the Puritans, including those who were ejected from the Church of England in 1662. Ryle's writings have often been reprinted and are readily available.

The merit of the Reformation was that it went right back to Christ and the apostles for its teaching. The tragedy of the Oxford Movement was that its members turned their backs upon the Reformation and the principles for which Cranmer, Latimer, Ridley and Hooper, great bishops of their own church, had died at the stake. Instead, they returned to the erroneous ideas of the Middle Ages.

Roman Catholicism in the nineteenth century

In France, the military genius and force of character of Napoleon soon raised him to the highest pinnacle of power. Since the French Revolution, the Roman church had passed through many bitter experiences. Many thousands of the priests had been driven from the country, and many were put to death. Religious freedom was restored in 1795, but the pope refused to recognize the French Civil Constitution of the Clergy, and thereupon, in 1796, Napoleon marched on Rome and drove the pope into a humiliating acceptance of French demands.

Soon the Gallican Articles of 1682 were restored and the pontiff was forbidden to interfere in the affairs of the French church without governmental sanction. This led to much discontent among the clergy, who looked more and more to the pope across the Alps, and were therefore called 'Ultramontanists'. Protestants were given full religious freedom and their ministers were paid by the state.

In 1806 Francis II renounced the title of Emperor of the Holy Roman Empire that was first given to Charlemagne in 800. In spite of eagerness on the part of Pope Pius VII to placate Napoleon, a French army entered Rome in 1808, annexed the papal territories and took the pope prisoner. The latter, however, returned in triumph to Rome in 1814 when Napoleon abdicated. With the final defeat of the emperor of the French at Waterloo in 1815, there began a new era of prosperity for the papacy. The ungodliness of the revolutionary period had produced a strong reaction against atheism and in favour of the Roman church.

The Jesuits had been busy propagandists in this period, alleging that all the evils that had overtaken the nations were due to the worship of reason, disloyalty to the Catholic faith and, in particular, the suppression of the Jesuit order. On 7 August 1814 Pope Pius VII revived the order that Pope Clement XIV had suppressed in 1773. The Jesuits were welcomed back with open arms, and not only regained their position of power in Roman Catholic countries but also found a footing in Protestant lands such as the Netherlands, England and the USA. They exercised a great influence through their tremendous grip on schools and colleges, and implanted a hard intolerance in many minds.

For centuries, the Roman church had claimed to be infallible, and there had been much debate as to where this infallibility lay. The Jesuits insisted, for their own ends, that infallibility rested in the pope alone. They persuaded Pope Pius IX in 1854 to promulgate, without consulting his council, the doctrine of the Immaculate Conception of the Virgin Mary – the doctrine that she was born without original sin. In taking this line, the pontiff had practically claimed infallible authority. The next step was taken at the Vatican Council of 1869–70 where, again through Jesuit influence, the doctrine of papal infallibility was decreed on 18 July 1870. This teaches that when the Roman pontiff, speaking 'ex cathedra', defines a doctrine regarding faith or morals, 'he is infallible, by virtue of his supreme apostolic authority'. In the council, there was a great weight of learning against the proposal. Nevertheless, the arguments of those in favour of the declaration of infallibility easily prevailed. From then on, the Jesuits had more power than ever at the Vatican.

Because of the immense number of immigrants who entered the USA in the nineteenth century from the Roman Catholic areas of Europe and from Ireland, the Roman church became very powerful there. As the nation developed and became prosperous, so did the church of Rome. In Britain also there was a marked increase in the numbers and strength of this church, and the century witnessed the removal of the political disabilities under which its members formerly laboured. In Latin America, where Protestants were very few, the Catholic Church grew in strength as the various states developed politically, economically and numerically. Liberalism was, however, very strong in Latin American universities and, in most Latin American lands, there developed eventually a strong anti-clerical undercurrent, especially among the educated classes.

Nineteenth-century revivals

As one looks at the Protestant churches in Britain and North America in the second part of the nineteenth century, the impression given is one of abounding vitality. It was an age when rationalism and scepticism were spreading in many sectors of the population. Nevertheless, for the mass of the people loyalty to the gospel call and to the church was a notable feature of the time. It was an era of great theologians and great preachers, and the churches were excellently attended. It is questionable whether the power of the pulpit on such a wide scale was ever so marked in the English-speaking world as it was in the years from 1840 to 1890. There were, indeed, great Christian leaders in that period, and we have only to think of some of the prominent names to realize how influential was their appeal. It has never been adequately realized, however, how much this period owed to the great revival movements that took place. This is particularly true of the 1857–60 revival. As a result of this work of the Holy Spirit, at least one million converts were received into the church of God in the USA alone – a large proportion of the population in those days. From America, it spread first to Ulster and then to England and Scotland. In Britain, as in America, it was seen to be a work of God, not of man, and in the UK also a million new members were added to the churches.

The tremendous effect of this can scarcely be exaggerated. It came to many congregations as life from the dead. One of the great results was the effect produced upon William Booth and his wife that led to the founding in 1865 of the Salvation Army, which has brought so much blessing to many countries. This organization was strongly opposed at first, but is now recognized in most countries as a powerful force in evangelistic and philanthropic work. As it does not practise the sacraments of baptism and the Lord's Supper, the Salvation Army has often not been classified as a 'church'.

Again, it was through the influence of the revival that Thomas Barnardo was converted in 1862. The story of the establishing of his orphan homes is typical of the great upsurge of philanthropic activity during this period that derived its vitality and earnestness from the evangelical convictions of those who shared in it. Much of this activity was directed towards helping children, and, as the century progressed, many societies were founded that had as their objective the promotion of the physical and spiritual welfare of boys and girls. In 1844 George Williams, a young draper's assistant, had founded the Young Men's Christian Association (YMCA). Its branches furthered the revival and in their turn were greatly stimulated by it. In 1859, for example, a conference of provincial and London delegates resolved to emphasize anew one of their early principles – that all members of branches should have experienced 'a decided and well-authenticated conversion to God'. This was the spirit underlying many of the great movements of the century.

Looking back, one of the most notable events of the revival movement in North America was the conversion of Dwight L. Moody at Chicago in 1857, when he was 20 years old. He entered a business career in the Midwest but later felt called to become an evangelist. He began his great work among the wildest and ungodliest young men of Chicago. In 1870 he was joined by Ira D. Sankey, whose power as a singer profoundly touched people's hearts. In 1873 the two men came to Britain and held meetings in most of the large cities, and even in some small towns, with astonishing results. There was no sensationalism about Moody's presentation of the gospel. Its most remarkable feature was the way in which it affected men and women of all classes, educated and illiterate, rich and poor. The evangelists made several visits to Britain at intervals of some years and always with the same results: vast numbers professed conversion. In North America, also, their influence became immense.

As a result of the spiritual quickening of this period, there arose the Keswick movement, closely associated with the work of D. L. Moody but scarcely the result of it. In 1874, and again in 1875, a number of evangelical leaders who had been influenced by the writings of three Americans, T. C. Upham, Asa Mohan and W. E. Boardman, on the importance of the Spirit-filled life, arranged conventions at which special teaching on this subject was given. Among those who were greatly influenced by these early gatherings were the Revd T. D. Harford-Battersby, Vicar of Keswick, Cumberland, and Mr Robert Wilson, a Quaker, who lived at Workington in the same county. They resolved to call a convention at Keswick, and the first small gathering was held in 1875. Since then the Convention has met every year in the same place, except for the period of the two World Wars, and its influence has become worldwide. Thousands gather every year in the small lakeside town, and similar conventions have come into being, often with the name 'Keswick', in all parts of the world. Starting with the motto 'All one in Christ Jesus', the Keswick movement stressed the need for Christians to experience the victorious life through the Holy Spirit. This teaching, which was practically calling for a two-stage conversion process, has gradually receded, and now the Keswick movement is much more representative of mainstream evangelicalism.

22

The turn of the century

The evangelical awakening of the eighteenth century made a tremendous impression on British society. Shortly after John Wesley's death, the separation of Methodists from the Church of England took place, and, in spite of divisions in their ranks, the Methodist movement grew fourfold between 1800 and 1860. Methodism appealed to ambitious middle-class workers and also to skilled workers, and by 1850 was exerting a strong influence both religiously and politically. Other Nonconformist bodies, such as the Congregationalists and Baptists, were also growing. Although the Tractarian movement was beginning to take effect in the Church of England, evangelical Anglicanism remained strong. All in all, England remained fundamentally religious and Protestant, while Scotland had continued to experience an increase in evangelical life.

By the middle of the century, pressures were beginning to be felt that gradually, by the end of the century, lessened the continuing impact of the Great Awakening and subsequent developments. However, the revivals that occurred throughout the English-speaking world in 1857–60 injected new vigour into Protestant church life, and because of the large numbers of conversions many came into the fold of the Christian church at that time. This meant that whereas church attendance was decreasing in Europe, and unbelief had become prevalent, in the English-speaking world there were, for some years, increased church attendance and a general quickening of religious life in the population as a whole. The Baptist Church, in particular, grew quickly as a result of the second evangelical awakening, and Baptist preachers, such as Charles Haddon Spurgeon in London and Alexander Maclaren in Manchester, drew vast congregations. The peak in attendance and influence was probably in the period 1870–90.

Witness in the universities

Reference was made earlier to the outstanding work of Charles Simeon of Cambridge (see pp. 144–5). He was one of a group of evangelicals in the Church of England who left an indelible mark upon it. While he was vicar of Holy Trinity Church in Cambridge (1782–1836), it became a centre of evangelical life and Simeon exercised a powerful influence upon students. This was through his lectures (or sermons) on Sunday evenings, and also through the tea parties he gave that provided a more informal opportunity to present biblical teaching. The result of Simeon's ministry lasted long after his death, and it was not surprising that organization of Christian students into societies should have had its origin at Cambridge.

Throughout the nineteenth century, the impact of students upon Christian life and witness in general was considerable. This was as true of the Scottish universities as of Oxford and Cambridge, and a similar phenomenon was apparent on the North American scene. Informal meetings of students had long been a feature of university life, but student Christian societies were organized at Cambridge (1877) and Oxford (1879), and soon Christian Unions in other British universities and colleges were formed. A national grouping of these unions occurred with the formation in 1894 of the British College Christian Union (the name was later changed to the Student Christian Movement [SCM]). It became a powerful influence in British religious life prior to the First World War. Later it was to contribute to the movement towards ecumenicity, and through its publishing branch (SCM Press) became an important element in the field of religious literature. The liberal trend in the theology of the period affected the SCM, and in 1910 the Cambridge Inter-Collegiate Christian Union (CICCU) withdrew from membership. After the war, an attempt was made to heal the breach, but the broadening outlook of the SCM prevented cooperation. As new Christian Unions were formed in the 1920s, they remained unaffiliated with the SCM, while their evangelical stance drew them into close association with one another.

The part played by students in the area of missions was enormous, and the formation of the Student Volunteer Movement in 1886 brought an organized arm of missionary enthusiasm into existence in both North America and Europe. Two years previously, the call to missionary service of the 'Cambridge Seven' (of whom C. T. Studd [1862–1931] is best known) symbolized the start of a new era in missions, in which university graduates would take a prominent part. These seven graduates were from upper-class families and had already made their mark, some because of sporting prowess. Their offer to go to China as missionaries created great interest and was directly responsible for an upsurge in student concern for missions.

The impact of D. L. Moody on the missionary vision of students was considerable. He had conducted a mission at Cambridge University in 1882 that resulted in many conversions, and stimulated interest in missionary societies. In 1886 he presided over a conference at Mount Hermon in Massachusetts from which the Student Volunteer Movement had its origin. Already students, such as Robert P. Wilder of Princeton and others, had been meeting to pray for missions, and the interest aroused was such that, at the conference, a hundred students offered for the mission field. Wilder made several visits to the UK, and helped to stimulate further the missionary interest of students that had already been awakened by the Cambridge Seven. He coined the expression 'the evangelization of the world in this generation', and this became the major theme of the movement. A conference at Edinburgh in 1892 marked the official commencement of the Student Volunteer Movement in Great Britain. Thousands of students were eventually to offer for missionary service through its auspices. The Student Volunteer Movement was a vigorous organization until the 1930s, but eventually faded entirely in the 1940s.

The effects of rationalism

For some time, the influence of the revival movements counteracted strong trends in a different direction that were becoming more prominent by the late nineteenth century. Ultimately, views already being propagated on the Continent would have a tremendous effect in Britain and elsewhere. The closing decades of the century saw this strong Continental influence on religious thought open new paths that, in time, brought about marked changes in religious thought and practice. The development of these views and their impact require description.

Rationalism had come into prominence in the previous century. Originally, this term did not mean a viewpoint opposed to Christianity, but one that assumed that in all matters of religion the human reason was supreme. Positions adopted by philosophers such as Descartes and especially by Kant began to find expression in theological writings. Kant was opposed to the idea that God worked directly in the world and revealed himself to men. The Bible, he believed, must not be used to give direction to our morals. Many writers on biblical and religious topics followed this approach and questioned the reality of the supernatural elements in the Bible. The publication of Charles Darwin's *On the Origin of Species by Means of Natural Selection* (1859) strengthened this trend, and created doubts in the minds of many Christians regarding the biblical narratives. Religion and science came to be commonly regarded as incompatible, and incipient unbelief started to sap the spiritual life of churches.

It was on the Continent that rationalism first expressed itself widely in writings that threw doubt on the contents of the Bible, and that questioned the manner in which the Scriptures had been composed and transmitted. During the eighteenth century, Jean Astruc in France and J. G. Eichhorn in Germany popularized views on the composition of the Pentateuch that were adopted and refined by many others in the following century. While Alexander Geddes in Scotland and Bishop John Colenso of Natal were proponents of the position that Moses was not the author of the Pentateuch, the most lasting development of critical views on the origin of the Old Testament came through Abraham Kuenen in the Netherlands and Karl H. Graf and Julius Wellhausen in Germany.

The view generally accepted up to this period was that Moses had composed the Pentateuch around 1400 BC, and then the historical, prophetic and poetical books came later. The only books placed in the post-exilic period were the prophets Haggai, Malachi and Zechariah, and the historical narratives of Ezra and Nehemiah. The significance of the views of Graf and Wellhausen was twofold. First, to a concept of documents underlying the Pentateuch that could be isolated by analysis of the text, they added the idea that there was development in the religious life of Israel and that the documents reflected this development. Hence, there arose both the designation of the major postulated sources of the Pentateuch and their chrono-logical order using the letters J, E, D, P. In addition, it was asserted that in fact the Prophets came before the Law, and that many of the books of the Old Testament (such as the Pentateuch) were from the post-exilic period. Second, this approach was also accompanied in many cases by an alteration in attitude to the inspiration of the Scriptures and to the formation of the canon. The classic Christian view was that God had breathed out the Scriptures (2 Tim. 3:16) and that the Holy Spirit had borne the writers along as they penned their words (2 Peter 1:21). By this supernatural influence of God's Holy Spirit, the human writers wrote what he wished to be written and preserved for communication to others. In contrast, the new approach was very often linked with a denial of the supernaturalism that dominates the biblical outlook. Instead of being regarded as the product of divine inspiration, the Scriptures were now regarded by many as human and secular products that were later brought together and made part of the canonical Scriptures. By concentrating on the human origins of the biblical text, the church's awareness of the divine origin of the Scriptures was blurred, and the radical approach to sources and their chronological order tended to weaken trust in the reliability of the Scriptures.

The popularization of this position on the Continent was largely due to Kuenen. By the 1860s, it had started to penetrate the English-speaking world. Younger UK and US scholars studied in Germany and on their return began to propagate the new approach. Developments in Scotland were important both because the Continental approach made inroads in evangelical and conservative circles, and also because of the tensions that resulted from its introduction.

A. B. Davidson of Edinburgh, and more particularly his brilliant pupil William Robertson Smith of Aberdeen, began disseminating the new views. Davidson to the end of his life never managed to harmonize his critical approach with his earlier evangelical convictions. Robertson Smith's position was both more unified and less influenced by traditional views. He forced his position on his church, and after several years of controversy was removed from his post as Professor of Hebrew at the Free Church College, Aberdeen. Earlier, Bishop Colenso of Natal had come under ecclesiastical discipline in 1862 for his critical opinions. In the USA, C. A. Briggs of Union Theological Seminary, New York, was suspended in 1892, and the seminary, having severed its links with the Presbyterians, became the leader of liberal theology.

The new approach soon became influential. Scholars such as William Robertson Smith and A. B. Davidson in Scotland, T. K. Cheyne and S. R. Driver in England, and C. A. Briggs, W. R. Harper and C. H. Toy in the USA popularized the position. Clergy were affected, but church members also came to know and accept the new approach. This acceptance was linked to the general trend towards liberal theology, and, by the end of the century, the influence of the earlier revivals was fading and critical views were in the ascendancy. George Adam Smith's judgment at the end of the century was very perceptive: 'Modern criticism has won its war against the traditional theories. It only remains to fix the amount of the indemnity.'

German scholarship was also very significant in New Testament studies throughout the nineteenth century. The Tübingen school, represented particularly by D. F. Strauss (1808–74) and F. C. Baur (1792–1860), exerted a strong influence, with more sceptical writings, such as Renan's *Life of Jesus* (1863), making a considerable impact on the general public. While making some concessions to modern trends, English scholars such as the triumvirate of J. B. Lightfoot, B. F. Westcott and F. J. A. Hort maintained a tradition of close biblical and textual study and left an enduring mark on subsequent New Testament literature. Towards the end of the century, the impact of a new method of approach being adopted in Old Testament study was applied also to New Testament studies. Form criticism, which was largely the work of the German scholar Hermann Gunkel, sought to isolate the forms that underlie biblical books and to reconstruct the way in which the final form of those books was reached. Although form criticism was also applied to the books of the New Testament, it was not until after the First World War that German scholars such as K. L. Schmidt, Martin Dibelius and Rudolf Bultmann made it of major importance in New Testament criticism.

Developments in the USA

It was in the USA that Christianity made some of its greatest gains in the nineteenth century. In the largest of the new nations created by European migration, Christian churches were transplanted into a new setting, and the main British and Continental churches quickly established their presence. Two new factors present were the deviations from orthodox Christian teaching that resulted in the formation of new Christian sects, and the creation of an African-American section of the church. The Mormons were founded by Joseph Smith, who claimed that the Book of Mormon, which proclaimed him as a prophet, was supplementary to the Bible. Brigham Young led the Mormons on their march west to Salt Lake City, Utah, where their headquarters have been ever since. The Seventh-Day Adventists (1863) arose out of the earlier movement based on the prophetical interpretation of William Miller. The Jehovah's Witnesses, another outgrowth of the Adventist teaching, had their origin in the 1870s. Before the civil war, Christians had initiated programmes to free the slaves and to improve their social conditions. What these programmes failed to achieve, the civil war accomplished. African-Americans soon gained emancipation, citizenship and the franchise. Their churches grew rapidly, partly because they were already in existence and were the only social institutions prior to emancipation totally under African-American control. Now with greater freedom these churches assumed even greater importance in African-American life. By 1900, almost one-half of African-Americans were church members. The 'negro spiritual' developed out of Christian songs that were current among the whites in the South before the civil war. The African-Americans took over this means of expressing their religious faith and devotion, stamped it with their own genius and from them the spirituals have become part of Christian music worldwide.

The Christian churches were at the forefront of education in the USA. Numerous church colleges were established, and, by 1850, fifty theological seminaries were operating. After the civil war ended, most denominations saw increased demand for a better-educated ministry. Enlargement of some of the older seminaries helped to meet the demand, but many new ones came into existence, so that, by 1900, the number of Protestant seminaries had doubled. These seminaries provided graduates for the home ministry and also trained many who were to serve abroad in the rapidly expanding missionary projects of the US churches.

23

The early twentieth century

The outbreak of the First World War caught the church and the world unprepared. Great advances in learning had taken place at the end of the previous century. New trends in theology, especially from German sources, had been embraced eagerly. Liberal theology, such as that presented by Adolph Harnack (1851–1930), had caused Christians to look for a progressively better world. Evolutionary philosophy, coupled with emphasis on the divine fatherhood and universal brotherhood, was a controlling influence. War was no longer considered an appropriate instrument of policy among the great nations. Even the crises leading up to 1914 were not taken seriously as indicative of an impending cataclysm.

Changes in Western society culminating in this period also contributed to the optimistic outlook. Industrialization had altered the traditional patterns of living. Improved transport overcame the barrier of distance. Commodities were cheaper and social experience more varied. Politically, the working classes were released from traditional relationships with ruling castes and encouraged to expect greater power in the future. Scientific and religious thought brought a new emphasis on humans as children of nature. Technical discoveries opened new possibilities in areas such as communications.

The coming of war in 1914 was far more devastating in its moral and spiritual consequences than any later conflict. The ideas of progress were shattered, and the barbarism and futility of war took their toll on the world. Platitudes could not explain to people the tragic events of the war, nor help prepare them for participation in finding solutions for the resultant problems at its close. Both

Christians and non-Christians alike were stunned, and groped for new answers.

The war was European in its central focus, but involved most of the developed nations. It resulted in tremendous cost and loss of property, and took the lives of more than eight million. The loss of so many of the rising generation of Christian leaders was also to have a profound effect on Christian developments in the post-war period. The consequences in political terms were also disastrous, as the new political conditions in countries such as Germany, Italy and Russia had a marked influence upon the life and witness of the church.

Moreover, the post-1918 period was characterized by unrest and financial crises, coupled with the fear of renewed armed conflict. The spirit of the church was more one of conserving what it already held, rather than making new advances. Relative to comparative strengths in the previous century, Roman Catholicism fared better than Protestantism in the post-war period and, with considerable additional support from the USA, made advances especially in the East. Meanwhile, after a post-war surge, Protestant missions remained relatively static. In the area of new thought and religious movements, the Protestant churches made significant advances that were to exercise considerable influence.

Theological trends after the Second World War

A new direction in theology emerged at the end of hostilities. A young Swiss pastor, Karl Barth (1886–1968) published a commentary on Romans in 1919. This provided a turning point in modern theology, and Barth became the most influential Protestant theologian of the twentieth century. After holding professorships in several German universities, he took a prominent stand against the Nazi regime and was dismissed from his chair at Bonn in 1935. From that year until his retirement in 1962, he taught at Basel.

What Barth emphasized in his teaching was not altogether new. The British theologians John Oman (1860–1939) and especially P. T. Forsyth (1848–1921) had already advanced views that were to become much more popular by Barth's advocacy. Barth first criticized the prevailing liberal theology from a pastoral standpoint, and then proceeded to develop an emphasis on divine revelation in a way that had affinities with orthodox Christian belief. Hence, the movement begun by Barth was later to be called Neo-orthodoxy.

Barth is best known for his massive *Church Dogmatics*, during the publication of which he modified and refined his early views. He placed great stress on God's transcendence and the fact that knowledge of God is only by revelation of the Father, through the Son by the Spirit. The Word of God cannot be an object, for it is God's speaking. He maintained that one encounters that Word in a threefold form in the incarnation, Scripture and proclamation. There is, therefore, no place for any natural theology that arrives at a concept of God by means other than God's own revelation.

Barth's greatest impact was in the 1930s, but he served as a catalyst for more recent theological trends in both Protestant and Roman Catholic circles. From conservative theological standpoints, Barth's doctrine of Scripture was defective in that it did not adequately deal with biblical statements on the origin and nature of the Scriptures. To many others, Barth was not radical enough in setting aside older views on the Scriptures. It is significant that many of the latter critics, ultimately disillusioned with Barthian theology, themselves went much further and have been involved in the 'death of God' movement.

The ecumenical movement

The word *ecumenical*, coming from the Greek word meaning 'the inhabited world', was originally applied to the church councils of the fourth and fifth centuries AD. They were characterized by the presence of bishops from the 'whole world'. In modern times, the word has come to mean the bringing together of people who are in different churches or denominations. It has become the common word to use in describing joint activities that cross denominational boundaries or efforts to unite specific churches.

The modern ecumenical movement dates from 1910. However, its roots go back a long way in Protestant history, and various movements in the nineteenth century paved the way for its development. There had already been considerable cooperation in missionary situations, and interdenominational missionary organizations existed in both Europe and North America by the turn of the century. Youth activities provided another area for interdenominational activity, and the YMCA, Student Volunteer Movement for Foreign Missions and the Student Christian Movement were led by those who were later to become important figures in the ecumenical movement. Another formative influence was the development of worldwide groupings of churches holding to a similar doctrinal position. The Lambeth Conference of Anglican Bishops (1867) was the precursor of other associations such as The Alliance of Reformed Churches Throughout the World Holding the Presbyterian System (1875), the World Methodist Council (1881) and the Baptist World Alliance (1905).

The Edinburgh Missionary Conference (1910) marked a turning point in ecumenical relations. More than 1,300 delegates participated in this conference chaired by J. R. Mott (1865–1955), who was to become the dominant leader of the ecumenical movement in the following thirty years. Discussions concentrated on mission strategy, with emphasis on conveying the gospel to the whole non-Christian world. This was the first such conference that was so clearly interdenominational in character. It provided the stimulus for many to aim at greater interchurch cooperation. Many of the later leaders of the ecumenical movement in both Europe and the USA had been delegates to it.

In practical terms, the outstanding outcome of the Edinburgh Conference was the formation of the International Missionary Council at Lake Mohonk, New York, in 1921. It was intended to be a council of councils, with no direct participation by missionary societies. With stimulation of cooperation as its main aim, this council organized major conferences. These were at Jerusalem (1928), Madras (1938), Whitby (1947), Willingen (1952), Ghana (1957) and New Delhi (1961). While very few representatives from Global South countries were at the Edinburgh Conference, by 1938 many non-Western delegates took part. By the 1947 meeting, the question of parity between missionaries from mother and daughter churches had become a major issue.

In addition to interdenominational activity and growing missionary cooperation, two other lines of development also played a major role in the ecumenical movement. The first of these was the Life and Work movement. Though founded after the First World War, it was the outcome of concern to see the Christian faith applied to human life in general. Due largely to the efforts of Nathan Söderblom (1866–1931), who was later to become Archbishop of Uppsala, the first conference was held in Stockholm in 1925. The second conference, at Oxford in 1937, gave careful attention to the theological basis for the church's role in the world.

A parallel line of development took place contemporaneously in connection with the World Conference on Faith and Order. At the Edinburgh Missionary Conference, it became clear that doctrinal issues would have to be faced if cooperation between churches was to advance. These issues centred around the Lord's Supper, the nature of the ministry, and the organization of the church. The First World War necessitated delay, but conferences were held at Lausanne (1927) and Edinburgh (1937).

Suggestions were made that Life and Work should merge with Faith and Order. Proposals to this effect were approved at the 1937 conferences, and a provisional structure for a world council was drawn up. Implementation had to wait until 1948, when the World Council of Churches was inaugurated at Amsterdam. Its basis was, 'The World Council of Churches is a fellowship of Churches which accept our Lord Jesus Christ as God and Saviour.' This was later altered at New Delhi (1961) to read:

The World Council of Churches is a fellowship of churches which confess the Lord Jesus Christ as God the Saviour according to the Scriptures and therefore seek to fulfil together their common calling to the glory of the one God, Father, Son and Holy Ghost.

The first half of the twentieth century saw considerable momentum towards organic union of churches. These were of two kinds. First, there were those within a family of churches holding similar doctrinal positions. In Scotland, the majority of the Free Church of Scotland united with the United Presbyterian Church in 1900 to form the United Free Church of Scotland. In turn, the majority of this body united with the Church of Scotland in 1929 to bring together a large percentage of the Scottish population. Both unions left behind minorities that form the present Free Church of Scotland and the United Free Church of Scotland respectively. The divisions in British Methodism were caused in the main by differences over church government, and plans for reunification of the branches were set in motion before the turn of the century. Three bodies united in 1907 as the United Methodist Church, and then in 1932 joined with the Wesleyan and Primitive Methodists to form the present Methodist Church of Great Britain and Ireland. Similar intra-confessional unions took place in the USA. These included the formation of the United Lutheran Church (1918) and the American Lutheran Church (1930), while the Northern Presbyterian Church united with the majority of the Cumberland Presbyterian Church in 1906.

The second type of union was one that crossed previous denominational barriers and brought into being a new united body. The formation of the United Church of Canada stands out as an example of this kind. Negotiations between the Methodists and Presbyterians began officially in 1902, and in 1925 the new church came into being. It also included the Congregationalist Churches in Canada, but about 40 per cent of the Presbyterians continued as the Presbyterian Church in Canada. In China, the mid 1920s were the high point of missionary penetration. More than 8,500 Protestant missionaries were then working in China. Discussions were initiated that led to the formation of the Church of Christ in China, embracing Presbyterians, Baptists and Methodists. In India, protracted negotiations of more than twenty years led eventually to the formation of the Church of South India (1947). The first step was taken when the Presbyterians and Congregationalists formed the South India United

Church (1908). A conference of ministers of that church and of Anglicans in 1919 was a further step, and the addition of Methodist negotiators in 1925 added another dimension. Anglo-Catholic opposition in England to the proposed basis of union retarded progress in the 1930s, but eventually the new church came into being in 1947. The Church of South India (and the content of the protracted negotiations) has provided a basis for other similar proposals. The stature of men associated with it, such as Bishops Lesslie Newbigin and Stephen Neill, has also served to draw attention to it.

Religious trends in America

The end of the nineteenth century saw considerable theological turmoil in North America. Especially in Presbyterian circles there were heresy trials, such as those concerning Professor C. A. Briggs (1841–1913) of Union Theological Seminary, New York. Liberal theology was in the ascendency. However, to set out clearly the basic doctrines of orthodox Christianity, a series of booklets was published in the years 1910–15 called *The Fundamentals*. These were written by prominent US churchmen and theologians, such as B. B. Warfield of Princeton and the Anglican theologian W. H. Griffith Thomas. Many British authors also contributed, including James Orr (1844–1913) of Scotland. Free distribution was organized, so that all leaders in the English-speaking Christian world, such as every pastor, missionary, theological professor and theological student, received copies. More than three million individual copies were made available in this way. From the title of these books has come the term *fundamentalism*, though it was later to assume cultural and theological connotations that originally it did not have.

The tension between conservative and liberal tendencies in US church life came sharply into focus in the 1920s. The Presbyterian churches (especially in the north) had become so alienated from their own creedal statements that more than 1,300 ministers could sign the Auburn Affirmation (1924), which asserted that the General Assembly of the previous year had acted unconstitutionally when it insisted that all candidates for the ministry had to subscribe to five 'essential and necessary' doctrines. The Auburn Affirmation was basically a claim for toleration in theological standpoint. Opposition to this type of theology was led by men such as C. G. Macartney (1879–1957), J. G. Machen (1881–1937) and other professors at Princeton Theological Seminary. Reorganization of the seminary by the church resulted in the formation of Westminster Theological Seminary in 1929. Dissatisfaction over the theology of missionaries of the church led to a new independent missions board being established and the expulsion of Machen and others from the church.

This period of church life saw the US churches assuming a leading role in various areas of the church's witness – missions, theological education and social concern. Not only was this true of the Protestant churches but also in the Roman Catholic Church a similar shift was evident. In missions, there was a swing away from traditionally denominational missions to those that were interdenominational in character. While the US churches provided increasing numbers of missionaries, there was a change in recruitment patterns. The Student Volunteer Movement, which had provided more than 20,000 students for foreign missions, gradually faded, and the last major convention was held in 1936. Other sources amply compensated for this loss, and the increasing dominance of the USA in the world political arena had as its parallel the vision and achievement of US churches in the field of missions.

State of the church between the wars

The interwar period was not an easy one for the Christian church. There were many factors that militated against church life and made missionary work difficult. First, there were consequences of the war and the economic problems associated with recovery. These were being overcome just when the financial collapse of 1929 ushered in years of severe economic depression on a worldwide scale. Second, the rising fascism was casting its shadow over Europe, and the premonition of the coming catastrophe of the Second World War was impressing itself on the world. Mussolini came to power in Italy in 1922 and Hitler in Germany in 1933. Third, the Russian

Revolution of 1917 created another perplexing factor that has had immense repercussions for the Christian church to the present day. Not only was a large section of the Orthodox community cut off from the Christians in the West, but the gradual extension of communist ideas, including anti-Christian sentiment and practice, was soon to impinge on Christian life and witness. Fourth, the rise of nationalism and patriotism, exemplified in India and Japan, brought to the fore a movement that was to blossom after the Second World War. This was important for Christianity because it was basically a reaction to the Western world, with its colonial dominance, and hence, in many cases, against the faith that Westerners had brought with them.

In spite of the problems, considerable advance was made in the interwar period, especially in Asia, Africa and Latin America. Missionary activity in China reached its peak in 1928, and in 1929 circulation of the Scriptures in China exceeded 4.5 million. That figure remained fairly static until the outbreak of the war with Japan in 1936 severely affected all forms of missionary enterprise in the East. Throughout the Pacific islands the number of Christians doubled between 1914 and 1939. Consolidation took place in many African countries and, in regard to both personnel and Scripture distribution, 1937 marked the peak of activity prior to the outbreak of the Second World War. Central and South American countries received significant missionary input, though the predominance of North American missionaries was to have unfortunate consequences after the war. In many countries, the Christian faith was linked with US political and cultural influence.

Distinct advances were made in certain spheres during this time. One of these concerned Bible translation. W. Cameron Townsend had gone to Guatemala as a missionary in 1917. He saw the need for specialized training in order to produce translations of the Bible in all languages. In 1934 Camp Wycliffe was held to train intending missionaries in the field of linguistics. The later formal organization saw two branches develop. The Summer Institute of Linguistics is concerned with the scientific and cultural aspects, while Wycliffe Bible Translators is devoted to the religious aspect, as well as encouraging support from churches. The application of scientific linguistic principles was a major step forward, and the creation of such a dedicated team of translators led to many more, as well as more accurate and colloquial, Bible translations. Another application of modern technology to the communication of the gospel came in 1931 when the first missionary radio station, HCJB in Ecuador, went on the air. Its range was hardly beyond the city of Quito, but it was soon joined by many more transmitters owned and operated by missionary agencies. Christian programmes on commercial radio added another dimension to the churches' proclamation of the gospel in their home areas.

The rise of totalitarianism

The developments relating to totalitarianism require further comment, as they not only impeded Christian witness between the wars but also left a legacy that continues to affect the progress of Christianity in the world. The entry of the USA into the war in 1917 sealed the fate of Germany. The Paris Peace Conference that followed the final surrender of Germany in November 1918 was dominated by the prevailing nationalism and a desire to see Germany duly punished. The Treaty of Versailles (1919) dictated a settlement upon Germany, which resented the harsh terms. Not only was Europe affected but provision also had to be made for former German and Turkish spheres of influence. In the Middle East, France (Lebanon and Syria) and the UK (Palestine and Transjordania) were given mandates in an area destined to become a major tension point in international politics for the next hundred years. The provision of the Peace Conference for the establishment of a League of Nations was an expression of the aspirations of many. However, the exclusion of Germany and Russia, and the refusal of the USA to participate, meant the conference was doomed from the outset.

Of the totalitarian regimes that came into existence, that in Russia was left-wing communism, while those in Italy and Germany were right-wing fascist regimes. The Russian Revolution of 1917 brought about a complete upheaval in the life of the country, and from the outset the church was affected. The revolution was not engineered by the communist leaders. It arose from the bankruptcy of the old regime and the breakdown of government in the three years of war. The communists took advantage of the situation and seized power under the leadership of Lenin. He was a convinced atheist and his influence against the church was seen very quickly. It was obvious that the Russian Orthodox Church would be attacked, as it stood in such a close relationship with the previous tsarist regime. It held enormous wealth and appeared allied to those who were oppressing the poor. Many of the criticisms of the church were indeed valid. Action was soon taken by the new regime, and church property and schools were nationalized without compensation. The permitted use of church buildings was for worship only, and priests and monks were disenfranchised. Some change in policy took place after 1921, but while direct attack lessened somewhat, an intense propaganda campaign commenced. Militant atheism obtained a convenient tool with the formation of a Union of Godless in 1925. By its activities, together with the anti-religious propaganda of the Communist Party itself, a concentrated attempt was made to eradicate the religious belief of the Russian population.

Lenin's death in 1923 created a power struggle that was won by Joseph Stalin (1879–1953). He had been a theological student at Tiflis from 1894 to 1899, but at some point during his course became an atheist and espoused the Marxist philosophy. While Lenin had a real love for the poor and downtrodden, Stalin was more obsessed with a hatred for the middle and upper classes. Many suffered oppression and death during his regime (including former friends and allies), and for Christians it was a period of intense persecution. In 1929, as part of the five-year plan, new provisions were introduced to see that communist ideology was fully accepted and practised. This involved harsh restrictions on religious activities, whether of the Orthodox, Roman Catholic, Lutheran or the smaller evangelical bodies. No religious propaganda was permitted, and this meant that Christian education for the rising generation was virtually impossible.

Although the new Soviet constitution of 1936 did restore some rights to priests (such as the franchise), the brutal persecution decimated the Christian church in the period just prior to the war. Leaders were placed either in concentration camps or liquidated. From the Revolution until the outbreak of war, the number of Orthodox churches and priests fell by 90 per cent. The Roman Catholics suffered for their adherence to the Catholic Church, and also because of their church's intense opposition to communism. Pope Pius XI in 1937 issued an encyclical condemning communism, and by that year there were only ten Roman priests still functioning in the Soviet Union. The extension of Russian territory on the outbreak of war brought several million Roman Catholics living in Poland, Lithuania and Latvia into the Soviet Union.

Many of the upper and middle classes fled from the Soviet Union in the interwar period. They organized congregations in exile, and especially found in France a congenial home. In Paris, a theological seminary was established, with Nikolai Berdyaev (1874–1948) as its most distinguished teacher. Many non-Orthodox Christian emigrants also went to Western Europe or to Canada and the USA. Twenty years of harsh persecution had failed to extinguish the Christian faith and in turn gave rise to an incipient underground church in the Soviet Union.

Totalitarianism appeared in a completely different form in Western Europe. The roots of fascism and the conditions for its growth existed in the years immediately following the First World War. The impending world economic crisis provided another important element. Italy and Germany became the main countries with fascist governments, and in both there was conflict between the government and Christian churches.

In Italy an uneasy relationship between the Roman Catholic Church and the Italian government had existed from 1870. When Louis Napoleon withdrew his troops from Rome in that year, the Italian armies took Rome. The pope was deprived of his temporal possessions except for the restricted area around the Vatican. He refused the offer of financial compensation and non-interference by the government, becoming virtually a prisoner within the Vatican. This situation altered in 1929 when the Church came to an agreement with Mussolini's government. Mussolini, after serving in the Italian army in the First World War, organized the Fascist Party in 1919. He skilfully used nationalistic feeling and opposition to communism to impose totalitarian measures on the country. A reign of terror was instituted as the party consolidated its hold. The accession of Pius XI in 1922 brought about a new relationship between the Vatican and the Italian state. In 1929 two documents were signed formally sealing the relationship. The first acknowledged the Vatican to be a sovereign state and also granted compensation for loss of other income and territory. The second regulated affairs between church and state in Italy, and afforded special privileges to the Roman Catholic Church. That this was really an uneasy truce between the two soon became apparent, as Mussolini tried to bring the youth movements of the church under the control of the Fascist Party.

It was not only the Roman Catholic Church that suffered at the hands of the fascists in Italy. The Protestant churches, although numerically much smaller, were also hampered in their activities. Many of them were funded from abroad, and progressively restrictions were placed on them. The indigenous Waldensian church, which had its stronghold in the north of Italy, was regarded with disfavour, mainly because its foreign connections were regarded as a danger to the state.

The emergence of totalitarianism in Germany took longer than in Italy but, when it did emerge it was even more radical in its outworking. There were many similarities between Mussolini and Hitler. Their family backgrounds were lower class; they had each served as a non-commissioned officer in the war; and both were conscious of the need to appear as a man of the people. They had learned from the methods of democratic parties, and knew how to utilize mass meetings and parades as a propaganda technique. However, the vigour with which Hitler carried through his basic policies, coupled with his territorial ambitions and anti-Semitism, ensured that Germany was to experience an even more radical regime than Italy.

The churches in Germany were affected severely. In the country in which the Reformation had been born, the church was to endure the most violent attack upon it since that time. Protestantism suffered most, as it comprised more than 60 per cent of the German population, yet Roman Catholicism was also attacked. This was in spite of the fact that Hitler had been brought up as a Roman Catholic and was never excommunicated. On leaving the German army in 1920, Hitler immediately took over the propaganda section of the National Socialist Party. He was able to use the party to achieve his aim of political power, and the period of economic and political instability from 1929 onwards provided the conditions for him to become Chancellor in January 1933. A considerable section of Christians in Germany welcomed the rise to power of Hitler and found in his views support for their own nationalistic and racist traditions. In some respects, they held to a liberal theology with nationalistic overtones, coupled with a rejection of the Old Testament and the Jewish element of New Testament Christianity. Even when democracy was overthrown, many Christians still supported Hitler because they viewed him as a bulwark against communism. To these Christians, Hitler gave the name 'German Christians'.

The desire to carry over National Socialist policy into the realm of the church ultimately resulted in the provincial churches of both Lutheran and Reformed persuasion coming into one centralized organization under a Reichsbishop. This bishop, Ludwig Muller, was an ardent Nazi and his election was evidence of the massive strength of the German Christians. Opposition to these moves came from theologians and pastors such as Karl Barth, Martin Niemöller (1892–1984) and Dietrich Bonhoeffer (1906–45). Barth was already well known as a theologian. Niemöller was pastor of a church in a fashionable suburb of Berlin, while Bonhoeffer had been pastor of German congregations in Barcelona and London. From movements such as the Pastors' Emergency League, there developed the Confessing Church in Germany. Its theological basis was set out in the Barmen Declaration (May 1934), which was largely the work of Karl Barth. This declaration proclaimed the uniqueness of God's revelation in Jesus Christ and, in so doing, set itself in opposition to the position of the German Christians. The Confessing Church was harassed from without and suffered from tension within. Barth was removed from his teaching post in 1935, while Niemöller was imprisoned from 1937 to 1945. Bonhoeffer was first responsible for training pastors for the Confessing Church, and then after the Nazis forced the seminary to close, he travelled abroad. His itinerant ministry did much to alert Christians in other countries to the real conditions in Germany and of the true nature of Hitlerism. Returning to Germany in 1939, Bonhoeffer became involved with the resistance movement, and after spending two years in prison was executed in April 1945. The Confessing Church was an embarrassment to the Nazi regime, but, as Niemöller and other leaders acknowledged after the war ended, it should have been more vocal in direct opposition to the main thrust of the Nazi policies.

In spite of Hitler's Roman Catholic upbringing, moves were also made to place severe restrictions on the Roman Catholic Church and its organizations. The Centre Party had been viewed with suspicion by the National Socialists because its membership consisted mainly of Roman Catholics. When it voluntarily disbanded in 1932, opposition was directed to church organizations such as Catholic Action. Negotiations were carried out between the Vatican and the Nazi leaders that resulted in a concordat being signed in September 1933. On the face of it, the concordat seemed to retain for the Church many of its privileges, though certain limitations were placed on the clergy, and the bishops were required to pledge loyalty to the state. It soon became clear that a totalitarian state could not allow any church to possess such independence, and soon rigorous attempts were made to restrict the freedom of pulpits, to force Roman Catholic youth into Nazi organizations and to ensure that Roman Catholic children were forced to attend state schools so that they would be indoctrinated with Nazi beliefs.

By 1937, it was clear to the Vatican that while Hitler was anti-communist, he was also anti-Christian. The papal encyclical *With Deep Anxiety*, read in all Roman Catholic churches in Germany on 14 March 1937, was the first major church document to express resistance to the new cult of the state that had arisen, and to call for opposition to moves that were contrary to basic Christian doctrine and morality.

While church dignitaries were allowed some liberty, every pressure was brought to bear on the rank and file within the Roman Catholic Church. Even in Roman Catholic Austria, annexed to Germany in 1938, severe repression occurred and many schools and monasteries were closed, while ecclesiastical properties were appropriated by the state.

Persecution may drive the church underground, but never destroy it. Thus, in Nazi Germany, in spite of all the repressive measures adopted by the regime to make the church but an arm of the state, religious life continued and, in some circles, flourished. For example, in spite of all the Nazi propaganda, sales of the Bible in Germany far outstripped sales of Hitler's *Mein Kampf* and actually increased between 1930 and 1939. However, the emphasis was on personal faith and not on the application of Christian principles in the areas of social life or government policy. Hence, in general, the Christian community in Germany did not openly oppose National Socialism and the resistance offered was minimal. Most sections of the church failed to oppose the anti-Semitic measures, but Christian mission agencies and many individual Christians continued giving aid to the Jews in their plight.

24

The Second World War and its aftermath

The outbreak of war

The tensions in Europe in the 1930s finally erupted in 1939. Germany's territorial designs included the Danzig corridor, and after issuing farcical ultimatums to the Polish government, the German invasion of Poland took place in September of that year. The UK (and all the British dominions) declared war on Germany. In its early stages, the war was a European conflict, intensified by the German occupation of Norway, Belgium, the Netherlands, Denmark and most of France in early 1940. Italy entered the conflict in June of that year by declaring war on the UK and France. The aim of the Allies was to restrain the Nazi dictatorship that now ruled over the whole of the western coast of Europe from the Bay of Biscay in the south to the Arctic in the north.

The new phase of the war, which was to turn it into a global conflict, took place when, on 22 June 1941, Germany suddenly attacked the Soviet Union, with which it had signed a secret pact in 1939. The entry of Japan into the war in December of that same year, with her unexpected attack on British and US bases (notably Pearl Harbour), ensured that the war would encircle the whole world. Germany and Italy declared war on the USA, and this meant that no major power was isolated from the conflict – every ocean and continent was part of the battleground.

The Second World War had immediate effects on the Christian church, and its consequences helped to mould the subsequent history of the Christian churches and the scope of Christian missions.

As with the First World War, the conflict absorbed the energies of millions, and Christian work suffered from lack of personnel and money. In the areas of armed conflict, Christian work was rendered difficult, if not impossible. Missionary candidature was brought to a standstill, and many mission fields were cut off from their traditional home churches. Temporary help was provided from other sources for German and Norwegian missions.

Within Europe, the trends in Nazi policy towards the churches evident in the 1930s became more pronounced, and, wherever German control extended, harsh measures were used to control religious activities. Though the majority of German Protestants and Roman Catholics supported the German cause, the Nazi leaders worked towards the elimination of the churches. Influential leaders such as Niemöller were kept in prison, and others executed or sent to concentration camps. The German churches failed to perceive the inherent anti-Christian element in Nazism or openly to oppose National Socialism. As Niemöller famously wrote:

> First they came for the socialists, and I did not speak out –
>   Because I was not a socialist.
> Then they came for the trade unionists, and I did not speak
>   out –
>   Because I was not a trade unionist.
> Then they came for the Jews, and I did not speak out –
>   Because I was not a Jew.
> Then they came for me – and there was no one left to speak
>   for me.

In Eastern Europe, Christian churches suffered severely at German hands, and particularly in Poland drastic attempts were made to break the hold of the Roman Catholic Church on the populace. More than 90 per cent of the Roman Catholic clergy in Poland were imprisoned or exiled. Christians in occupied territories in western and northern Europe faced severe persecution. In the Netherlands, for example, Roman Catholics and Protestants alike suffered for their outspoken opposition to the Hitler regime and for their valiant efforts to help provide food and shelter for the hounded Jews. In almost all the occupied territories, the churches formed the main opposition to the Germans, and were the focal points for national and spiritual resistance to their oppressors.

For Christians in Russia, the war brought some alleviation of the pressures against them. As early as 1939, some anti-religious activities were curtailed and priests were given the right to vote. The church supported the state when Germany invaded in 1941, and Stalin sensed the need to conciliate a large section of the population that continued to adhere to religious belief. The Russian Orthodox Church was permitted to elect a patriarch in 1943, and seminaries were reopened. Freedom of religious activity was not restored, but some degree of toleration became government policy.

The post-war period

The years of war left a heavy legacy. In the UK and on the Continent, massive reconstruction of bombed cities had to occur. Millions of service men and women had to be reintegrated into a civilian workforce that was adapting to post-war needs. The war had been one in which machines, not men, were predominant. Industries directed to the supply of war material had now to be redirected to peace-time needs and conditions. All of this provided intense economic problems, for, as William Cowper puts it,

> War lays a burden on the reeling state,
> And peace does nothing to relieve the weight.
> (*Expostulation*, I.306)

The fact that the USA and parts of the British Commonwealth did not suffer direct damage in the war meant that assistance was available for Europe. Massive financial commitment by the USA prevented major starvation in the post-war years, and provided the capital necessary for financing the reconstruction programmes. The UK, which before the war had been in a strong economic position, was forced to borrow heavily from the USA and Commonwealth countries, and her exports were only 40 per cent of their pre-war level.

The changes engendered by the war created new problems for Christian witness, but also opened new possibilities. The altered world political scene closed doors to traditional areas of missionary activity. However, the effect was to redirect missionaries into new areas of service and to produce new emphases in Christian witness in the world. While the traditional geographical areas remained, there was a significant emergence of Global South Christian leaders and increasing influence of the churches they represented. While the proportionate strength of Christianity decreased in Western countries, the Christian church became represented in far more countries, and also showed spectacular growth in some areas. This broadening of the scope of Christian presence on the international scene has been one of the most striking changes since the end of the Second World War.

The political boundaries at the close of the war and the extension of communist power in both Europe and Asia forced changes in Christian strategy. Severe restrictions were placed upon church life behind the Iron Curtain. In spite of many hindrances and persecution, the church showed remarkable vitality in the communist countries: evangelical churches increased and church life had a vigour often lacking in the West. The Orthodox and Roman Catholic churches maintained their positions, even with heavy restrictions on education of the young and theological training of the clergy. There was an accommodation in church–state relations that brought the established churches under greater state and political control. From the West, it appears that this, in some cases, permitted communist philosophy to be joined to Christian doctrine. In other cases, especially in Roman Catholic areas, the tension between church and state revealed the concern to ensure that the church did not conform to an alien viewpoint.

Japanese expansion in Asia before the war brought problems for churches and missionaries, especially in Korea and China. Japan's territorial gains in the war years stopped missionary activities, as well as introducing persecution for Christians. Her defeat in 1945 reopened some doors, but effectively closed others as communist power spread in Asia. The surrender of Japan and the resulting Allied occupation saw the reintroduction of missions to Japan and a new openness to Christian teaching. However, despite the steady growth of churches, Christianity has still not succeeded in penetrating the cultural pattern of Japanese life. In South Korea, the reverse is true, in that the Christian faith has gained wide acceptance. Many influential educators and politicians are Christians, and some of the largest churches in the world are located in South Korea. In higher education, many Christian institutions and universities have a significant presence there.

Resurgence of communist activity in China led to the formation of the People's Republic of China and the expulsion of Christian missionaries in 1950–51. From 1958 onwards, stricter government control of the churches within China occurred and, with the closure of its borders to foreigners, little information was available. With the reopening of contacts in the late 1970s, encouraging signs of growth in Christian witness in China emerged. Absence of Western missionaries did not impede strengthening of congregations, nor did rigid controls prevent evangelization.

Communist influence caused radical changes in Christian work in other Asian countries. It disrupted activities for several years in Malaya immediately after the war. The years of battle in Vietnam restricted missionary work, and the eventual communist victory in 1975 resulted, for a decade or two, in persecution for Christians and separation from Christian contacts abroad. In other South-East Asian countries, restraints were placed on mission work but, in general, the response to the gospel was encouraging and indigenous churches were well represented.

The end of the colonial era

The whole panorama of Christian work altered drastically after 1945 with the demise of Western colonialism. In that year, there were 51 members of the United Nations, but in 2020 this number had increased to 193. These figures tell their own story. Progressively,

Western countries with large colonial empires, such as the UK, France, the Netherlands, Portugal and Belgium, have had to grant independence to former colonies. Nowhere is this seen so dramatically as on the continent of Africa. This change has brought with it many political overtones, not only in terms of voting power in the United Nations, but also in terms of influence of the major powers by provision of military and economic assistance.

For the Christian church, the change has been far reaching. Wherever Western imperialism went there were openings for missionaries. The inherent danger, however, was that people would link acceptance of the Christian faith with adherence to a Western lifestyle, and view the faith as an adjunct of the imported political and economic systems – the Bible and flag went together. With the coming of independence for so many countries, several important factors relating to Christian work have emerged.

No longer can the accusation be made that Christianity and colonialism go hand in hand. That was true previously, and missionaries were often identified with Western exploitation and dominance. The introduction of the Christian faith was frequently seen as an intrusion and viewed as an inseparable part of expanding colonial empires. The missionaries, and the churches they helped to establish, are now free from connection with a colonial power. The stigma of such an association is gone, and the indigenous church has the opportunity to show that it has vitality without the need for government support.

Though colonialism created special problems for the Christian church, it often meant that societies were touched with many of the influences Christianity brings with it. Thus, the gospel had an impact far beyond the boundaries of the organized church. Many of the new nations have inscribed religious freedom into their constitutions, even if the practice at times falls short of the ideal. The way opened for Christians both to evangelize and permeate further into their countries with Christian influence.

Independence for nations has often been accompanied by independence for the national churches. This move is good, as ecclesiastical imperialism inhibits the natural growth of churches and hampers their evangelistic outreach. It will take years, however, to eradicate the mentality of dependence and also, in many cases, continued economic aid from foreign church sources.

The role of the missionaries has also altered. They stand alongside national workers as invited helpers in the activities of the indigenous church. With special skills, they are able to serve the church, and to train local leaders to fill the positions that missionaries for so long occupied.

The end of colonialism also produced a resurgence of ethnic religious life. This is as true of the Eastern religions as it is of militant Islam. These religions, while reasserting themselves in their traditional geographical areas, are also engaged in propaganda activities in Western countries. Migration of their followers has provided a ready base from which to operate. While this whole change has created a new problem for the Christian faith, it has provided yet another opportunity for the message of the gospel to be presented.

Ecumenical developments

The end of the war opened the way for renewed ecumenical contact and activity. Finally, in Amsterdam in 1948, the World Council of Churches (WCC) was established. One hundred and forty-seven churches from forty-four countries approved the Basis and entered membership. The majority of the major Protestant denominations in Europe, the British Isles, North America and Australasia joined, but the Roman Catholic Church and a large section of the Orthodox community abstained. Many of the younger churches from Africa and Asia were participants as well.

The council has no direct authority over member churches. Its executive committee meets every year and the General Assembly normally every seventh year. Successive meetings of the Assembly have been held at Evanston (1954), New Delhi (1961), Uppsala (1968), Nairobi (1975), Vancouver (1983), Canberra (1991), Harare (1998), Porto Alegre (2006) and Busan (2013). Significant milestones have been reached at some of those meetings. At New Delhi, as the culmination of long discussions, the integration of the International

Missionary Council with the WCC was achieved. For many, this meant that world evangelization was now to have the wholehearted support of the major Christian denominations, but in practice this has not occurred. This meeting also saw further progression in ecumenical relations in that the Orthodox churches were fully represented for the first time.

Other trends soon became apparent in the WCC that seemed to direct attention away from mission (in the sense of evangelization with the gospel) to service. The location of the 1961 Assembly, New Delhi, focused attention on the hunger and poverty of much of the world. Many of the younger churchmen participating in discussions were out of sympathy with the older discussions on faith and order. They wished to pursue one of the major reports of the 1961 Assembly on 'Reshaping the Witnessing Community'. This trend became even clearer after conferences in Geneva (1966) and Beirut (1968). Emphasis was placed on social action of a radical kind to correct the imbalance between rich and poor in society and between nations. Attention was given to the revolutionary nature of the gospel and the effect it should have on freeing those suffering from oppression. By the Nairobi Assembly, there was enough support for this approach to ensure that the Assembly approved of financial aid for civilian guerilla activity.

The Roman Catholic Church, though still not a member of the WCC, has drawn closer to it, and has participated in various activities. The issuing of the Decree on Ecumenism by the Second Vatican Council (Vatican II, 1962–5) marked an about-turn for the Roman Catholic Church. Previously, non-Roman Catholics had been encouraged to return to the fold of Roman Catholicism as the only true church. Now there was at least the recognition that there was sin on both sides, and the Vatican Council called on the faithful to participate in the ecumenical movement. In 1965 a joint working group was set up between the WCC and the Roman Catholic Secretariat for Promoting Christian Unity. The Uppsala Assembly signalled the growing rapport between them when, for the first time, there were official observers from the Roman church. While still not a member of the council, the Roman Catholic Church showed its desire to draw closer to non-Roman Catholic churches and to engage in cooperation with them.

In the area of organic union, the post-war period witnessed some significant moves. This is as true of intraconfessional unions as of those that crossed previous denominational barriers. Unions in the USA in the early 1960s brought together the majority of the Lutherans in three churches. The American Lutheran Church (1960) united four separate churches, while the formation of the Lutheran Church of America (1962) created the largest of the American Lutheran Churches, and the one most receptive to modern trends in theology. The third major Lutheran Church in the USA, The Lutheran Church, Missouri Synod, was organized in 1847, and is noted for its strongly confessional theology. It also has a high reputation for its system of parish schools, its theological seminaries and mission programme. Similarly, the largest Presbyterian Church in the USA was formed in 1958, when a merger created the United Presbyterian Church of North America. In turn, it commenced discussions with the Presbyterian Church in the USA (commonly called the Southern Presbyterian Church) and in 1983 these churches united. Unions such as these have been typical of many such mergers within denominational streams.

Mergers in different parts of the world also drew together churches from differing traditions into organic union. Some examples of these can be cited. In England the Congregational Church of England and Wales joined with the Presbyterian Church of England in 1972 to form the United Reformed Church, and in 1982 the Churches of Christ became part of this body. The formation of the Church of North India in 1970 merged six denominations. Some of the difficulties experienced by the Church of South India were avoided by recognition of existing ministers in a service of laying on of hands, though the service was capable of more than one interpretation. The Church of North India also avoided some of the problems over baptism by permitting adult or child baptism, and the mode could be by immersion, pouring or sprinkling. In the USA, four different denominations were represented in the union that produced the United Church of Christ in 1961. Australia was the scene of a major ecumenical experiment with the formation of the Uniting Church in 1977. It consisted of the former Methodist Church, a considerable number of Congregational churches and a majority of the former Presbyterian churches. In New South Wales (NSW), another grouping of evangelical Congregational churches has been formed since the union. The Presbyterian Church is still represented in all states but particularly so in NSW, where more than half of the congregations voted to remain within the Presbyterian Church.

The ecumenical movement has not been without its critics. There have been continuing objections to the WCC from an evangelical standpoint because of the brevity of its doctrinal basis and the consequent theological inclusiveness of its membership. Opposition to its formation prompted the formation of a militant rival, the International Council of Christian Churches (ICCC). Like the WCC, it began in Amsterdam in 1948, with Dr Carl McIntire, a US Presbyterian minister, as the main driving force. It has been marked by strong doctrinal convictions, and opposition to ecumenism and communism. While it has a considerable denominational membership, many of its constituent churches are small. The ICCC has had difficulty maintaining its own unity and its negative stance does not attract many evangelicals. Especially since the death of Dr McIntire, the ICCC has had a decreasing influence.

Other evangelicals have felt that alternative groupings, either with a distinctive theological framework or a particular aim in Christian witness and service, are the best ways in which to express true Christian unity. The Reformed Ecumenical Synod (RES) was an illustration of a doctrinal grouping, with major support coming from North America and the Netherlands. Theological changes within the Reformed Churches in the Netherlands and the Christian Reformed Church in the USA created tensions, with more conservative churches seceding, before the RES merged with the World Alliance of Reformed Churches in 2006. Interdenominational missionary societies and agencies have provided for many a common meeting point and an avenue for service in Christ's kingdom.

For others, discussions over participation in the ecumenical movement have brought tensions. This is so in the case of evangelical

Anglicans in England, whose situation has to be viewed both in relation to the general position of their church in England and its place in the ecumenical movement. While retaining its parochial ministry, the Church of England has adapted it to meet modern needs. Changes also have been made both in regard to the introduction of more modern forms of worship and to alterations in the pattern of Sunday activities to meet the demand for parish Communion as the main service. The influence of the charismatic movement has been strong and, through younger clergy in particular, its impact has been felt widely. Parishes have been changed dramatically through it, and while some laypeople have been drawn outside the orbit of the Anglican Church because of it, many have remained within it. The Church of England has maintained its dominant position in the country, and attendances such as at Easter Communion showed a remarkable consistency over most of the twentieth century.

The Church of England has been at the forefront in moves towards Christian unity, and with able leadership has pioneered approaches in relation to various other branches of the Christian church. Vatican II recognized the special position of the Church of England, which, with its Roman Catholic and Protestant elements, is clearly viewed as being in a unique position in the ecumenical movement. Participation in ecumenical endeavours has created tensions for the evangelicals within the Church of England. Over the years, there has been a growing presence of evangelicals, and several (including the late David Sheppard and Maurice Wood) have been appointed to the episcopate. The tensions result from a desire to participate in the ecumenical movement while retaining the Protestant character of their church. The Keele Conference of 1967 proved to be a watershed for the evangelical Anglicans, who in general had been attempting to maintain a position of involvement without compromise. Other English evangelicals have been unable to share this approach to the problem, and unresolved tensions remain.

Similarly, for other evangelicals whose churches are members of the WCC, there has been a time of reassessment. In some cases, there has been enough support to withdraw from the WCC (the

Presbyterian Church in Ireland and the Presbyterian Church of Australia are examples). Two factors have increased the criticism of the WCC from within. First, the shift in emphasis from biblically orientated mission to social action has left evangelical Christians deprived of opportunities to assist in cross-cultural evangelism. From the Uppsala Assembly onwards, while token emphasis has been given in WCC circles to bringing sinners into reconciliation with God and into service of his kingdom, programmes to implement this emphasis have been lacking. Second, at the Nairobi Assembly the stress was placed on the struggles for liberation and the creation of a new society. The decision to fund civilian guerilla programmes was widely criticized from within as well as from without the WCC. Further erosion of support for the WCC can be traced directly to this decision, though recently indications have suggested that a more balanced approach is emerging in the WCC that may arrest this trend.

Within countries there has often been a national grouping that affords a meeting place for evangelicals, as well as an opportunity for concerted action. In the UK, the Evangelical Alliance, formed in 1846, has served to draw together in fellowship Christians from many denominations and to unite them in working on specific projects. Since the Second World War, the Evangelical Alliance has sponsored large evangelistic crusades (such as those of Dr Billy Graham in 1954–5 and 1966–7), organized conferences and initiated the formation of the Evangelical Missionary Alliance (1958). A very significant move was the establishment of The Evangelical Alliance Relief Fund (Tearfund), which consolidated evangelical Christian relief work and provided gifts and equipment for relief activities in many parts of the world. For those who felt that the Evangelical Alliance was too broad in its outlook, the British Evangelical Council has provided an alternative association without links with the wider ecumenical movement. It had over 2,000 local churches linked into its network of evangelical churches in 1981, though it lost ground in the final two decades of the twentieth century. In 2004 it was renamed Affinity, and has since regained some strength, linking evangelical denominations and groupings, such as the Evangelical Movement of Wales, in a strong organization.

In North America, the National Association of Evangelicals (NAE) stands in direct line of descent from the Evangelical Alliance, though it was organized only in 1942. It has denominations, churches and individuals as members, and its various commissions deal with areas such as missions, evangelism and social action. Along with the British Evangelical Alliance and evangelical groups from other countries, the NAE participated in the formation of the World Evangelical Fellowship (WEF) at Woudschoten, the Netherlands, in 1951. Its membership is restricted to national evangelical fellowships, and its main concerns are theological education, relief programmes and Bible ministries.

Trends in Roman Catholicism

Some dramatic changes took place in Roman Catholicism during the twentieth century, especially in the period after the Second World War. At the beginning of the century, there was a strong modernist movement led by such men as Alfred Loisy in France and George Tyrrell in England. The pope at the time, Pius X, countered strongly in 1907 with a decree and an encyclical, condemning much modern historical criticism and new methods of biblical interpretation. The First World War provided Roman Catholics with an opportunity to display humanitarian interests through their charitable institutions. The involvement of US Roman Catholics in the war helped to make the Roman church truly part of American life.

The period between the wars was marked by continuing missionary interest and theological activity. Relations between the Vatican and the fascist states resulted in agreements with Italy (1929) and Nazi Germany (1933), both of which were broken by these governments. The conservative theological stance of the Church, and its centralized government, continued after the Second World War. In 1950 Pius XII strengthened existing trends by promulgating the dogma of Mary's bodily assumption into heaven. His encyclical of that same year contained a warning against deviation from the established philosophical and theological position of the Church.

The unexpected change in direction for the Roman Catholic Church came not from below but from above. It was prompted by the election of John XXIII as pope in 1958. Though many felt that his pontificate would be of an interim nature, it was to produce the most dramatic results. Shortly after his election he announced that he was calling the twenty-first ecumenical council. Three years of preparation preceded it, and this council (Vatican II) met in four sessions from 1962 to 1965. John XXIII did not live to see its work completed, for he died in 1963, but his successor, Paul VI, implemented his plan and brought the work of Vatican II to completion.

Two aspects of the council's work were highly significant, apart from the documents produced. Although they did not take part in the proceedings, Protestant and Orthodox observers were present. This was an attempt to stress the ecumenical aims of the council. John XXIII had in 1960 established the Secretariat for Promoting Christian Unity, which gave the Vatican a formal means of communication with other churches on ecumenical concerns. The council's decree on ecumenism was to formalize the developing ecumenical interests of the Roman church by referring to non-Roman Catholics as 'separated Churches and Communities', and encouraging the faithful to share in the ecumenical movement. The second significant aspect was the forum that the council gave to elements within the Church who wanted major theological changes. The opening speech at the council by John XXIII paved the way unintentionally for progressive members. He made a distinction between the ancient deposit of the faith and the manner in which that deposit is presented. The presence and participation of theological advisers, especially those from Northern Europe and North America, introduced progressive theology into the debates. The tensions surfaced between conservative elements and those desiring change, and Paul VI had himself to intervene in order to avoid too radical a change or excessive polarization.

Sixteen documents were issued by the council. Some dealt with practical matters such as missions and education, but several were on major doctrinal issues. The one on divine revelation reasserted the traditional Roman Catholic position that there are two sources of revelation – Scripture and tradition. However, a new note was sounded, in that easy access to correct translations by the faithful was encouraged. In keeping with the ecumenical spirit of the council, the view was expressed that such translations could be produced in cooperation with separated brethren so that all Christians could use them. Vatican II took up discussions on the Constitution of the Church that had been started during the course of the First Vatican Council (Vatican I, 1869–70). An important element was the stress on a college of bishops to guide the Church collectively. While giving certain power to the bishops, the traditional place of the pope as the supreme authority was maintained.

The impact of Vatican II was quickly seen. Liturgical changes came, with the Mass often taking on a more communal aspect than previously, and vernacular languages being used instead of Latin. Bible reading was encouraged, and homilies on biblical passages reintroduced. The ecumenical contacts with the WCC were increased on an official level, and also at national and local levels. Expression of radical theological views have become more common since Vatican II. Steps had to be taken by the Vatican to curb outspoken critics such as Edward Schillebeeckx (1914–2009) and Hans Küng (1928–). While many welcomed these changes (and the movement initiated by Vatican II seems irreversible), others have been dismayed by them. Because the changes have been so rapid, and have reversed entrenched positions of centuries, many of the faithful have been bewildered. The Church has lost many of these, as well as those who considered that the change was neither as radical nor as rapid as desirable.

Another factor affecting modern Roman Catholicism occurred in 1966 when charismatic influence began to be felt. This was a direct consequence of the Protestant charismatic movement. While the early leaders were laymen, nuns and priests later participated. The Roman Catholic phase of this movement has many similarities with its Protestant counterpart. There is a stress on prayer, Bible study and personal evangelism. It is significant, though, that those participating in the movement are retained within the Roman church, often with a heightened devotion to the Mass and the veneration of the Virgin Mary.

The tensions within Roman Catholicism that were clearly visible in the mid 1960s continued. Pope John Paul II (1978–2005), with his Polish background, brought a new dimension to the pontificate, and his experience gave him an excellent understanding of communism. He continued the pattern of extensive travel set by his predecessor, John Paul I. In theology and church practice, he was conservative, though progressive trends within the Church seemed to be dominant. Modern Roman Catholicism is not as monolithic as it once was. While its essential doctrines appear unchanged, trends within it, including Bible reading by the laity, have brought it somewhat closer to Protestantism. Many joint services have been held and various cooperative ventures undertaken. However, until there is alteration to tenets essential to Roman Catholic teaching (revelation and tradition, the sacraments, the way of salvation, the worship of Mary), there is little possibility of fuller unity being achieved.

Trends in evangelical life

Evangelicals have continued to play a full role in modern church life. Church membership has waned in the UK and other Western countries, but the number of evangelicals has remained high or increased, particularly in the USA. It is estimated that at least 30 per cent of the population of the USA adhere to evangelical beliefs and participate in the life of churches. This fact helps to account for the relatively high church attendance in America compared with other Western countries.

There has been a considerable diversity of approach to biblical teaching and practice within evangelicalism. In the USA, funda-mentalism commands large support. The term is in general applied to those holding strongly to evangelical beliefs, maintaining a separatist position and living a lifestyle they regard as required of all true believers. While many other evangelicals share the same basic beliefs, they feel a different approach is required. From 1950 on-wards, a group of Americans preferred to be called neo-evangelicals (the phrase was coined by Dr Harold Ockenga). Holding to a conservative Christianity, they also wished to show their concern for social issues and for cooperation in wider Christian activities. Carl F. H. Henry and E. J. Carnell took a prominent part in the development of this approach, and the periodical *Christianity Today* was an influential exponent of it. Tendencies in the movement have brought severe criticism, especially in relation to biblical inspiration and inerrancy. Harold Lindsell, in his book *The Battle for the Bible*, opposed views on the doctrine of Scripture that he claimed were contrary to biblical belief, and initiated a continuing discussion on the nature and authority of biblical revelation.

Since the late 1950s, another feature of modern evangelicalism has been the resurgence of a strongly Reformed influence. Many of the English and Scottish evangelicals of previous generations had shared a common Calvinistic system of doctrine. Their adherence was either to the Thirty-nine Articles or to the Westminster Confession of Faith, both of which were in direct line of descent from the Reformation creedal statements. In the USA, in addition to Presbyterians both in the north and the south, many Baptists had held to Calvinistic beliefs. They included the Southern Baptist leader E. Y. Mullins (1860–1928) and the famous Greek scholar A. T. Robertson (1863–1934). In the UK, the ministry of Dr Martyn Lloyd-Jones at Westminster Chapel, London, from 1938 to 1968 provided a focal point for many concerned with the lack of biblical exposition in modern pulpits and lack of appreciation of the lessons of church history from the Reformation onwards. The formation of the Banner of Truth Trust in 1957 introduced a publisher concentrating initially on republication of older Reformation and Puritan literature, but later broadening its scope to embrace many contemporary authors. The effect of this movement has been to rekindle a deep interest in Reformation and post-Reformation history and theology, and their application to modern church life. Its influence has crossed denominational barriers, and annual conferences for ministers, such as the Leicester Conference in England (and similar ones in the USA), have become very influential. In the USA, the effect has been most notable in non-Presbyterian circles. It has effected a return to systematic biblical exposition from the pulpit, challenged defective evangelistic practices that had become standardized and, in line with its Reformation emphasis, stimulated missionary outreach and concern for the lost.

Many evangelicals make their ecumenical contacts by cooperating in evangelistic outreach and in participating in parachurch organizations. The student Christian societies organized at Oxford and Cambridge in the 1870s were the forerunners of many others in the UK. Annual conferences of evangelical student leaders, especially after the First World War, encouraged the desire for closer links between individual Christian Unions, and in 1928 the Inter-Varsity Fellowship of Evangelical Christian Unions was formed (renamed the Universities and Colleges Christian Fellowship in 1975). For students in many parts of the world, the Inter-Varsity Fellowship offered stimulus to their spiritual lives through biblical teaching and fellowship, coupled with opportunities for service. The 1930s saw the creation of many more Christian Unions in the British universities and colleges, and the foundation of similar bodies in other countries. Visits by Dr Howard Guinness stimulated Christian students in Canada, Australia, New Zealand, India and South Africa. Links were created with similar organizations in Europe, while the early missionary emphasis was maintained. In the USA, the InterVarsity Christian Fellowship was organized in 1941. Its missionary impact is notable, especially through the Urbana Missionary Convention held every three years. The InterVarsity movement in general has been responsible for providing large numbers of volunteers for missionary service. The trend in the 1930s of those with tertiary qualifications taking up missionary appointments became even more pronounced after the Second World War.

Evangelical life among students since the war has been marked by vigorous activity and tremendous growth. The post-war period saw the rapid development of new universities and colleges, and Christian Unions were formed in many of these. In the UK, the number of tertiary students increased by more than 500 per cent between 1948 and 1978, and there was a similar percentage increase in the number of Christian Unions. Similar situations were reported from many countries, not only in the Western world but also in the Global South. Discussions immediately after the war led to the formation of the International Fellowship of Evangelical Students, which now has more than forty national associations affiliated with it. Other movements have also impinged on evangelical student life and added another dimension to it. The work of Dr Francis Schaeffer (1912–84) and his associates at L'Abri in Switzerland (and through related organizations elsewhere) has brought many young students both to an intelligent appreciation of the Christian faith and to a personal experience of its reality. The integration of those influenced by L'Abri into student life has brought new vitality to many groups, and given a deeper understanding of the Christian's task in relation to the current unbelief. Other organizations such as Navigators and Campus Crusade for Christ provide further opportunities for Christian students to meet for study and witness.

Christian businessmen unite in organizations such as the Gideons, which aim at winning individuals to Christ, especially through free distribution of Bibles. Since it was formed in 1899, it has become an international Christian organization and, through its efforts, millions of Bibles and New Testaments have been given to individuals or placed in public places without cost. The proliferation of parachurch organizations poses its own problems for the church, for there is the danger that they may assume many of the functions of churches and also draw people away from involvement in their local church setting.

Evangelistic campaigns, often in buildings other than churches, have been a feature of evangelicalism since the time of Moody and Sankey. In the post-war period, they took on a new significance with the large-scale campaigns by Dr Billy Graham (1918–2018). After a brief pastorate and the experience as the foundation evangelist for Youth for Christ, Dr Graham conducted his first major mission in Los Angeles in 1948. His prominence as an evangelist and Christian leader stems from the Greater London Crusade of 1954, which saw many conversions and created a deep impression throughout the British Isles. Following these crusades, he conducted large-scale missions in all parts of the world, including behind the Iron Curtain. Through his Billy Graham Evangelistic Association, radio and television broadcasts have been used most effectively for presentation of the gospel, and the monthly magazine *Decision* has an extensive readership. While there have been many other modern evangelists, none has been as effective as Dr Graham, who was a powerful teacher with a gospel message directed towards personal conversion. He utilized his personal ability and the skills of his organization to reach millions with the gospel.

On the British scene, Tom Rees (1911–70) stands out as an eminent post-war evangelist who conducted campaigns in British cities, especially at the Royal Albert Hall, London, and established conference centres. Rees also campaigned extensively in North America. Using the same method, Luis Palau conducted major mass crusades in Latin American cities, and later in the UK and the USA. The effectiveness of mass crusades has been questioned, as well as the legitimacy of some of the methods employed. While there is a renewed stress on local-church evangelism, major crusades, such as Mission England in 1984, continued as a part of current evangelistic activity.

In order to reassess evangelistic priorities and to plan for reaching the untouched millions, the Berlin Congress on Evangelism was organized in 1966 by the US evangelical magazine *Christianity Today*. Chaired by Dr Billy Graham, its 1,200 participants came from more than a hundred countries, and critical areas of concern were probed. An even larger conference was held at Lausanne in 1974, when 2,400 visitors took part, of whom more than one third were from Global South countries. The Lausanne Covenant, while stressing loyalty to the inspired Scriptures and evangelism as a mandate contained in them, also emphasized the social concerns of the gospel. Many subsequent regional and national congresses have been held, especially in Latin America, Africa and Asia. The conference at Pattaya in Thailand in 1980 maintained the strong evangelistic emphasis of Lausanne.

Post-war missionary activity

Many aspects of missionary work have altered since 1945. Clearly, nationalism has forced changes on Western churches and missionary societies, which have had to adapt to the altered circumstances. Missionary recruitment from the UK decreased, with a commensurate increase from the USA and British Commonwealth countries. In general, major denominational missions suffered a severe reduction in staff. For example, in the five years from 1971 the major US denominations (with the exception of the Southern Baptists) reduced the number of overseas missionaries by one third. The fact that the Southern Baptists increased their missionary involvement also testifies to the fact that theological factors play a significant role in commitment to missionary programmes. In many cases, the slackening of interest in missions in major denominations tied in with changes in theological emphases, and in particular with a universalism that undercuts the impulse to proclaim the gospel to all. However, other factors have contributed as well, for the slackening in missionary interest has taken place even where no apparent theological change is discernible.

As major denominations have had a smaller share in world missions, so has the task devolved more and more on interdenominational missionary societies. Some of these stem from the middle of the nineteenth century, while others are of much more recent origin. Several of the older societies have changed their names, as their focus of interest has been redirected since the Second World War. The Zenana Bible and Medical Mission became the Bible and Medical Missionary Fellowship, while the Middle East General Mission, the Lebanon Evangelical Mission and the Arabic Literature Mission merged to become the Middle East Christian Outreach. After the expulsion of missionaries from China, the work of the China Inland Mission was redirected to other Asian countries and its name altered to the Overseas Missionary Fellowship. Many of the policies applied in China with such good results have been given a new application elsewhere in Asia. This mission has retained its commitment that its missionaries identify as closely as possible with those to whom they minister, and that other activities do not override the essential aim of diffusing knowledge of the gospel as widely as possible.

The length of each term of missionary service has been shortened considerably in recent years. With the advent of modern air transport, furlough times need not be lengthened by sea voyages. Air travel has also meant that missionaries' absences from their tasks are not so disruptive because of the shorter time away. The sending churches also benefit by more frequent contact with those they have commissioned for service overseas. Another important change has been the introduction of short-term missionary programmes. Traditionally, mission work was a lifetime commitment. Now it is possible to go for a short time, and some missions are making such a term of service mandatory, prior to final acceptance as a career missionary. This scheme enables participants to gain insight both into the missionary task and into themselves, and allows the mission to judge their suitability for the task.

In the post-war period there has been greater need for missionaries to possess technical skills. Partly, this has been dictated by the immigration policies of many countries, which are refusing visas to those who possess training in only Bible teaching and evangelism. It also has been demanded by the changing role of missionaries and the introduction of new technology into many missionary programmes. The areas of communication are a good illustration of this change. Typical programmes may involve radio broadcasting, correspondence Bible courses, biblical translation and production of high-quality literature. All these require specialized skills and often the use of complex and costly equipment. The trend in the 1930s towards a predominance of college- or university-educated missionaries has continued, as the demands made of missionary staff have also increased. In the area of theological training, many colleges developed into graduate and postgraduate institutions, and the competence of staff has had to be upgraded accordingly. Numerous opportunities still exist for Western missionaries with advanced theological training to assist in such programmes.

Two other aspects of modern missions need emphasis. The first concerns the financial cost of missionary work today. No longer are missionaries working predominantly in areas where costs are minimal. Many are operating in large urban centres of developing countries that have borrowed the lifestyle of the West and its economic problems. The training of missionaries, their travel, housing, equipment and support are imposing an ever-increasing burden on sending churches. The second aspect is that of the geographical spread of mission. While some doors have been and remain closed to missionaries, many others have opened. At no previous stage in the history of the church has the influence of the gospel been as widespread. Moreover, none of the other world religions has been able to penetrate every continent as Christianity has done and establish its presence there. The fluctuation in Christian witness from country to country causes reassessment of priorities, and, in the post-war years, there was the realization that vast areas of the West required re-Christianization. Hence, there is far greater involvement now with European missions than before, and the recognition that there has to be revitalization of churches there if the full impact of the biblical faith is to be felt.

25

The global church

Global South Christianity

In the turmoil of the modern period, the most significant change for the Christian church has been the shift of emphasis from Western to Global South churches. At the same time, as there has been a spiritual decline in the West (with the USA being a partial exception), there has been a change in leadership roles, missionary involvement, areas of church growth and application of Christian principles to life in general. During the years of rapid growth in newly independent nations, the churches in those countries also asserted their independence from mother churches, and often sensed the complacency and spiritual decline beginning to affect these older churches. Reassessment of traditional roles created tensions, but the indigenization process for the church strengthened the position of local Christians to evangelize and play a true role in national life.

Advances in Asia continued to be more among animistic peoples than among adherents of the major faiths. The latter have religious faith that is coupled with a distinctive cultural pattern, and often the presentation of the gospel to them has not been adapted to this problem. But throughout Asia the Christian church is well established, it has able leadership and is poised to make further advances.

At first, the transfer of Hong Kong back to China in 1997 did not seem to affect the status of churches there. However, in 2019 mass protests were initiated by a bill proposing extradition of offenders to mainland China, and these protests extended more broadly to failure to implement further changes for Hong Kong in accord with the agreement with the UK in 1997. It is uncertain how far this unrest will impinge on the liberties Christians have enjoyed in Hong Kong.

As of April 2020, it remains a strong regional centre for Christian outreach.

The Christian message came to Indonesia early in the sixteenth century and a large church community was established in the midst of an Islamic population. Since Indonesia achieved its independence in 1949, there has been some spectacular growth of the church there, especially in the 1960s. Just as there had been historically in these islands, there were mass conversions, for which the church was unprepared, and that it could not adequately absorb. Christians now number about 10 per cent of the population. The leadership is strong and well trained, and there are several theological colleges of a high standard. Some militant Islamic groups have aroused opposition to the Christian presence, and sporadic destruction of church buildings has taken place.

Around the Pacific Islands, as a result of missionary work in the nineteenth century, the Christian presence is evident.

Government immigration policy in India restricts the entry of foreign missionaries, though Commonwealth subjects can enter as visitors and are free to engage in voluntary service. In some Indian states, there is legislation relating to conversion. As in other parts of the world, Indian Christians have been adjusting to a new stage in the life of their country and churches and now have the opportunity to strengthen their position. The social outreach of the Indian churches is prominent, with many famous medical institutions under church control or connected with bodies such as the Emmanuel Hospital Association. The initiatives for Christian advance in India now rest with national Christians, as the Indian government has imposed severe restrictions on mission work, especially disallowing entry of missionaries from overseas or foreign financial aid to be received and utilized by Indian church organizations.

Throughout the Middle East the church remained small. Jewish believers began to make a significant contribution to Christian life in Israel, with expatriates taking a less prominent role in the organization of Christian witness there. While overseas mission agencies (such as the Scandinavian Jewish missions, the Church Mission to the Jews, Christian Witness to Israel, from the UK, and

US Baptist missions) remained in Israel, their role was no longer as prominent. Congregations of Hebrew Christians began to develop as a regular feature of Israeli life and witness. Ha-Gefen Press, situated in Rishon LeZion, was set up to translate evangelical literature into Hebrew and to publish regular magazines in Hebrew that contain indigenous writing. Orthodox Judaism in Israel was still able to make it difficult to purchase land and erect buildings for Christian congregations, and exerted constant pressure on the government to outlaw conversions from Judaism. Neighbouring Lebanon has been war-torn since 1958 and promising Christian expansion there has been stunted. The North African Islamic states have small Christian communities, with those in Egypt being by far the largest. This is because of the survival of the ancient Coptic Church in considerable strength, as well as the presence of churches resulting from Protestant and Roman Catholic missionary activity. Fundamentalist Muslims have attempted to prevent conversions to Christianity and have been responsible for damage to Christian church properties. Through the response to radio ministries it has become known that there are many individual believers in Islamic countries who are unable (or unwilling) to identify with any organized Christian group.

The rest of Africa after the Second World War presented a far different picture. While the growth of the church was slowest where Islamic penetration was greatest, over the continent there was a dramatic increase in the Christian population. Between 1900 and 1950, the Christian population in Africa increased sixty times, and the rate of growth since has been higher. Missionary work by Western and South African churches continued in many countries. The most dramatic development, however, was in the realm of indigenous, independent churches. This was not a recent phenomenon. In the early part of the twentieth century, there were several significant African preachers. The best known of these was William Harris, who came from Liberia to the Ivory Coast. Between 1913 and 1915, thousands were converted under his preaching, and English Methodist missionaries were able later to gather many of these into their churches. More recently, there was a proliferation of African churches, especially in South Africa. The phenomenon is in part a reaction to white dominance, and its many African features are less commonly seen in churches associated with Western missions. These African churches usually have a formal church structure, yet have spontaneity in worship (often with stress on prophecy, revelations and healings) more akin to the Western charismatic groups. These churches occur where there is a considerable Christian presence, and while accurate statistics are not available, the total number of people associated with them runs into millions.

In contrast to them are the established churches in South Africa. They represent the older British and European churches (especially those from the Netherlands). Theological change in the churches in relation to apartheid policies was one significant factor in the political changes that led to multiracial elections in 1994, resulting in the election of Nelson Mandela as Prime Minister. New opportunities have opened up for the churches in South Africa within their own country and they are now able to take part in mission programmes abroad with greater ease. The change in the country has also meant that South African representatives were able again to take their place in international Christian forums. Politics in South Africa post-1994 has been tainted by corruption, and support for the ruling African National Congress has receded. The emigration of many Afrikaners has weakened the Christian presence in the country, though it has brought an influx of Christian influence to other countries, especially the UK and Australia.

The Christian presence in Africa has been stimulated by the revival movement that began in Uganda in 1929. Commencing through the experience of an English missionary and a Bugandan believer, a spiritual awakening spread throughout Uganda and into Kenya and Tanzania, then into central Africa and north into the Sudan and Ethiopia. While there were features in the movement that led to problems (e.g. open confession of all sin), in general it proved to be a purifying and strengthening factor in the life of the church, and its influence is still present. Persecution was also very real, and mass murders occurred in the Sudan, Ethiopia, Chad, Kenya, Burundi, Zaire and especially in Uganda during the reign of Idi

Amin (1925–2003). Rather than slowing the rate of growth of the church, this quickened it and added impetus to the Christianization of Africa.

If Africa provided so much encouragement for Christians during the twentieth century, then Latin America even more so. To borrow Bishop Stephen Neill's apt expression, 'this [was], above all else, the Evangelical century in South America'. The Roman Catholic Church was the dominant nominally Christian group in Latin America from the time of the Iberian conquest. It managed to suppress many of the early Protestant missionary efforts but, from the middle of the nineteenth century, Protestant missions, both denominational and interdenominational, have operated throughout the region. In 1900 there were 50,000 evangelicals (as the Protestants are generally called) in Latin America. By 1995, this had grown to more than thirty million. Much of this increase came in the years immediately following. The new attitude of the Second Vatican Council (Vatican II, 1962–5) towards Protestants meant that Roman Catholic persecution lessened. Missionaries and national Christians have been very active in evangelism, and in particular Pentecostal churches have led the advance. They have the ability to bring the gospel to the working classes especially, and identify more easily than other churches with the Latin American cultural pattern. From the outset, the Pentecostal churches have been largely indigenous and have not been dependent on foreign funding.

Latin America has produced its own problems for Christianity, but has also stimulated innovative thinking and the production of programmes to meet specific needs. Social conditions have dominated the horizons and forced Christian theologians to wrestle with the inherent problems of so many of the Latin American republics – foreign economic control, unequal distribution of wealth and dictatorial regimes. Both Protestant and Roman Catholic theologians were involved in the formulation of a 'theology of liberation'. For them, Western theology had little to say regarding poverty, racial discrimination or oppression. Roman Catholic leaders such as Helder Camara of Brazil and Gustavo Gutiérrez of Peru stressed the aspect of liberation, and the person-to-person dimensions of the biblical faith. Many evangelical leaders in Latin America expressed sympathy with the aspirations of 'liberation theology' but felt its emphasis was too radical. They wanted to preserve the stress on the relationship between God and humans, and the need for sinners to be reconciled to God. They recognized that the Christian faith must apply to life in its entirety, but sensed the dangers of adopting a stance that differs little from radical Marxism.

Two innovative programmes had their beginnings in Latin America and have been borrowed by Christians elsewhere. Presbyterian missionaries in Guatemala were faced with the difficulty of supplying enough pastors for rapidly expanding churches. Traditional training methods could not cope, nor was the finance available to support full-time students. Hence, in 1962 they devised the scheme of theological education by extension (TEE). In this scheme, the students worked in their home situations on studies provided by the seminary, and were paid occasional visits from trained teachers to help and encourage them. It has proved to be a highly effective method and has been widely implemented, especially in Latin America, Asia and Africa. The other major innovation has been evangelism-in-depth. Robert Strachan of the Latin America Mission devised a scheme whereby the total Christian community in a country is mobilized in a year-long campaign of saturation evangelism. It operates under national leadership, and trains believers in how to reach their neighbours for Christ. The method was first used in Nicaragua in 1960 and has since been employed widely in Latin America and elsewhere, though with decreasing frequency.

The growth of Global South Christianity marks the most significant development of Christianity since the Second World War. Increasingly, Western Christians have been recognizing this fact. The list of centres at which major conferences were held in the last decades of the twentieth century reveals this shift. Moreover, leaders from the Global South were taking a prominent place in such conferences and, on the general world scene, were respected and becoming increasingly influential.

Theological training and writing are other areas in which there has been rapid advance in Global South countries, and the literature being produced is influencing Western thinking. Another part of Christian work where there has been an increasing Global South commitment is in missions. By 2000, there were approximately 4,000 missionaries from Global South countries working in cross-cultural situations. This trend accelerated as the younger churches reached maturity.

Pentecostalism and the charismatic movement

The twentieth century saw the growth of Pentecostal churches. Some of the features exhibited by this development had already been seen earlier. This was so of some of the physical manifestations that had appeared in some revival and holiness meetings. A new phase began around 1900 in the USA when, in addition to orthodox evangelical belief, it was asserted that Spirit baptism and its accompanying sign of speaking in tongues was a necessary addition to a conversion experience. From Topeka, Kansas, the movement spread to Los Angeles. A convert from Houston, Texas, an African-American by the name of William J. Seymour, brought the teaching when he founded the Apostolic Faith Gospel Mission in Azusa Street, Los Angeles, in 1906. From there, it spread throughout the USA and to other countries. As early as 1907, it had come to both the British Isles and Scandinavia, and soon established itself in Latin America. The early supporters of the movement had no intention of forming new denominations, but when opposition to their teaching arose they formed new groupings. Of these, the Assemblies of God (1914) is the best known and the largest. They proclaim that they are 'Pentecostal in experience, evangelical in outlook, and fundamental in [their] approach to the Bible'. The Assemblies of God are marked out by their generally Presbyterian type of church government, their ministry being better trained than in many other Pentecostal churches, and their strong missionary programme. The greater emphasis on theological scholarship in these circles is exemplified in the publications of G. D. Fee (1934–), noted for his work on the New Testament text and exegesis.

The spread of Pentecostalism has been greatest in Latin America. Within the first decade of the movement's history, Pentecostalism had established itself in Chile and Brazil, and spread throughout the region. While there has been considerable growth of Pentecostalism in other areas (e.g. East and West Africa), nowhere else has it been as rapid as in Latin America. Nor does Pentecostalism elsewhere represent such a high proportion of the Christian community as it does in Latin America. It is estimated that it constitutes more than two thirds of the evangelicals in that region. The Pentecostal churches have a special ability to make the gospel intelligible to the poor and oppressed. Moreover, the conversions that occur have both social and economic, as well as religious, consequences. Reception of the gospel also means reception of a new lifestyle, and Latin American Pentecostalism has brought major social changes in numerous communities.

In the last half of the twentieth century, a phenomenon closely related to Pentecostalism emerged with the appearance of the charismatic movement. The word 'charismatic' comes from the Greek word for a free gift of grace. All the New Testament occurrences of the word (except for 1 Peter 4:10) occur in Paul's letters, and the plural form of the word (*charismata*) is used by Paul to indicate the variety of spiritual gifts given to the church. The charismatic movement is not uniform; hence, it is difficult to generalize regarding its characteristics. In some circles, there is stress on the more spectacular gifts, such as healing, prophecy and speaking in tongues. But the place of the other gifts in the life of the body of Christ is also recognized, such as the nine gifts listed in 1 Corinthians 12:7–11. While some regard the gift of tongues as the initial sign of the baptism of the Holy Spirit, this is by no means the universal view.

Early in the 1960s, the charismatic movement appeared in the mainstream Protestant churches. Suddenly, in churches where there was little stress on the work of the Holy Spirit in regeneration and sanctification, many came to experience the power of the Holy Spirit. This meant that new vitality was infused into congregations and it produced spontaneity in worship, along with a deep desire to share the gospel message with others. The movement commenced on the west coast of America and spread rapidly. While not within the mainstream of charismatics, the 'Jesus People', who often adopted a communal lifestyle, were influenced by it. They arose in the late 1960s and were part of a generation disillusioned with the society that endorsed the Vietnam War, and who chose to opt out of it. Their strength faded in the 1970s as their membership was absorbed into regular denominational churches. The charismatic movement spread from the USA and became well established in many churches of the Western world. Its influence is exerted by individuals who have had a charismatic experience, but also by conferences, publications and extensive recordings ministries. From 1966 onwards, the charismatic movement began to have a significant impact upon the Roman Catholic Church. The fact that leading ecclesiastics such as Cardinal Suenens of Belgium approved of it helped to secure its firm place within the Roman Catholic Church. The common factors between Protestant and Roman Catholic charismatic experience have resulted in many ecumenical gatherings where the 'gifts' are exercised. Clearly, the bond between the participants is more in terms of subjective experience than of commitment to objective doctrinal beliefs. While Roman Catholic charismatics may pay more attention to Jesus' redeeming work than many of their fellow Roman Catholics, in the main they still give allegiance to traditional Roman belief, including the intercession of Mary and the Mass.

Though many have been brought to a personal relationship with Christ through the charismatic movement, this movement has not been without its critics among those who do not share its emphases. Classic Pentecostalists have been wary of it, especially as they find it reformulating the theology of the Pentecostal experiences. Others have opposed it on doctrinal grounds or because it has created tensions in many congregations. As those involved in charismatic experiences did not in the main separate from their original congregations, a divisive element was often introduced into local fellowships. Some have separated, and in various countries house churches unaligned with any denomination have been established. Factors other than charismatic tendencies have in some cases contributed to their development. The charismatic movement has certainly prompted theological discussion on the question of the continuity of all of the charismatic gifts after the apostolic age. Clearly, some expressions of the charismatic gifts seem at variance with the New Testament pattern, which stresses not their individuality but their usefulness for the edification of the whole body. Those who oppose the idea of a continuation of apostolic gifts point to the lack of need for them in the light of the finality and sufficiency of Scripture. The New Testament also regards the gifts as a sovereign bestowal by God upon the recipient. There can be no doubt, however, as to the vitality of the Christian experience of many within the charismatic movement, nor of their love and devotion to Christ.

New trends in the charismatic movement appeared in the 1980s in the growth in churches associated with the ministry of John Wimber (1934–97). Starting from his pastorate of the Anaheim Vineyard church in California, Wimber began a national and international 'signs and wonders' ministry, and the Association of Vineyard Churches grew to number more than 250 churches. In the 1990s specific physical responses, including unusual prostrations and laughter, marked out meetings of the Toronto Vineyard church and these (known popularly as the 'Toronto Blessing') spread internationally. Wimber finally distanced himself from these phenomena.

Bible translation and distribution

The period since 1945 has been one of intense activity on the part of the Bible societies, missionary agencies, churches and interdenominational groups in translating the Bible. The impetus has continued from earlier periods of providing mission churches with the Bible in their own language. Emphasis on this has led to missionary societies seeking better-trained staff to join these programmes. Knowledge of cross-cultural communication and linguistics are now regarded as prerequisites for the task. Foremost in interdenominational work has been the Wycliffe Bible Translators. It is currently represented in more than forty countries and, with a staff of over 5,000, this organization has developed as an indispensable aid to mission outreach. Parts of Scripture are now available in approximately 3,000 living languages. It is estimated that there are still more than 440 million people, speaking at least 3,800 languages, who have no part of the Bible translated into their own language.

The coordination of biblical translation and distribution has been facilitated by the formation of the United Bible Societies (UBS). The excellent work of individual Bible societies was often lessened because of duplication of activities. After discussions in the 1930s, immediately after the Second World War the UBS was formed. It is divided into four regions (the Americas, Asia, Africa and Europe), with consultants able to help at all stages of Bible translation, printing and distribution. This unified structure meant that resources could be pooled and more effective use could be made of skilled personnel. The UBS is concerned also with publishing Scripture in the original languages, and its Greek New Testament is widely used. Close contact has been maintained with Roman Catholic translation programmes since Vatican II, and an agreement made in 1968 between the UBS and the Roman Catholic Church has controlled this expanding cooperative effort. Never before in the history of the church have so many resources been available for Bible translation work. With the expansion of literacy in the Global South, there is an urgent need for Bibles and other Christian literature to be provided in large numbers, and through the UBS, Wycliffe Bible translators and many other church and mission agencies, there is every prospect that this challenge will be met.

The last forty years of the twentieth century saw a tremendous number of modern versions of the Bible published in the major languages of the world. For more than three centuries, the translations from the Reformation and post-Reformation periods were dominant, but were joined by translations in contemporary idiom. Paraphrases have served to introduce many to the Scriptures or deepen their understanding of them. In English, J. B. Phillips, especially through his *Letters to Young Churches*, was a significant interpreter of the New Testament, to be joined later by Kenneth Taylor and his Living Bible. A revision of Taylor's work (of which more than forty million copies are in print) was made by a team of evangelical scholars and published in 1996 as the New Living

Translation. This revision has both improved the Living Bible's accuracy and also widened its usefulness.

Several major revisions of the Authorized (King James) Version (AV), have appeared. In the USA, the International Council of Religious Education authorized a revision of the American Standard Version (1901) with the intention of staying as close to the Tyndale–King James tradition as possible. The New Testament of the Revised Standard Version (RSV) was published in 1946 and the complete Bible in 1951. It was an elegant revision that won wide acceptance throughout the English-speaking world. In the historical books of the Old and New Testaments, it is hard to better, but in the poetical and prophetical books of the Old Testament more than necessary conjectural readings were introduced. While minor modifications were made to the RSV over the years, a full revision called the New Revised Standard Version appeared in 1990. Its major changes included addressing God as 'you' and, more contentiously, attempting to avoid sexist language. In the latter regard, its efforts have not won general support as they alter the cultural setting of the original text. The result is a revision that has moved further away from the AV and which is less suitable for study purposes than the original RSV. Another revision of the American Standard Version was made by the Lockman Foundation and published in 1962 as the New American Standard Bible. It is a useful study Bible because it keeps very closely to the phrasing of the Greek and Hebrew. This characteristic is also its greatest limitation in that it lacks the smooth flow of some of the other versions. A further attempt at revision was made by the publication in the UK and USA of the New King James Version in 1982. It aimed at preserving the thought flow of the 1611 Bible and its precision, while modernizing the English. For those who have been brought up on the AV, these versions provide a choice of a modern translation made in the same tradition.

Several significant new versions have also appeared. The most widely used modern Roman Catholic version, the Jerusalem Bible (1966), is based on the work of French Catholic scholars at the École Biblique in Jerusalem, and it has found acceptance by many Protestants as well. Just after the end of the war, a move from the

Church of Scotland resulted in the formation of a committee of representatives from the major denominations in England and Scotland to work on a new translation. The committee was later widened to include other churches in the British Isles and the British and Foreign Bible Society and the National Bible Society of Scotland. The decision was made to work on a fresh translation in contemporary English. The New Testament of the New English Bible (NEB) was published in 1961 and the complete Bible in 1970. Several factors have militated against its wide acceptance. On the one hand, it broke too radically with the tradition of biblical translation, but on the other hand it often was not sufficiently modern in style. At times, the influence of the joint directors (Professors G. R. Driver and C. H. Dodd) seems too apparent on the translation. Some of the major defects of the NEB were removed in the revision published in 1989 as the Revised English Bible.

Another two of the modern versions are the Today's English Version (Good News for Modern Man) and the New International Version. The former is the most colloquial of the modern versions. While it has often captured the sense of the texts, the principle of dynamic equivalence is carried too far and a lack of accuracy is the result. Similar Good News Bibles have now been published in the major European languages. The New International Version, published as a whole in 1978, attempted to stay in the long line of English translations while bringing the Scriptures in clear and natural English. It soon won widespread support, establishing itself as one of the major English Bibles for personal and church use.

Theological and biblical study

The period after the war was marked by intense theological activity. The influence of Karl Barth (1886–1968) and Emil Brunner (1889–1966) was strong up to the late 1950s. Despite their differences, their combined views represented a position that, while stressing God's sovereignty in revealing himself to men, moved away from the emphasis in evangelical orthodoxy on the concept of the Bible's containing objective truth. Many welcomed this approach, but others felt that Barth and Brunner were still too bound by traditional concepts. These critics were themselves to move much further from traditional views. The most radical form of this development was the appearance in the USA of a group holding to the thought of the 'death of God'. Writers such as Harvey Cox, Paul van Buren and, in particular, T. J. J. Altizer popularized the notion that the word 'God' was meaningless. In many ways, their expression of belief had little in common with Christian doctrine, even though they drew upon the thought of Dietrich Bonhoeffer (1906–45). He had been influenced by Karl Barth (1886–1968) and Rudolf Bultmann (1884–1976), and spoke of 'religionless' and 'worldly Christianity' and of man 'come of age'. The 'death of God' theologians took up and applied these ideas in ways that went far beyond what Bonhoeffer had intended by them. In the UK, views that had some similarity to these radical US views were espoused by Bishop John Robinson. His book *Honest to God* sparked off a controversy by his speaking openly of his doubts and difficulties with the traditional Christian view of God, though his later writings on the New Testament were much more conservative.

German theologians were seminal thinkers during the twentieth century. The work of Rudolf Bultmann had a profound effect on both New Testament studies and theology. His popularization of the method of approach to the biblical text called 'form criticism' has deeply affected biblical studies. His assertion that the Bible has to be demythologized before we can apply its teaching has helped to undermine further the confidence of many in the realities of which the Bible speaks. As a reaction to his position and similar viewpoints, a new quest for 'the historical Jesus' developed, with German and US scholars being the main participants. Once again, the historical figure of Jesus was in the foreground. More recently, the German theologians Wolfhart Pannenberg (1928–2014) and Jürgen Moltmann (1926–) have stressed the future action of God, and the elements of hope and promise are dominant in their presentation. Roman Catholic theologians such as Hans Küng (1928–) and Karl Rahner (1904–84) succeeded in bringing Protestant and Roman theology into greater interaction.

Ecumenical initiatives after Vatican II led to the setting up of the Anglican–Roman Catholic International Commission (ARCIC) that met between 1970 and 1981. The result of the dialogue was published in 1982, claiming substantial agreement on eucharistic doctrine and ministry. Before official responses had been made to this report, a second commission (ARCIC II) was established to deal with outstanding doctrinal differences. Its report, *Salvation and the Church* (1987), dealt with the doctrine of justification. Varied responses have been made to it, but it is clear that it places Anglican theology in a midway position between Reformation teaching and traditional Roman Catholic theology. Further progress in Anglican–Catholic relations may well depend upon other disputed points, and in particular the question of women in ministry. Progress towards reconciliation has come up against a serious barrier at this point.

Two main trends are observable in relation to modern critical studies. A new phase of the quest for the 'historical Jesus' was under way between 1980 and 2000. This is in marked contrast to the studies for the greater part of the century that dismissed any idea of recovering the 'historical Jesus'. Some scholars have asserted the Jewishness of Jesus, while others emphasized the Hellenistic background of his teaching. Whichever background has been adopted, there is a separation between the reconstruction of Jesus' life and Jesus Christ, God's Son, who has been confessed and preached by the church over the centuries. Most of these critical studies challenged the uniqueness of Christ, which was under attack from another angle by writers such as John Hick. He and others asserted that Jesus is not the only way to God the Father, and this teaching has made inroads among evangelicals. Clark Pinnock emerged as a leading proponent of the view that the vast majority of people who have ever lived on the earth will not be excluded from salvation.

The second major trend is that there has been a notable shift away from investigation of the possible sources behind the biblical text. This is partly the result of the work of Brevard Childs (1923–2007), with his stress on canonical criticism. By this, he meant the study of the books of the Bible in their canonical setting and in their completed form. There was also a strong tendency towards literary criticism of the Bible by both Jewish and Christian scholars. The biblical books are considered as literary works in their own right, and their form and function are analysed to assist the process of interpretation. The way literary criticism is applied depends on the theological and historical pre-understanding of scholars, but it has shown its benefits and is much more congenial to an evangelical position than the older source criticism.

Much attention has been given to biblical studies, and fruitful gains have been made. To the earlier archaeological finds of Ugaritic tablets at Ras Shamra in 1929 (which have shed light on the Hebrew language and given a fuller understanding of Canaanite beliefs) have been added the striking discoveries of the Dead Sea Scrolls. While these scrolls (uncovered from 1945 onwards) and the community that originally possessed them are of significance for New Testament studies, their major impact is on the study of the text of the Old Testament. This one find has taken the textual history of the Old Testament back more than a thousand years, as the biblical manuscripts from the Dead Sea are the earliest extant Old Testament texts and come from the intertestamental period. There has been considerable delay in the editing and publication of these texts. When they are fully published, further light will be shed on the Old Testament text, intertestamental Judaism and the theological views of the community that preserved them. In northern Syria in 1974 tablets were discovered at ancient Ebla that illumine the patriarchal period. The discovery of Gnostic manuscripts at Nag Hammadi in Egypt in 1945–6 has thrown light on both the New Testament and early church history. The close attention that scholars are giving to the biblical text is manifested in the translations, books and commentaries that are appearing in greater numbers than ever before.

While general theological trends since the war have been basically antagonistic to the orthodox viewpoint, evangelical scholarship consolidated its position. Organizations such as the Tyndale Fellowship in the UK and the Evangelical Theological Society in the USA have fostered devout scholarship, and publications from these circles have been widely welcomed. Series of commentaries such as the

Tyndale and the New International enjoy a high reputation, while books such as the *New Bible Commentary* and *New Bible Dictionary* have aided many Christians. Scholarly reference tools (e.g. the *New International Dictionary of New Testament Theology* and the *New International Dictionary of Old Testament Theology and Exegesis*) show the strengths of evangelical scholarship. In the UK, scholars of the calibre of F. F. Bruce, D. J. Wiseman, I. H. Marshall and Alan Millard have done much to further evangelical scholarship. Other scholars, such as J. I. Packer, Alister McGrath and D. A. Carson, have been influential on both sides of the Atlantic, while their books have wide distribution throughout the world. In the USA, the Princeton tradition has been maintained since 1929 at Westminster Theological Seminary, and scholars such as E. J. Young, Meredith Kline, Cornelius van Til, Ned Stonehouse, John Murray, Edward Clowney and John Frame have made valuable contributions to theological literature. Many colleges and seminaries in the USA and Canada (e.g. Wheaton College, Fuller Theological Seminary, Trinity International University, Trinity Evangelical Divinity School, Gordon-Conwell Seminary, Regent College, Reformed Theological Seminary, Dallas Theological Seminary, Southern Baptist Theological Seminary and Denver Seminary) have been noted for their evangelical stance, and their staff and graduates have strengthened theological enterprise. Continental scholarship, of which the monumental series of studies in theology by G. C. Berkouwer of the Netherlands are a notable example, has also made its mark. However, evangelical scholarship on the Continent tends to be directed more to the European scene, and due to a lack of translations does not have a strong impact on the English-speaking world.

26

Into the new millennium

Global trends

Changes in the overall strength and direction of the Christian faith were evident late in the twentieth century, but the trends discernible then have accelerated in the twenty-first century. New pressures have had a great impact on the Christian church. The shift of the centre of Christianity from Europe to Africa, North and South America and Asia has continued unabated. In past centuries, areas of Christian dominance retained their prestige but lost their vigour, which was taken over by other areas. This happened in the seventh to the ninth centuries, when the Eastern church retained its status but was lacking in the zeal of the church in the Netherlands, northern France, England and Germany. Starting in the twentieth, but extending into the twenty-first century, there has been a notable shift to other continents. Prominent leaders now come from the Global South, and the size of churches in these countries often dwarf those of mother churches in Europe. For example, the Anglican churches of Nigeria and Uganda are far larger than the Church of England or the Episcopal Church in the USA.

With this shift of centre has also come another change: the dominance of strong denominations in Europe has been replaced by innumerable smaller churches. The growth of Pentecostalism has encouraged this trend, while a desire to adapt to local traditions and beliefs has frequently been the driving force behind the development of new churches in Africa. Expressions of the Christian faith have taken on very diverse characteristics, as dominant personalities lead their followers into expressions of Christianity that blend local religious beliefs with elements of the Christian faith.

Even in the West there has been the splintering of denominational loyalties. Mission programmes of major denominations are no longer strongly supported, as many independent agencies compete for money and support. Many of these are aimed at niche missionary targets, but in effect divert funds away from denominational goals. Fundraising has become a major task for many aspiring missionaries, before they can be recognized by mission agencies. Some large, older mission agencies, such as Wycliffe Bible Translators, Overseas Missionary Fellowship and Pioneers, have maintained their positions as leading bodies claiming support from a wide spectrum of denominations.

Rapid technological change in the world has made a great impact on church life, and also on church outreach and missions. Computer equipment has become the norm in churches for record keeping, communication with members and projection on to screens for worship services. Although the use of social media has opened new avenues of contact, sometimes, because of its use by individuals, it adversely affects social interaction. For countries in which minorities have restrictions placed on them, these means have created new ways of maintaining relationships with isolated Christians, and have been very effective in the distribution of Christian teaching material.

Global political changes have also made an impact on the life of the church. This is notably so in relation to the former USSR, which, after considerable political turmoil and a coup, was dissolved on 31 December 1991. Twelve independent states subsequently assumed their place on the world scene. At first, many Christian agencies took advantage of what seemed to be new openness to Christians in these countries, but later these countries imposed greater restrictions, severely limiting evangelism and even public meetings of Christians.

Shift to the Global South

The focus of Christianity that had begun to shift from Europe to the Global South in the final decades of the twentieth century became more evident in the twenty-first century. This shift is very evident within Anglicanism. In 2008 the Global Anglican Future Conference

(GAFCON) was formed to guard and proclaim biblical truth globally and provide fellowship for orthodox Anglicans. The leaders of the majority of the world's Anglicans felt it was necessary to take a united stand for truth, because of moral compromise, doctrinal error and the collapse of biblical witness in many parts of the Anglican communion. More than a thousand people, including primates, archbishops, bishops, clergy and lay leaders gathered in Jerusalem. Later, conferences were held in Nairobi (2013) and Jerusalem (2018). The numbers attending the last conference show the breadth of support it has. Official numbers reveal attendance by 1,292 men and 670 women, from 53 countries. These numbers include 993 clergy, among whom were 333 bishops, and 973 laypeople. The first chairman of GAFCON was Archbishop Nicholas Okoh, Metropolitan and Primate of All Nigeria, while the deputy chairman was the Most Reverend Stanley Ntagali, Archbishop of Uganda, who succeeded Okoh as chairman.

Another significant trend is the number of scholars from the Global South who are contributing to academic theology. Important contributions are being made in journals and books by theologians who are able to bring insights from their own backgrounds to bear as they discuss the Christian faith and its practical outworking. This input is evidence of the maturing of Christian communities and the development of fine institutions in many Global South countries.

Ecumenical developments

The formation of the World Council of Churches in 1948 opened the spectre of many mergers of Christian groups in the quest for unity. However, that has not happened. The Uniting Church of Australia, formed in 1977, deliberately chose its name to indicate that it was in the process of merging with other Christian traditions, though no such unions have eventuated or even seem likely. The World Council of Churches has achieved some success at a theological or intellectual level, but little real progress has been seen at the ground level. The great hopes predicated on the formation of the Churches of North and South India have not been replicated elsewhere. While discussions have involved the Roman Catholic and Orthodox Churches, they still are not members of the World Council. Other factors have more recently had an impact on union possibilities, such as the ordination of women and the admission of practising homosexuals to the ministry, which have both inhibited discussions between churches that hold opposing views on these issues.

Resurgent Islam

Since the last two decades of the twentieth century, Christianity worldwide has been influenced by a resurgent and aggressive Islam. This has been coupled with political moves that have led to extended clashes between the USA and her allies, or sometimes by the USA alone, and Islamic groups. Various events in Islamic countries since the 1990s, mainly though not exclusively in the Middle East, have had a profound effect upon the day-to-day work of the Christian churches. The Iraqi invasion of Kuwait in 1990, which led to the intervention of Western forces and the overthrow of Saddam Hussein, was one of them. On 9 September 2001, three US airliners were hijacked by Islamic suicide bombers and deliberately crashed into the twin towers of the World Trade Center in New York, and the Pentagon in Washington. A fourth plane crashed in Pennsylvania when passengers thwarted the plans of the hijackers. These attacks, perpetrated by the Muslim terrorist group Al Qaeda, claimed more than 3,000 lives and destroyed both tower buildings. They led to the US decision to challenge the power of the Taliban in Afghanistan, where the Al Qaeda influence was very strong. This antagonism increased when suicide bombers struck in many different countries.

In 2011 a movement started in the Middle East that was given the name 'the Arab spring', though the inappropriateness of this name was recognized later when some began to call it 'the Arab winter'. A series of anti-government uprisings took place in Muslim countries in North Africa and the Middle East trying to end oppressive regimes and resultant corruption and food shortages. However, by mid 2012 it became clear that these developments were not going to solve the problems, and regime change did not occur. The causes that led to the start of the movement still exist. Another movement of strict Islamic control commenced in 2015, with the declaration of an Islamic caliphate centred on Syria by a group calling itself the Islamic State of Iraq and Syria (ISIS). The resulting conflict took four years to regain territory lost to ISIS, and, while some think the battle has been won, it seems that terrorist activity elsewhere will be the outcome.

The gospel in the Middle East and the Indian subcontinent

The Middle East

World focus has been on the Middle East in the first two decades of the twenty-first century. Events and ideology emanating from there have had a serious impact on Christian churches. While 'the Arab spring' brought some relief from oppressive rule, it did not achieve what many Christians and non-Christians expected and desired; namely, freedom of speech and religion. It and succeeding events led to some of the worst violence against Christians that has been experienced for centuries. It has also seen the Christian churches decimated in countries such as Iraq and Syria. In 1987 Christians made up 8.5 per cent of the Iraqi population (16.5 million), whereas now it is estimated that only 250,000 Christians remain.

In spite of appalling persecution, Christian witness remains in Muslim countries, and access through website, email and smartphones has created new avenues disseminating the Christian message across the region. Organizations such as Middle East Reformed Fellowship (MERF), based in Cyprus, have done much to propagate the gospel in Arabic, to bring leaders out of their home countries for periods of training and to administer fine diaconal projects that have alleviated the pressing needs of many in Muslim communities.

Strident Islam, and decades of warfare, have reduced the numbers of Christians in many other countries in the Middle East. The Coptic Church in Egypt has suffered repeated attacks on personnel and buildings. Many institutions founded by evangelical Christians no longer maintain their earlier vision, and the Turkish occupation of Northern Cyprus has virtually extinguished the Christian presence there. One country in which progress has been made is Israel, for, while many orthodox Jews strongly oppose evangelistic endeavours by expatriate Christians, the number of Hebrew-speaking congregations has increased. Christian Witness to Israel established a bookshop in Ha-Gefen Street in Haifa, and from that developed Ha-Gefen Publishing, which produces a variety of gospel materials in modern Hebrew. As many modern Israelis cannot understand Biblical Hebrew, Ha-Gefen has produced a five-volume text of the Old Testament in modern Hebrew, as well as material for evangelism and instruction.

The Indian subcontinent

On the Indian subcontinent considerable expansion of Christian witness took place in the latter part of the twentieth century, despite restrictions being placed on the entry of new missionaries to India following independence in 1947. The very old Mar Thoma church in Kerala (which reputedly had its origins after Thomas the disciple came there in about AD 50) has held its position, and even extended overseas to the USA, the Middle East, Malaysia, Singapore, South Africa, Australia and New Zealand. It has about 700,000 members. Catholic and Protestant churches in India have seen growth, largely it would seem because of their indigenous leadership. Rising Hindu nationalism has impeded growth in some areas, while Western charities, such as Compassion International, have been restricted in their operation. Pakistan continues to be a safe haven for Islamic terrorists, and Christian activities can be carried on only with the greatest caution and sensitivity.

Christian churches in Asia and the Pacific

Many Western Christians expressed great hope that resurgent Christian belief and practice in China would be allowed to have a public face. Underground churches had flourished, but the desire was for open expression of the faith to take place in church buildings. For a time it seemed that this was going to happen. However, although the Chinese constitution guarantees religious freedom, a tightening of control over churches (and over Muslims) occurred after President Xi Jinping came to office in 2014. The claim is made repeatedly that the churches are a means whereby the West is able to subvert social stability in China. Hence, efforts have been directed towards eliminating Western influence and replacing it with Chinese culture and tradition. This programme of Sinicization (*sino-*, from Late Latin *sinae*, the southern Chinese) has included destruction of churches, unless they are part of officially sanctioned Christian groups registered with the government-approved Protestant Three-Self Church, China Christian Council and the Chinese Patriotic Catholic Church. Harsher measures have been taken against the Uighur (also spelled Uyghur) Muslims in the west of China, and many of them have been taken to indoctrination camps. Some Western expatriates have also been forced to leave at very short notice.

Strong churches exist in major centres such as Hong Kong, Kuala Lumpur, Singapore and Jakarta. Many missionaries still work in Asia, though much greater care has now to be taken due to sensitivities in relation to overt evangelistic activities in many countries. The Christian churches in South Korea remain extremely strong, though the rapid rate of growth seen late last century has now tapered off. The Korean churches retain a high sense of mission awareness and, in many parts of the world, Korean missionaries are busy with gospel ministry. It is not unusual to find Chinese and Korean speakers forming churches in Western countries to which they have gone for either temporary or permanent residence. Japan still remains a difficult country to penetrate with Christian missions, and a recent estimate is that Christians form approximately only 1 per cent of the total population.

The Philippines remain a stronghold for Catholicism. After Brazil and Mexico, it is the third largest Catholic country in the world. Indonesia, the most populous Islamic nation, with a population of 264 million, is 87 per cent Muslim, with Christians comprising almost 10 per cent. In the cities, ethnic Chinese often constitute a major part of the church membership. The churches in Indonesia are well served by seminaries and Bible colleges. Violence against Christians by Muslims has been sporadic, but in general Islam is not as extreme as in the Middle East. Most of the South Pacific countries are strongly Protestant, largely as a result of nineteenth-century missionary activity. Roman Catholic orders and Protestant missions entered Papua New Guinea at about the same time, and now 95 per cent of the population claim to be Christian, with Protestants far outnumbering Catholics. Countries such as Samoa, Tonga, Vanuatu and the Cook Islands have large Christian populations, and when people from these countries move to Australia or New Zealand they retain their national identity and Christian affiliations.

The gospel in Africa

North Africa was once a prime geographical area of Christian influence. That is so no longer, as it is now a stronghold of Islam, and from there aggressive and militant Islam is seeking to push further south, especially into Nigeria. But for the rest of Africa, the prospects are brighter, as much of the population has a Christian majority. However, to the long-standing traditional groups – Protestantism, Roman Catholicism and Orthodoxy – has been added African independent churches. These had their origins more than a hundred years ago, and came into existence for a variety of reasons. Sometimes they were a response to Western domination of church life or a feeling of dispossession, or arose from a desire to blend indigenous religious life with the Christian gospel. Pentecostal distinctives are often blended with African religious beliefs, and hence it is hard to predict where such diverse expressions of Christianity are going to go in the future.

Nowhere has the development of African independent churches been seen so clearly as in South Africa. Higher standards of education and greater wealth there might have contributed to the proliferation of these new expressions of the Christian faith. Approximately 80 per cent of South Africa's population claim allegiance to Christianity, but this includes those with very syncretistic beliefs and practices. Afrikaner churches have been weakened due to the continued loss of many due to emigration, but also because of the close links between these churches and the political processes. The lingering effects of the apartheid era still militate against the witness for the gospel by the Dutch Reformed churches.

Vigorous expansion in Latin America

For centuries, Latin America has been a nominally Christian region, dominated by Roman Catholicism, which, as the official religion in most countries, often persecuted Protestants. However, a massive change took place in the twentieth century that continues through to the present day. Millions became Protestants, and Pentecostals accounted for more than half of these. Though at first the influence of North American Pentecostal missionaries was significant, later developments were not constrained by imported church structures, and so indigenous developments have been dominant in the rapid growth of more recent times. In just a century, Pentecostalism has become more Latin Americanized than Roman Catholicism has in four centuries. Social issues were not at first a major concern, but now are being confronted, just as they are in Africa. In addition to Pentecostalism, Anglicanism, Seventh-day Adventism and Presbyterianism (especially in Brazil) have a strong hold in Latin America. Present indications are that strong growth of Protestantism in Latin America is continuing.

Roman Catholicism

The effects of the Second Vatican Council (Vatican II, 1962–5) continue to be felt in the Roman Catholic Church worldwide. There is greater variation in theology within it, and a willingness to disagree with official doctrinal statements. Entry into the priesthood, and into both male and female orders, has declined markedly in developed countries, and subsequent vacancies have been made up from Global South countries such as India, Sri Lanka, Nigeria and the Philippines. Even in such a nominally Catholic country as the Republic of Ireland, overseas priests are participating in parish life to compensate for a greatly reduced flow of new entrants into the priesthood. The Church has also been engulfed in scandals relating to sexual abuse by priests, and prosecutions in civil courts have reached to the highest levels in the Roman hierarchy, including Cardinal George Pell of Australia. While other churches and mission agencies have been embroiled in similar scandals, the supposedly celibate priesthood has been under close scrutiny for offences going back decades.

The Roman Catholic Church differs from Protestantism in that one of its greatest strengths is its worldwide dimension. Despite differences between dioceses and orders, there is a commonality in that the Church is orientated towards Rome. While its official doctrines have not changed, there is now a greater similarity between Roman Catholicism and Protestantism in that various influences, including the charismatic movement and the use of Protestant hymnology, have brought many aspects of their Christian expression into closer alignment.

The role of the pope continues to undergo change. Paul VI (1963–78) began the practice of travelling overseas, and this was greatly increased under John Paul II (1978–2005), who visited 129 countries. Under the rule of Benedict XVI (2005–13), greater prominence was again given to the Tridentine Mass, and the use of Latin was promoted. He voluntarily relinquished the papacy, and the election of this successor, Francis (2013–), brought a much more liberal pope into office. He is the first pope who was a Jesuit and also the first from the Americas. Many Catholics now question papal authority, and agitation for change in areas such as the role of women in the church and the abolition of celibacy of the clergy has noticeably increased.

Bible translation

The work of Bible translation is an ongoing priority for Christian missions. Dedicated groups such as Wycliffe Bible Translators, aided by various Bible societies and many other missionary organizations, continue to produce an amazing range of Bible versions year by year. It is hard to get an accurate estimate of the number of languages spoken throughout the world, but certainly it is at least 6,800. Of these, approximately 3,000 have at least a portion of a Bible translated. The situation in Papua New Guinea (PNG) highlights the need for increased work on Bible translation. There are 838 living languages in PNG, which amounts to 12 per cent of the world's languages. Of these, 462 still do not have any Scripture translation.

In English, the New International Version (NIV) for thirty years or more occupied a prominent place among those looking for a faithful translation of the Hebrew and Greek scriptures into modern dignified English. The 2011 update to the NIV is the latest fruit of a process allowing for regular revision. By working with input from pastors and biblical scholars, by grappling with the latest discoveries about biblical languages and the biblical world, and by using cutting-edge research on English usage, the Committee on Bible Translation updated the text to ensure that the New International Version of the Bible remained faithful to its original vision. However, the decision to adopt more inclusive language has meant that quite a percentage of readers have switched to other versions, especially the English Standard Version (ESV). Suited for personal reading, public worship, in-depth study and Scripture memorization, the ESV is available in more than 200 print editions, and free digitally via mobile applications or online. Published in 2001, the ESV Bible has been widely accepted and is used by numerous denominations and organizations, and by millions of individual Christians around the world.

Moral issues

The past decades have witnessed several moral issues in which the churches have been deeply involved. Abortion has been a very prominent issue. In the USA, the *Roe* v. *Wade* decision of 1962 opened the way for the widespread practice of abortion, and this decision has often been referred to in other countries as well.

However, in the USA and elsewhere, there have often been strong opponents among Christian people to the practice. On the one hand, many supporters of abortion argue that it is the right of a woman to control her own body, and hence abortion is a permissible form of birth control after conception. On the other hand, from a Christian perspective, it is argued that human life according to Scripture begins at conception, and that it is only morally right to permit abortion under carefully controlled circumstances. In the USA, there has been a considerable legislative move against abortion in several of the states in the past few years.

While abortion rates decreased in the two decades until 2010, largely due to the widespread use of birth-control methods, the number of abortions has increased again since then. Many maternal deaths occur in Global South countries (estimated at 47,000 per year) due to unhygienic practices and conditions. The total number of abortions worldwide is hard to calculate, but prominent medical journals such as *The Lancet* have given the massive number of 56 million per year. Christians have taken a prominent part in opposing induced abortions, and legal battles have been fought over protests outside abortion clinics. In the main, Protestants and Roman Catholics have taken the same approach to abortion, arguing on biblical grounds that human life begins at conception.

Sexual differentiation issues have also been prominent. While some churches right through the twentieth century had at least some women ministers or priests, most did not until later in the century. In 1992 the Church of England approved the ordination of women to the priesthood, and now more than one third of Anglican priests are women. The majority of denominations have women pastors. Opposition to the ordination of women to the priesthood or ministry continues to come in Anglican or Episcopal circles from two different directions. Those of 'High Church' persuasion generally quote the absence of women in Christ's apostolic band, while those of 'Low Church' sympathies cite the biblical injunctions against women taking part in leadership roles in the local church (1 Cor. 14:32–35; 1 Tim. 2:11–12). By 2018, of those entering training for ministry in the Church of England, 54 per cent of them were female. In Australia, the large evangelical diocese of Sydney has had women deacons for twenty-five years or more, but does not ordain women as priests. Three other dioceses of the Anglican Church in Australia (Armidale, Murra and North West Australia) also do not ordain women. While Anglican and Episcopal churches have had women priests for many years, it has taken much longer for women to be appointed as bishops or archbishops. Most larger Presbyterian churches, such as the Church of Scotland or the Presbyterian Church (USA) do, though the more strongly evangelical and reformed Presbyterian churches do not. This applies to the Presbyterian Church in America, while the Presbyterian Church of Australia revoked its approval of women ministers in 1991, and there is no move to have them restored.

Probably the greatest shift in public morality in the West has concerned approaches to homosexuality. A concerted campaign to press for gay rights brought an alteration in public opinion, and then a change within churches. Many countries repealed legislation that had made homosexuality a criminal offence, and then proceeded to permit gay and lesbian marriages. Reaction within churches has brought to the fore the differences between liberal and evangelical approaches to Scripture. Conservative Christians have based their opposition on the express teachings of the Bible, while liberals have not felt constrained to adhere to the statements of Scripture, arguing that they are time-bound and are not intrinsic to current Christian belief. It was significant that in 1998, when the attempt was made within Anglicanism to get the Lambeth Conference to accept ordination of homosexuals, the greatest opposition came from the Anglican provinces in Kenya, Uganda and Nigeria. However, the election of Gene Robinson, an openly gay priest, as Bishop of New Hampshire in the USA in 2004, opened the way for other similar appointments.

Euthanasia

Arguments relating to euthanasia are not new, for it was practised in ancient Greece and quite a few other countries. Last century, much debate took place in the UK, Europe and the USA regarding the ethical expediency of legalizing voluntary euthanasia. Even where such legislation has come in, no country has laws permitting non-voluntary euthanasia. The Nazi programme in Germany of killing those with retarded mental capacity or belonging to specific racial groups, such as the Romany or the Jews, was abhorrent to the rest of the world. In practice, if not in law, medical means of ending life have been available in Switzerland since the 1980s, while in the Netherlands legislation came into effect in 2002 permitting euthanasia and physician-assisted suicide under specific circumstances. In the UK the issue has been widely debated, but no change to the current law has been introduced to date. A number of states in Australia have now legislated to permit euthanasia.

The Roman Catholic Church has always condemned euthanasia and assisted suicide, as have the Orthodox Churches. A very wide spectrum of Protestant churches also take the same stance, particularly those of evangelical commitment. For example, in the USA this includes churches such as the Assemblies of God, the Evangelical Lutheran Church in America, the Seventh-Day Adventist Church and Southern Baptist Convention. Some from a more liberal viewpoint, and not holding to the final authority of the Bible, are prepared to allow the practice to take place in hospitals and other institutions they control, while not supporting its introduction.

On these issues, and many others, including world hunger and poverty, climate change and the treatment of refugees, the churches have had to assume a prominent role in public life. Often in the past, single issues loomed large in the social conscience of Christians, such as the abolition of slavery, the working conditions of children or universal suffrage. Now the range of issues is much wider; and as the churches battle strong secularist agendas, they have to convince the public and legislators that the Judaeo-Christian ethic is still relevant for modern society.

Trends in theology

Modern theology is vigorous, and continues to cover the whole range of traditional theological topics. This is evidenced by the numerous theological and philosophical journals, websites and blogs, and the continuous stream of new publications. The doctrine of Scripture and questions relating to interpretation continue to occupy attention, but perhaps less so among the evangelical community than in the last two decades of the twentieth century. While Roman Catholic scholars nominally adhere to the traditional views of inspiration, the document *Dei Verbum: The Dogmatic Constitution of Divine Revelation*, which emerged from Vatican II, entrenched openness to historical-critical methods. The methods had been used before in Roman Catholic circles, but now they were given prominence in an official document.

The atonement

From the days of the early church, discussion has taken place concerning the death of the Lord Jesus, and repeated mention of his work in the creeds calls for a response. Also, the fact that the death of Christ is so central in services of the Mass or Eucharist or Lord's Supper encourages theological reflection on the significance of the atonement. Two questions that have constantly been faced are, 'Why did Jesus die?' and 'What was achieved by his death?' These questions are still behind current writing on the atonement. Many positions may seem novel when presented, but very often can be seen as virtually identical with positions put forward by theologians such as Friedrich Schleiermacher, John McLeod Campbell, Albrecht Ritschl, Karl Barth or Jürgen Moltmann. That is to say, much modern writing on the atonement is derivative, and the antecedents can be traced. Modern liberal theologians frequently object to the ideas of sacrifice, satisfaction and substitution. In their place, they want to propagate a non-violent atonement, in which Christ by his incarnation atones, or, as with the Edinburgh theologian T. F. Torrance, Christ atones through his whole being and life, including his death and resurrection.

Defenders of the traditional evangelical understanding of the atonement have not been absent from the discussions. Leon Morris (1914–2006) in his book *The Apostolic Preaching of the Cross* gathered the evidence to refute the earlier arguments of C. H. Dodd (1884–1973) that speaking of God's wrath is only a figure of speech, not a real expression of the divine nature. Morris did not retreat from his arguments, and published many later studies on the cross that upheld his position. His advocacy in support of the view that Christ suffered in the place of his people was taken up and defended with great vigour on the Anglo-American scene by J. I. Packer (1926–) and John Stott (1921–2011). Packer had stated his position as early as 1973 in a Tyndale Biblical Theology lecture ('What Did the Cross Achieve? The Logic of Penal Substitution'), and reiterated and expanded it in many later writings. In recent times, there has been a shift both in the UK and North America towards Reformed theology among younger evangelicals, and this has produced substantial books that defend the traditional view that it was in our place that Christ suffered on the cross.

Justification

One issue dominated theological discussions late in the twentieth century, and this has still been the case into the twenty-first century. That topic is the doctrine of justification. While many other theological conversations have branched out along new lines, the doctrine of justification has been dealt with in relation to long-standing theological traditions, especially those that arose at the time of the Reformation in Europe. The Roman Catholic Church did not accept Luther's teaching that righteousness is a gift of God's grace to the individual believer. The Council of Trent (1545–63) came to findings that rejected Luther's teaching, insisting that righteousness must *inhere* in the individual, and not merely be imputed or reckoned.

Vatican II proved to be a watershed in relation to the doctrine of justification, for it led to ecumenical discussions resulting in several accords between Rome and individual Protestant churches. The most significant of these is the *Joint Declaration on the Doctrine of Justification* by the Lutheran World Federation and the Roman Catholic Church in 1999. While this declaration makes it clear that justification is not based on individual merit, it is unclear on other issues, such as the place of 'by faith alone' in the justifying process, or how the Lutheran position can be reconciled with that of the Roman Catholic Church. Other discussions have taken place between the

Roman Catholic Church and the Anglicans, and also with evangelicals. The documents resulting from these discussions are of a different nature from the *Joint Declaration*, in that they do not have any binding authority. Catholic–Orthodox discussions have also taken place, but the doctrine of justification has not been part of them.

The New Perspective

What later became known as the New Perspective on Paul can be traced back to the work of E. P. Sanders entitled *Paul and Palestinian Judaism* (1977). His central thesis was that the Judaism of Jesus' day was not concerned with justification of the individual as taught by Luther, but with keeping the stipulations of the covenant so that the Lord would remain faithful to Israel. This point of view was taken up and expanded in various ways by others, but especially by the British scholars James Dunn and N. T. Wright. Dunn has argued strongly that the phrase 'the righteousness of God' in the New Testament refers to God's faithfulness to his covenant with Israel. The work of Wright is more nuanced, but he insists that the apostles would have understood the events of the first century over against the Torah, the first five books of the Old Testament. This means that they would think of Jesus' mission in terms of a second exodus. Hence, Wright argues, Jesus' role was to bring his people back from exile so that they could live in God's presence, not that he suffered the curse of death for them.

The New Perspective is not a uniform movement, and embraces a wide variety of viewpoints. Nor is it by any means universally accepted. Among the spate of literature that has been generated by the discussions, there are many scholarly discussions challenging it, and arguing for the traditional Protestant doctrine of justification by faith alone. Its diverse elements will make it difficult to maintain a unified direction in future discussions.

Pentecostalism

The rapid growth of Pentecostalism in the Global South means that it now represents a larger proportion of Christian expression than ever before. In Africa and parts of South America, it has blended with non-Christian elements, and in this way has an appeal to the illiterate or those barely literate. In North America and Europe, not so many of the excesses of earlier Pentecostalism are apparent, and only an exuberant worship style at times differentiates between it and other forms of Protestantism. Some prominent Pentecostal leaders in the USA, especially those with TV programmes, have promoted a 'prosperity gospel', claiming that spiritual health leads to material blessings. Scandals affecting several well-known evangelists have dented the reputation of such evangelistic efforts.

The neo-Pentecostal movement, often referred to as the charismatic movement, affected many within mainstream churches. From the 1960s onwards, a succession of charismatic teaching and practice spread widely in North America and Europe. Radical worship and distinctive experiences characterized waves of the charismatic renewal, such as the 'restoration' movement, 'power evangelism' and the 'Toronto Blessing'. None of these lasted a great length of time, and have not been replicated in the past couple of decades. Many aspects of the charismatic movement have carried over into the wider church, including preference for new songs, distinctive instrumentation in worship and stress on the role of ministry by every member in the local church fellowship. While many have appreciated the freshness of the charismatic experience, others have been affected adversely, and often find that after coming to faith in Christ they move to more traditional churches in order to be fed by gospel preaching.

Changes in the Western countries

Moral changes in the West have also brought new challenges to Christian communities. Legislation disallowing discrimination has been utilized against Christians, with those refusing to provide services to homosexuals, for example, facing court challenges and subsequent penalties. This has caught many Christians unaware, as the alteration in public morals has suddenly taken on a new profile. The change has been progressing subtly for decades, becoming enshrined in legislation only as Christian moral standards have been replaced by secular ones. In many countries, the pendulum has swung so far that even propagation of Christian beliefs can be regarded as offensive to others, especially those of the gay and lesbian communities. This has brought together Christian communities as they form a united front to educate their own followers with what is at stake, to publicize their positions and lobby parliamentarians to ensure that safeguards are in place to preserve rights of belief and practice. Numbers of attendees continue to drop in European churches, so that the Church of England and the Church of Scotland have both recorded big drops in membership. The same applies on the Continent. As an example, German Protestant and Catholic churches lost approximately 440,000 members from their rolls in 2018. While the losses in North America are not so significant, it is clear that there is a noticeable downward trend in membership, including in evangelical churches.

Future prospects

The story of the church is the record of the ebbs and flows of the history of God's people over 2,000 years of human history. The Christian church is a continuation of the people of God in Old Testament times. It is another form of the covenantal relationship between God and his people, wherein he gives the assurance 'I will be their God, and they shall be my people' (Exod. 6:7; Jer. 31:33; 2 Cor. 6:16; Heb. 8:10). The church is a divine institution, and the promise of Jesus is that not even the gates of Hades can prevail against it (Matt. 16:18). He has throughout history taken care of his church, for he has special affection for the fellowship of his people, whom he purchased with his own blood (Acts 20:28).

The history of the church provides many surprising aspects. Beginning with twelve apostles and a small group who believed in Jesus as the Messiah, the church has spread in 2,000 years to every continent. It has been driven by the commands of Jesus himself and the instructions he gave to the early church. Its mission has compelled it to reach out to all peoples with the good news of the gospel, and its influence has been seen in many different aspects of society. Politics and legal institutions, health care and education, and many other facets of society have been blessed by its imprint, quite apart from the direct acquisition of members into God's church and kingdom.

No Christian should attempt to disguise the fact that many mistakes have been made both by individual Christians and church organizations over the centuries. Redeemed people will be perfect only when the Lord Jesus returns in glory, and by faith we can rightly claim, '[W]e know that when he appears we shall be like him, because we shall see him as he is' (1 John 3:2). God has used redeemed sinners to fulfil his purposes up to the present, and will continue to use them in the future for the glory of his name and the building of his kingdom.

This book is an attempt to outline the life of God's church over many centuries. The church has always been countercultural, and the gospel will always be confrontational because it challenges the basic presuppositions of non-Christians. The church of the present cannot hide itself from the problems facing it, some of which have been described in earlier chapters. Militant Islam has even learned to imitate some aspects of Christian practice, while there is a resurgence of Eastern religions as well. The West is dominated by secular humanism, and the church itself in many parts has not been able to isolate itself sufficiently from non-biblical influences.

But Christians of today should not be daunted by the challenges facing the church. Just as it has progressed in spite of many forms of opposition over the years, so in the future it will survive and progress by God's sovereign power and grace. Ultimately, the future of the church depends not on men but on God. He has promised in the Scriptures that he will never forsake it (Ps. 94:14), but will be with his people until the consummation of this present age (Matt. 28:20). For Christians, the task remains of being lights in the world, and seeking under the blessing of the Holy Spirit to bring others into obedience to the claims of Jesus Christ. The commands of Jesus to his church to go and make disciples are accompanied by visions of a vast number who will at last enter his presence (Rev. 7:9–14). He is the eternal king who must reign until all his enemies are subdued under his feet (1 Cor. 15:24–25).

Bibliography

General introductions

Bromiley, G. W., *Historical Theology: An Introduction* (T&T Clark, 1998).

Cairns, E. E., *Christianity through the Centuries: A History of the Christian Church*, 3rd edn (Zondervan, 2009).

Dowley, T. (ed.), *Introduction to the History of Christianity*, 4th edn (Fortress Press, 2018).

McGrath, A. E., *Christian History: An Introduction* (Blackwell, 2013).

Shaw, I. J., *Christianity: The Biography – Two Thousand Years of the Global Church* (Inter-Varsity Press, 2016; Zondervan Academic, 2017)

Walker, W., *A History of the Christian Church*, 4th edn, rev. R. T. Handy (Scribner, 2014).

Reference books

Cross, F. L., and E. A. Livingstone (eds.), *The Oxford Dictionary of the Christian Church*, rev. edn (Oxford University Press, 2005).

Douglas, J. D. (ed.), *The New International Dictionary of the Christian Church*, rev. edn (Paternoster, 1981).

Douglas, J. D., P. W. Comfort and D. Mitchell (eds.), *Who's Who in Christian History* (Tyndale House, 1992).

McGrath, A. E. (ed.), *The Blackwell Encyclopedia of Modern Christian Thought* (Blackwell, 1995).

McManners, J. (ed.), *The Oxford Illustrated History of Christianity* (Oxford University Press, 2001).

Noll, M. A., *Turning Points: Decisive Moments in the History of Christianity*, 3rd edn (Baker Academic, 2012).

Reeves, M., *Introducing Major Theologians: From the Apostolic Fathers to the Twenty-First Century* (Inter-Varsity Press, 2015).

Reid, D. G., R. D. Linder, B. L. Shelley and H. S. Stout (eds.), *Dictionary of Christianity in America* (InterVarsity Press, 2000).

Index

Index

Baur, F. C. 175
Baxter, Richard 140
Beaton, David, cardinal 115–16
Beghards 76
Benedictine order 47, 56; *see also*
    monasticism
Berlin Congress 213
Bernard of Clairvaux 56, 71
Beza, Theodore 99, 117
Bible, versions of 9, 104–5, 127–9,
    227–9
Bible societies 154, 227
Bible translation 186–7
biblical studies 229–33
Bishop of Rome 4, 13, 15, 25, 29–30,
    34, 43, 45–6, 64–5
bishops, use of the term 9, 13–14, 25
Bithynia, Christians in 15–16
Blandina 18
Bogomils 76
Bohemia 67, 79, 81, 123, 125
Boleyn, Anne 103
Bonaparte, Napoleon, emperor of
    France 146, 165–6
Bonhoeffer, Dietrich 191–2, 230
Boniface (Winfrith) 60
Boniface VIII, pope 74–5
Bonner, Edmund, bishop of London
    108
Booth, William 168
Borgias 84
Brethren of the Common Life 82
Brewster, William 130
Briggs, C. A. 175, 184
Britain, evangelization of 48–9
British College Christian Union 171
British Evangelical Council 205
British missions 150
Browne, Robert 130
Brunner, Emil 229
Bucer, Martin 95–6, 106
Buchanan, George 116
Buchlin, Paul 106

Buddhism 54
Bulgaria 67, 76
Bultmann, Rudolf 176, 230
Bunyan, John 131, 136, 140

Calvin, John 42, 92, 94–100, 102, 106,
    117–18
Calvinism and Arminianism 132
Calvinism in England 111, 143–4
Calvinism in Hungary 101
Cambridge Inter-Collegiate Christian
    Union (CICCU) 171
Cambridge Seven 172
Cambuslang, Revival of 145
Campbell, J. McLeod 248
canon, the 8, 24
canonical criticism 231–2
Canossa 70–71, 73
Canterbury 49, 102–3
Carey, William 151–2
Carlstadt, Andreas 87, 89, 92
Carolingian dynasty 65
Carthage, church at 4, 11, 22, 26–30,
    34, 41
Cartwright, Thomas 111–12
Catechetical School (Alexandria)
    30–31, 33
Cathari 76
Catherine of Aragon 102–3, 108, 110
Catherine de Medici 100
Catholic Emancipation Act 146
Catholicism, critical methods in
    247–8
Cecil, William 111–12, 118
celibacy 22, 40, 43, 56, 106, 121,
    243
Celtic church 45, 48–50, 52, 55,
    59–60, 115
Chalcedon, Council of 40, 43–4
Chalmers, James 153
Chalmers, Thomas 161
charismatic movement 204, 208, 220,
    223–6, 243, 251

Index

Index

Index

Index

Index

Index

Index

United Presbyterian Church 183
United Reformed Church 202
universities, Christian witness in
171–2
Universities and Colleges Christian
Fellowship 211
Urban II, pope 70–71
Urban VI, pope 75
Ussher, James, archbishop 129
Utrecht, Union of 101

Valentinus 20
Valerian persecution 30, 44
Vandals 42, 45
Vatican II 201, 204, 207–8, 221, 227,
231, 242, 248, 249
vestments 36, 53, 90, 109–10, 127
'Vicar of Christ' 48, 69, 125
Vienne 18
Vineyard churches 226
Visigoths 44–5
Vulgate 43, 78, 84, 124

Waldenses 76, 100–101, 190
Warfield, B. B. 184
Watts, Isaac 146–7
Wellhausen, Julius 173–4
Wesley, Charles 141, 147
Wesley, John 141–3, 147, 151, 170
Wessel, John 85
Westminster Assembly 111–12, 135
Westminster Confession of Faith 118,
135, 137, 210
Whitby, Synod of 50, 59
White, Robert 94
Whitefield, George 141–3, 145, 150
Whitgift, John, archbishop of
Canterbury 112

Wilberforce, William 153–4
Wilder, Robert 172
William I (the Silent), prince of
Orange 101
William of Occam 57, 78, 115
William of Orange, king of England
137, 161
Williams, George 168
Willibrord 60
Wimber, John 226
Wishart, George 115
Wittenberg 86–9, 91
Wolsey, Thomas, cardinal 103
World Alliance of Reformed
Churches 203
World Conference on Faith and
Order 182
World Council of Churches 182,
200–201, 204–5, 236–7
World Evangelical Fellowship 206
World Methodist Council 181
Worms, Diet of 88
worship in the early church 10–11,
17–18
Wright, N. T. 250
Wyclif, John 78–79
Wycliffe Bible Translators 186–7, 226,
235

Xavier, Francis 123–4

Young Men's Christian Association
(YMCA) 168, 181

Zealots 7
Zinzendorf, Count Nicolaus 151
Zoroastrianism 76
Zwingli, Ulrich 90–91, 93–4, 105